I0754021

THE

LIFE AND PUBLIC SERVICES

OF

DR. LEWIS F. LINN,

FOR TEN YEARS A SENATOR OF THE UNITED STATES FROM THE STATE OF MISSOURI.

BY

E. A. LINN AND N. SARGENT.

NEW YORK:
D. APPLETON AND COMPANY,
346 & 348 BROADWAY.
M.DCCC.LVII.

PREFACE.

THE present volume has been prepared in obedience to what seemed to the writer to be a call from those, "the pioneers of the great valley of the Mississippi and their descendants," between whom and Doctor Linn there was, during his lifetime, a long subsisting association, a mutual esteem and interchange of good offices, which from the beginning became more and more intimate and cordial, until the ties which thus bound them together were severed by the hand of death.

Few men were more thoroughly identified with "the Great West" than Dr. Linn, and no one took a livelier interest in all that concerned the great Valley of the Mississippi and its enterprising people, or labored with greater zeal to develope its resources, open and improve its highways, by land and water, with a view to expedite the occupation of its rich soil and inviting climate by the temperate sons of toil from the East, and to facilitate its commercial intercourse with other parts of the country.

It is gratifying to know that the subject of this memoir is remembered through the fruits of his labors, by thousands to whom he was not personally known, but of whose interests, while he occupied a seat in the Senate of the United States, he was never unmindful or neglective; and that his memory is still affectionately cherished by other thousands to whom he endeared himself in a personal intercourse of many years as their neighbor, friend, physician, and senator, in each of which relations he failed not to win and retain their love and respect.

There are still others who have not forgotten the persevering labors of Dr. Linn, in their behalf, and whose memory is held by them in grateful regard for his unceasing efforts to secure the noble country which is now vocal with the voices of civilized man, whose flocks and herds, fields and farms cover its green hills and fruitful valleys,—the pioneers of Oregon. It is in obedience also to their wishes that this memoir of him whose name is so intimately connected with Oregon has been prepared.

Aside from, and in addition to, these calls, it seemed to be proper that some record of the services of one who labored so faithfully for others and for his country, should be preserved for those who for years, perhaps centuries, hence, will enjoy the fruits of those labors. This task I have endeavored to perform, and to inscribe his name upon a tablet composed of his own good deeds; and I need not say that it has been to me a labor of love as well as of duty. If it has not been done with artistic excellence, I know that the kind indulgence of friends will see in the *will* all that is wanting in the skill. My endeavor has been less to present a finished picture, than to body forth a true portrait of one whose every feature, physical and moral, I have reason to know so well, and to remember with so much affection.

E. A. Linn.

Linwood Cottage, Boonville, Missouri.

LIFE OF DR. LINN.

CHAPTER I.

DR. LEWIS FIELDS LINN, the subject of this biography, was born on the 5th of November, 1795, near the present city of Louisville, in the State of Kentucky. He was the grandson of the heroic Col. William Linn of the Revolution. His parents emigrated from Pennsylvania at that early period of our national history when there were few white people living on the banks of the Ohio River. Those who had already pushed their hardy fortunes so far into the wilderness and upon its watercourses, dwelt in small settlements scattered over the forests, and far apart from each other. The prosperous and powerful States which now skirt both margins of the Ohio River, were at that remote day the hunting grounds and fastnesses of roving Indian tribes, against whose ferocity neither age nor sex was a shield—against the property and lives of the white inhabitants they waged a harassing and incessant warfare, and seldom if ever spared one or the other when fortune gave them the advantage in their incursions.

Both the grandparents of Dr. Linn, with seven members of their family, fell victims to the merciless and bloody scalping-knife of the savages. His intrepid and chivalrous grandfather, Col. Linn, espoused the cause of the Colonies and took up arms for their liberties at the dawn of the American Revolution; he constantly remained active in the service of his country throughout that long struggle, so perilous and sanguinary to the frontier and its infant communities; and then sealed a life of devotion and patriotism by his death in battle against the Indians. He lived, however, to behold the Independence for which he had striven for so many years secured to his country; and some years after its establishment fell, overwhelmed by numbers, in a conflict with the Indians near Louisville, on the Ohio River.

An accurate and eloquent annalist of the West, the gifted Mr. Mann Butler of St. Louis, Missouri, thus relates an achievement characteristic of the indomitable spirit of Col. Linn, and the race from which he sprung:

"While the pioneers were thus bravely defending themselves against appalling numbers of savage enemies, the government of the parent State was not inattentive to the interest of their Western children. By a stretch of diplomacy scarcely to have been expected in so young a State, just sprung out of colonial bondage, yet still used to much independent care of her wide and exposed dominion, the Executive of Virginia dispatched a mission to New Orleans for the purpose of procuring military supplies for her Western ports. The officers sent on this perilous mission were Colonels Gibson and Linn, the grandfather of the late Dr. Lewis F. Linn, the much-lamented senator from the State of Missouri. These gentlemen went from Fort Pitt, and descended the Mississippi River in 1776, to New Orleans, by order, it is presumed, from the Governor of Virginia. So extraordinary an adventure may well require particular confirmation for the satisfaction of the reader, and it can be furnished to a most remarkable degree. John Smith, lately, that is, in 1833, a resident of Woodford County, State of Kentucky, was, in 1776, employed in reconnoitring the country with James Harod, so eminently distinguished in the difficulties and dangers of Kentucky. On their return the companions separated; Harod to go to North Carolina, and Smith to Potter's Creek on the Monongahela. While travelling on the bank of the Ohio River, the latter discovered Gibson and Linn with their party descending the river; they hailed Smith and prevailed on him to embark on this, one of the boldest of Western adventures. The party succeeded in their object with the Spanish government at New Orleans by obtaining one hundred and fifty-six kegs of gunpowder. Mr. Smith helped to carry around the Falls of the Ohio River this powder to the mouth of Bear Grass Creek, in the spring of 1777; each man carried three kegs along the portage, one at a time; this gunpowder was delivered at Wheeling or Fort Henry, and thence conveyed to Fort Pitt." Independent of this particularity of circumstances, learned from an old and most venerable citizen of Louisville, (the late Worden Pope, Esq., long a clerk, with untainted reputation to the highest courts of law in Jefferson County, Kentucky,) it was solemnly deposed to in a suit of law by a very respectable party in the transaction; it was frequently mentioned by Col. Linn in his lifetime, and is still known in 1833, as his information in the family left by this gallant and most energetic man. To this may be well added the manner in which he met his death, and the heroic firmness of his last moments. A few years after the United States had gained their independence from the yoke of England, Col. Linn set out at the head of sixty armed men on a march against a body of hostile Indians who had foraged the White settlements and taken many lives. At a point near what was called Linn's Station, not far from Louisville, his party was met by a force of three hundred Indian warriors, who had received full intelligence of his approach, and mustered in strength to receive him. The savages were composed of the most daring and vindictive of the predatory bands infesting the great bend of the Ohio River; they were acquainted with all forms assumed by border warfare between the Red Men and the frontier settlements; apart from desultory affrays many of them had borne part in the most memorable engagement which had, as yet, taken place upon this continent between a regular army in the field, and Aboriginal warriors; within thirty years their tribes had fought under the French banner against Washington and Braddock, and they were now arrayed within a few days' march from that disastrous battle-ground. The Indians were inspired with furious animosity against Col. Linn—his knowledge of their character and stratagems, his superior sagacity and dauntless intrepedity, his genius in border warfare, and the frequency with which they had been defeated by him; the dread inseparable from his name; the confidence and courage with which his protection inspired the weak and isolated societies of his partisans; added to the frightful chastisements with which he had repeatedly visited their common enemy, combined to render him, for long years, an object of deadly hatred and hereditary revenge. This was the era of Indian combination and preconcerted movements; his destruction appeared inevitable, and would open the way to sweep every stranger from the land; but in order to glut every horrid passion of their swarthy race, they determined to take him alive; his death could have been easily effected as he led on and encouraged his men. Suddenly a cry arose in the English tongue, "Take him! take him alive! take him alive! we want to eat his heart!" Instead of aiming at the vital parts of his person, they fired volley after volley below his knees, until his feet were shot to pieces and the bones of his legs broken. When he fell the braves rushed in to disarm and bear him off alive; but they found him in his last hour the same avenging implacable foe they had dreaded through life. Gaining his knees, the dying hero grappled with his enemies, giving and receiving many a death wound before he expired. Of them he slew, hand to hand, seven, before his arm was rendered nerveless by death.

It is a just reflection, that the most extraordinary acts of fortitude and brilliant valor which excite our admiration in history, have been evinced in the retrograde and not onward course of armies. Gallant retreats and daring passages, whilst they warm our sympathies lead us to forget that certain destruction was willingly exchanged for the chances and probabilities of self-extrication, and that chivalry alone which dazzles the mind in the face of death can best explain the steady onward course of our early emigration to the barriers held by savage races, and the strange inflexibility with which they penetrated the fertile region and mountain labyrinths beyond them. The task was always to force new avenues and never to retreat by old ones. Reviewing the occupation of districts in ancient Virginia before their erection into separate States, we are arrested by the number of appalling murders in Massachusetts;—forts surprised; block-houses given to the flames; and other evidences of civilization and industry reduced to ashes. The heroic conduct of a vast number of our admirable countrywomen during those distressing times, must be a source of great pleasure to their descendants.

The mother of Dr. Linn, whose maiden name was Ann Hunter, when only fifteen years of age, conveyed provisions on two several occasions, into forts invested by the Indians, to save, not only members of her own family, but others who with them were suffering for food; young, active, and possessing great resolution, Miss Ann Hunter eluded detection from the keenest human vision, and with her own hands carried into the forts food for her suffering friends.

Mr. Asael Linn, the father of Dr. Linn, accompanied four young gentlemen from his father's residence near Louisville, on the Ohio River, in pursuit of wild game. Carried away with the ardor of the chase, they had gone some distance from home before they were aware of it, when they suddenly found themselves surrounded by a number of hostile Indians. Resistance was vain. After one of their party was wounded in the leg they were secured as captives by the savages, and forced across the Ohio River. The Indians travelled at a rapid pace, fearing pursuit from the white settlements. Lewis Fields, although suffering greatly from the wound in his leg, kept his place among the prisoners with the utmost difficulty. The savages cast looks of impatience and anger upon him whenever he relaxed the speed at which they were proceeding. Young Asael Linn, scarcely twelve years of age, pressed on before his wounded friend, and removed every obstacle in his power when he arrived at difficult passes; another companion made a rough crutch for Lewis, which enabled him to keep up with the captors and the captured. It was by the most strenuous efforts on his part and the aid of his friends, that his life was saved, for the Indians required but the least pretext to determine upon his instant death; for, whenever he attempted to rest for a moment, they grasped their weapons to kill him. Young Linn's efforts were solely to save his friend Lewis Fields. He felt convinced that his own death was resolved upon as soon as they should reach the village of their tribe; for, as the son of Col. Linn, the great white warrior, there was no hope for him. To watch his lingering death would be grateful to the savage wretches who had so often writhed under the blows of his father. At length, after journeying incessantly for three days, so great a distance had been put between them and the Ohio River, that they supposed themselves safe from pursuit. They made an encampment, binding their captives to trees, leaving two old Indians to guard them, while the young dispersed to hunt in the wilderness. They judged the youth of Linn and the presence of the old savages a sufficient security for his remaining at large near his companions. The sequel shows how much they had miscalculated the energy and nerve of a border youth, partaking of the blood of Col. William Linn. When the shade of night had descended, young Linn was made to lie down flat upon the ground: the two old Indians spread a blanket over him, placing themselves on the edge of it on both sides of the brave boy, wedging him in between them, compressed by the blanket with their weight upon it. In a short time the old men, overpowered with fatigue, fell into a deep sleep. Linn watched their movements with intense anxiety, and when convinced his captors were asleep, commenced with great dexterity and presence of mind to draw his person from under the blanket without disturbing those upon it; for if awakened, his death would not have been delayed one moment. When liberated from his painful situation, the first object

Linn beheld was one of his companions, Mr. Wells, bound to a tree near him; and seeing from the gleams of light sent forth from the watch-fire, a tomahawk near to his hand, he seized it, and soon cut the cords that bound his friend. Mr. Wells made him a sign to retain the weapon, and arming himself with another, they drew near to their blood-thirsty foes, and in an instant buried their tomahawks in the heads of the Indians. Weakened in frame, and of the most humane disposition, in spite of the justice and necessity of the act, Linn's heart recoiled from putting a sleeping enemy to death, and the wound he inflicted, although completely stunning in its effect, did not produce death, but left a hideous and distorting mutilation on the face of the savage. In a few moments the captives were liberated from the cords that were cutting into their flesh. Collecting in great haste a few fragments of food, securing all the hatchets and knives they could find for their defence, and concealing the guns, (as the Indians might at any instant be so near their path as to hear a report from them, and the weight of them would retard their flight,) before the light of day (a bitter cold morning in the month of November) these five boys, not one of them out of his teens (Linn not twelve years old), commenced their flight through the wilderness towards the Ohio River, half starved, almost naked, and bearing with them one of their number, wounded, sore and crippled. Poor Lewis Fields suffered so much from his inflamed wound in consequence of the great exertions he was compelled to make, that he frequently stopped and implored his friends to leave him to his fate, and save themselves by retreating more rapidly than it was possible to do while he continued with them; but the faithful little band of friends, deaf to his self-devoting proposition, urged him forward by every act of friendship and encouragement until, through indescribable suffering of hunger, cold and lassitude, they stood once more on the bank of the Ohio River. Fortunately they could all swim, and it was only necessary to construct from the limbs of trees and drift-wood on the shore, a raft large enough to bear their disabled friend, and push it before them while swimming across the river. Linn was so much exhausted that his friends feared he would perish in the water, and urged him to get on the raft with Fields; but the gallant boy declined their friendly offer, assuring them that his father had taught him to swim very well, and that he was still strong enough to assist in getting their friend across the river. At the moment the raft was launched into the water, the distant yell of the Indians in pursuit was heard. They had struck the trail of the youths and were now almost upon them. Straining every nerve, the gallant boys soon gained the middle of the river, while the frail raft appeared as if it would go to pieces under the slight weight of Fields. As the Indians arrived one after another at the water's edge, they fired at the fugitives, but fortunately the distance was so great they were unable to do them any injury; and the reports of their guns attracted the attention of some settlers working on the Kentucky side of the river, who immediately came to their relief. Although exhausted and half dead, Linn still retained his hold upon the raft, but entirely insensible, and at first it was thought he had expired. He was carried home, and after remaining for three days wholly unconscious, awoke to a sense of external things in the arms of his mother. His life was spared, and he grew up to a manhood of great energy and exalted worth. Many years afterwards, when the country had become peaceful, Linn met his old enemy the Indian, whom in his boyhood he had deprived of so large a portion of his face, and, touched with his horrid appearance, bestowed on him an annuity for life.

The mother of Dr. Linn was married twice. Her name, it has already been stated, was Ann Hunter. This admirable and courageous lady did not live to see an event unknown to the history of any other family in our country, both of her sons and one of her grandsons Senators of the United States Senate, at periods nearly simultaneous. Her first marriage was contracted with Mr. Israel Dodge, of Louisville, the father of the

Hon. Henry Dodge, United States Senator from the State of Wisconsin, and of Mrs. Nancy Sifton of St. Louis, Missouri. After the loss of her first husband, Mrs. Dodge was united to Mr. Asael Linn of Louisville, Kentucky. Lewis Fields Linn and Mary Ann Linn were their only offspring who survived to maturity.

Much might here be said of the half brother of Dr. Linn, but these are not the pages to narrate the eventful life of Senator Henry Dodge, for they are devoted to the memory of one whose being was derived from the same beloved mother, and among its dearest recollections may justly be inscribed the tender affection that bound her two sons together; yet there is one, who deems it her privilege to say that for long years, with thrilling pleasure, she has witnessed the truth, honor, magnanimity, and heroic firmness, so conspicuous in the character of a husband's only brother, and equally so in that brother's son, the Hon. Augustus C. Dodge.

The death of both their parents left Lewis F. Linn and his sister Mary orphans early in life; the latter being thirteen years of age and her brother twelve years old. Between the brother and sister a remarkable similarity of character and personal resemblance existed; both had the same resolution and precocious self-reliance, with the same elevated and fearless spirit; they both possessed great personal beauty, set off by gentle unassuming manners; both were equally endowed with guileless, generous hearts—ever anxious to perform for their friends the most liberal and unselfish services. Unhappily the cheerful and buoyant spirits which Miss Linn had at all times possessed, and which bore her up under the greatest misfortunes and afflictions, were frequently overcast and oppressed in the temperament of her brother. She was always animated and full of hope, while he at times from his infancy labored under a great depression of mind: the fatal disease of the heart which cut him off prematurely from a world, fast learning to love and admire him, affected his health and induced periods of the greatest despondency. The knowledge he attained of his profession in early life, informed him too surely of the tenure by which his existence was held. When these melancholy moments weighed him down, he never repined, but by his touching sweetness of temper, and unaffected gratitude to those around him for their kind attentions and sympathy, drew them still nearer to him, and opened too fully their hearts to the anguish of his own predictions. He was left, it has just been stated, at the age of twelve years, to struggle for the future. Resolved that it should be an honorable one to him, as soon as his fifteenth year was attained he commenced a course of self-education. Making use of every means in his power, he endeavored to compensate for that want of early academical education inevitable in all new countries, and commenced the study of medicine with Dr. Gault, of Louisville.

Among the predilections of his earliest boyhood Dr. Linn evinced a strong inclination to devote himself to the profession of medicine, and following his desires on this subject, his health became seriously impaired by unremitting application to his studies, and at the end of two years it became necessary for him to resort to some relaxation from his labor and enjoy a period of leisure and change of scene. He proceeded to St. Genevieve, in Missouri, to visit his sister Mary, (who was then married to Mr. McArthur,) and his half brother, Gen. Henry Dodge. During his residence with these relatives the war with Great Britain broke out. No surgeon being attached to the troops commanded by Gen. Dodge, he accompanied them in that capacity, and at the close of the campaign, with restored health and an increased desire to pursue his medical studies, he returned to Louisville, and continued some time with Dr. Gault, and ultimately proceeded to Philadelphia for the purpose of embracing the facilities and advantages that city has always afforded to medical students. The presence of his sister and half brother at St. Genevieve decided Dr. Linn to make that place his residence and the field of his professional pursuits. By his own energy and ability he had mastered one of the most honorable and benevolent callings of civilized society; and at the age of twenty-one found himself established as a physician in one of the most refined and intelligent communities of the West.

At the period Dr. Linn established himself in St. Genevieve, it retained the distinguishing characteristics impressed upon it by its original settlers. They bestowed the name of the "Glorieuse patronne de Paris" upon this, their new home in the "far west," and from the banks of the Seine transplanted thither, with their cherished faith, all the amenities of a high civilization, the attentive politeness, the cultivated and polished manners, and the chivalrous gallantry peculiar to the true son of France. These primordial blessings, now transmitted through many successive generations, are sparklingly salient over the surface of society in this and other quiet communities of similar origin, and cannot escape the notice of the least incurious observer. Perhaps it may be considered out of place in a narrative like this to present these facts, but there is so much misconception of the true character of these most estimable citizens; so much hateful prejudice, and almost inexcusable ignorance relative to them, that one who went among them a stranger, of other affinity, association, habits, education, and religion, vividly retaining a remembrance of the numberless kindnesses received at their hands during a long series of years, is impelled by a feeling of gratitude and a sense of justice, to endeavor, however feebly, to dispel these most erroneous, though commonly received opinions. A proper information would have prevented many, well-intended, from having been betrayed into speech and action, the impression of which they subsequently deemed necessary to erase by a mortifying apology. With a charitable intent, it is desired most gently to say to any young lady who may happen to peruse these lines, that, if it should be her fortune in the great assemblies of the Atlantic cities, to meet a young person of her own sex from these ancient towns on the river or prairie, that she should not treat her as a semi-barbarian, and refrain joining in the invidious remarks which the appearance of a "creole" may occasion. Let her receive some idea that this "creole" girl is better instructed in her duty to her Maker and towards her neighbor, than she is likely to be; and is at least her equal in all the proficiencies of a polite education. The unlady-like conduct intimated is related to have occurred, and though politeness and self-respect forbade retort, others heard the unfounded sarcasm, and made a comparison between its modest subject and the pretentious beauty who so incautiously uttered it, far from complimentary, though she was the favorite of a fashionable boarding-school, and the belle and toast of the locality. The very word "creole" as usually received and applied in the more Eastern

States, is a perversion of its meaning. The fair descendants of those who first landed at Jamestown, of those who were wafted in the "Ark and the Dove" to the land of Mary, those who came in the "Mayflower" to the bleak shore of the "Old Colony," or in the succeeding ships to the more inviting ports on the "Bay," are properly as much creoles (with the prefix of English) as their fellow countrywomen along the great Father of Waters. The term creole simply designs to signify the children of European parents born in America or the Indies, and their descendants. As usually applied, it is incorrect and offensive, and being so, should be disused by every considerate person.

The discovery of the Mississippi, as the remote initial point of interest to its settlers, was effected by Fernando De Soto in 1541; its shore was the terminus of all his mundane hopes, aspirations, difficulties and disasters; its depths received his, the first Christian corse, over which its waters sang its monody, and its current conveyed the disheartened and shattered remains of his unfortunate expedition to the Gulf of Mexico. The survivors made report of this acquisition to geographical knowledge, but from deficiency in the requisite science of that day, or loss of proper instruments to determine, or of leaders most competent to define it, the exact place of disemboguement for a long period was mystical. Subsequent events have shown the vast importance of this stupendous stream, and the advent of De Soto is appropriately commemorated on the canvas that adorns the rotunda of our national Capitol.

The next approach of the European was from the north through Canada, which appellation is said to have been formed by that given in disappointment by the first discoverers of the sterile coast leading thereto —"Capo di Nada," or the Cape of Nothing. It was named New France by Jacques Cartier, who ascended the Saint Lawrence in 1535 as far as the Isle of Orleans. Before that period the French had made several unsuccessful essays at settlement at different points upon this continent. A few years afterward, Cartier with La Roche Robertval attempted to plant a colony, which was not more fortunate; from time to time others followed, but the inhospitable climate and the hostility of the natives prevented all permanent settlement. It was not until 1608 that they were able to retain a residence. Champlain early in July of that year laid the foundation of Quebec, and to conciliate his immediate neighbors, the Hurons and Algonquins, aided them in their war with the Iroquois. He secured the friendship of the first named, and the enmity of the warlike Iroquois continued towards his countrymen for nearly a century, preventing their advance southward until after the occupation of New York by the

Dutch and English. Dangers, suffering, and privations in every shape attended the feeble colony for many years. In 1620 there were but 100 inhabitants in Quebec, men, women and children. But the French had penetrated a great distance northwardly and westwardly, and were sparsely settled on the trail to the valley of the Ottawa. The Jesuit Fathers Brebœuf and Daniel, had entered the wilderness as far as the southern shore of Lake Superior as early as 1634, by way of the Ottawa; and this dangerous and difficult route was the one followed by the missionaries and voyageurs for many years, the easier way by Lake Ontario being closed by the hostility of the Iroquois. In 1659 a bishop's see was created, and Francis de Leval, the proto prelate of North America arrived. In 1665 the government of France considered the colony of such importance as to deem it fit to send thither, for the first time, a regiment of soldiers for its protection. The French possessed a great excellency in their new country by having among them a number of the much-abused sons of Saint Ignatius. From these models of piety, prudence and discrimination, in any emergency, they could always obtain the best advice, and often, when within the object of their mission, received the invaluable aid of their personal assistance. These exemplars of true courage were ever in advance of the most venturesome voyageurs; the great American historian says of them: "The history of their labors is connected with the origin of every celebrated town in the annals of French America; not a river was entered, not a cape was turned, but a Jesuit led the way." Indeed, for many years they were the main stay of the feeble colony, and but for them, left as it was, almost entirely to its own resources, must have succumbed in their inclement climate to the hostile natives. The "*Black Gown*" proved a more powerful protection than a band of armed soldiery.

In 1667, Father Allouez, being on the mission among the Chippewas, Sioux, Potawatamies, Sacs and Foxes, by his influence had reconciled their animosities and established peace among them. He here received information of a large river, unlike any that was as yet known in their territory to Europeans, which rolled its waters in a southern direction. Anxious to acquire a correct idea of the topography of the immense wilderness which he had entered, he retained the rude map which the unlettered but observant savage had depicted, and noting the time stated as necessary to proceed from one indicated point to another, attained some approach to information as regards distance, as well as direction. These faithful symbols, with appropriate questioning, were placed before other succeeding parties of aboriginal friends of a more southern residence, and received additions and confirmation. The French were convinced of the existence of a river of great volume of water, but where it would lead them they could only conjecture:—would it afford them the much-coveted passage to the South Sea? or was it the lost river of De Soto? It was resolved to verify their information and dispel their doubts, and if possible, by an expedition to find and examine this flow of water, which seemed to promise such transcendent advantages. Father Allouez returned to Quebec in 1669; and Fathers Marquette and Dablon were sent to the mission at the Sault de Sainte Marie. At this distant point the Jesuits had assembled neophytes from almost all the tribes among whom their brethren labored; even at that early day was there present a representative of the only tribe of the Red Men on the Atlantic border that yet possess a portion of their paternal heritage; the long-suffering, faithful, docile, patient, and once powerful Penobscot. In thus collecting the youth of their charge there was more than one object in view, all worthy of praise and complimentary to the sagacity said to be peculiar to their society; they were desirous those they were instructing should be free from the allurements and distractions which their larger establishments might expose them to; they thought to bring the neighboring Pagans to terms of greater amity and confidence, by an exhibition of the mutual affection between them and their pupils; they desired also to be taught, and by teaching, learn themselves; they considered it was of primary importance that missionaries should acquire a knowledge of the various languages of the people to whom they are sent, and it was thought by assembling the different dialects and idioms in the new France, they might, by study and observation, discover the radix of them all, and perhaps construct a language intelligible to all. This last object they soon found to present insuperable difficulties. A philosophical writer whose attention had been drawn to this subject (if his personal and political enemies are to be credited), by a very different motive, asserts that there are twenty radical languages among the native Americans, for one in Asia.

After remaining at St. Marie for about two years, acquiring the idiom nearest the scene of his survey, and making himself master of the unspoken language which has since been so serviceable to many succeeding adventurers through the wilds and over the wastes of this continent, with a few select companions, Father Marquette commenced his arduous undertaking; the charge of the material of the expedition was intrusted to Joliet, an experienced trader among the Indians, and one variously well qualified to be of great service to the enterprise in which they were embarked. Their course was southwestwardly, and reaching Green Bay ascended the Neenah or Fox River; and over the portage, which, from the formation of the country, offered much less formidable obstacles than had been anticipated, they, through the River Ouisconsin, entered a great stream with a southern current, the object of their desire; they descended to what is now the Chickasaw Bluffs. Fully convinced they had attained the great object of their voyage, they commenced their arduous ascent against the current; they entered the Illinois, and from the head waters of that river crossed to the creek which enters Lake Michigan, near where is now the flourishing city of Chicago. The pious Marquette remained to satisfy the yearnings of his compassionate heart in devoting the best energies of his nature to the labor of his love—the conversion and instruction of the poor Pagans. Joliet returned to Canada with a report of the result, and the observations which had been noted at the different points of interest during their progress. The Canadians were much elated with Joliet's success, and for years it was thought that a way to the Indies was through their territory: there was a special service of thanksgiving in the Cathedral and the Te Deum chanted. But the government of New France had its attention occupied with matters of more immediate interest, and were without the means to follow the discovery with another and better appointed expedition. A private individual from his own resources was destined to effect the continuance of the exploration to the sea.

Robert Cavelier de la Salle, a native of the city of Rouen, a gentleman of great natural abilities and of competent education, who had been received as a novice in a house of Jesuits where he remained some years; but finding his vocation was other than that of the ministry, at his own request received his dismission, and with the written commendation of his superior entered into secular employments. He embarked for New France, and was there first established as a fur trader at La Chiné. The recital of Joliet moved his ardent temperament to action; he represented to the Count de Frontenac the governor, all the various advantages that must accrue to Canada and to France upon the completion of the discovery, and pressed the necessity of taking steps to secure the prize offered to them. Frontenac assented to his views, and eventually sent La Salle to France, recommending him and his purpose to the court. La Salle was favorably received at Paris. He was made commandant and proprietor at Fort Cataracoui, received a grant of land, the king's approbation, and his patent of nobility—but no money. For that powerful agent of good or evil he had to rely upon his own talents, industry, and fortune for supply. He engaged the Chevalier de Tonti, a Neapolitan, in his enterprise, and having purchased a large supply of goods suitable· for the Indian trade, which his previous experience had taught the value of in the new country, sailed with a company of thirty, among whom were the mechanics necessary for his purpose. He safely arrived, and at once proceeded to Cataracoui; this fort, afterwards called Frontenac, was built in 1670, and was of great service in securing the navigation westwardly by the lakes. The city of Kingston is now situated upon its site. He made his arrangements in the most prompt and business-like manner, sending parties to prepare the natives for his coming, and to barter his goods for furs, from the sale of which he mainly depended to secure the means of defraying the expense of his expedition. Having built a small vessel, he left Cataracoui in the middle of November, 1678, and after a tedious and tempestuous voyage reached the western side of the lake, and determined to winter near the Falls of Niagara. Sending some parties of his men in various directions among the Indians, and employing others in the construction of another and larger barque above the Falls, near the mouth of Tonnewanda Creek, he returned to Fort Frontenac for further supplies, with which he again arrived the following spring. Having launched and freighted "The Griffon" the first vessel that ploughed the great inland seas of America, equipped with artillery, he pointed the prow of his argosy to the regions of his hope and expectation on the seventh of August, 1679. Sailing over unknown waters, his progress was slow. Staying some time at Michilimacanac, he entered Green Bay in the early part of October, whence he sent the Griffon richly laden with furs upon her return voyage. He built a fort among the Miamies near the Saint Joseph's river, where he anxiously awaited the arrival of his vessel until December. Leaving there a small garrison, with instructions for the captain of the Griffon, he with the Chevalier De Tonti and thirty-three men departed, some in canoes upon the St. Joseph, and by portage to the Kankeekee, and others by land to the Illinois, which the whole party descended as far as a large Indian village near Lake Peoria, where they met a hospitable reception, and were freely furnished with supplies of provisions which they greatly needed. About sixty miles lower, with the consent of the natives, it was determined to build a fort and await intelligence from his vessel. Here his men became discontented and disheartened, a mutinous spirit was apparent, some deserted, among them were mechanics upon whom he relied for the construction of the boats necessary for the descent of the great river; the Indians who had been friendly, became jealous of his purpose among them, and charged him with being in alliance with their enemies, the Iroquois; and to fill the cup of calamity, news of the loss of his valued Griffon and cargo reached him in January. Yet under all these adversities La Salle's energy and courage was unbroken. By his personal influence the confidence of the natives and the fealty of his followers were again secured, when he determined to return to Frontenac Fort for assistance and supplies. Having planned an expedition to go up the great river towards its source, in his absence he left Fort Crevè Cœur, which he so named because of the adversities that beset him there, and with but three companions threaded his perilous way through the trackless wilds in safety to Canada. Here he met with new difficulties—his creditors were clamorous; the means by which he had expected to satisfy their claims had been ingulfed with his vessel: but he did not despair; his perseverance and energy gained him friends and assistance.

Among those who had accompanied him to Fort Crevè Cœur was Father Louis Hennepin, a Recollect; to him was intrusted the exploration of the upper portion of the river. It left the fort in a canoe near the end of February, 1680. Six men being the party with Father Hennepin, they descended the Illinois to the Mississippi, then full of running ice, which they ascended in despite of difficulty, delay and danger, to the falls, which received the name of Saint Anthony, to whose spiritual intercession the intent, progress, and consummation of the expedition from its commencement had been especially committed. Correctly inferring from the volume of water that it was the great drain of a vast extent of unknown territory, they intended further discovery, but were made prisoners by a band of Sioux Indians, and for a time held and treated by them as slaves. Escaping from their red masters they descended to the mouth of the Ouisconsin, and by the route of Father Marquette's coming, reached the mission at Green Bay. Ambitious of effecting La Salle's main design, he again entered the Mississippi, going as far down that river as the mouth of the Arkansas only, and not the ocean as has been asserted. Late in the autumn he reached the Illinois, and returned to Europe the following year.

De Tonti, who had been left in command at Fort Crevè Cœur, found himself in a precarious situation on account of the hostilities between the Illinois and the Iroquois. He was between the belligerent tribes, and it was no part of his purpose to side with either; and he deemed it prudent to retire to Fort Miami, which he reached in September. In the spring of 1681 La Salle rejoined him there, and peace being restored, they again reoccupied Fort Crevè Cœur. The summer of this year La Salle spent in visiting his different trading posts, and cementing the alliance with the Miamies and his new friends on the Illinois. In November, to complete his arrangements he again returned to Canada, and thence in January to Fort Crevè Cœur. On the 2d of February, 1682, he and his companions were floating with the mighty current of the great Father of Waters, occasionally stopping for amicable intercourse with the natives. They rapidly descended, every day dawning upon new wonders, and every night witnessing their watch of apprehension, until their vision was greeted on the 7th of April by the billowy expanse of the "American Sea," proving one of the surmises of Allouez to be a verity: indeed, there are those who think the other will not always remain as a mere conjecture; for men of cool heads and matured judgment, with a life-long acquaintance with the subject, and from a point of view which best enables them to make the declaration, are of opinion that the rich products of famed Cathay and furthest Ind will yet come westward, to be water-borne on the capacious bosom of the swift-rolling Mississippi. Le Page du Pratz says, that this name is the French contraction of the savage term *Meacht Chassippi*, which literally denotes the ancient Father of Rivers.

La Salle, with his little frail flotilla, exposed to all the influences of the elements, having achieved a discovery, extending on one continuous stream over more degrees of latitude than any yet accomplished, felt himself recompensed for all his previous labors, privations and disappointments; his great mind penetrated futurity, and comprehended the vast results. Ascending the river above the marshes, he landed upon the first firm ground, and took formal possession with all the solemnity of religious and military ceremony. A column was erected with the arms of France affixed, and the inscription:

"LOUIS LE GRAND,
Roi de France et Navarre, Regne;
Le neuvieme Avril, 1682,"

the whole party chanting the *Te Deum*, the *Exaudiat*, the *Domine salvum fac Regem*.

La Salle in a loud voice made the proclamation of possession and demanded the act of the notary. A cross was erected, the *Vexilla* was intoned, and they fondly hoped they had planted the germ of Christianity as well as their evidence of French sovereignty in the soil of the vast valley. A metal plate with an inscription in Latin was buried at the foot of a tree. The procès demanded was made and signed by La Metaire, the notary, and was also signed by La Salle, Father Zenobe Mambre, De Tonti, and ten others of the most prominent of the party. After staying a short time to refresh his men, he proceeded homeward, until he reached the Chickasaws, among whom on his downward voyage he had erected a small stockade which he called Fort Prud'homme, from the name of the person he had there left in charge; here he was taken ill, the result of excitement, anxiety, and fatigue he had encountered, and remained seven weeks with most of his men, sending De Tonti with the others to the Illinois to take charge of his various posts. In September he himself reached there, and some of his followers, attracted by the beauty of the country, and rightly judging they would soon be joined by more of their kindred when the result of their exploration should be known, preferred remaining; and the date of the first European residents in the great valley of the Mississippi may be stated to commence in the year 1682;—they settled at Kaskaskia and Cahokia. La Salle sent Father Zenobe to France with his report of his discovery. The first great political event consequent thereto was the claim of his Most Christian Majesty, Louis XIV., to the territory on the east bank of the river to the western limits of Spanish Florida, the English Carolinas and Virginia to the Illinois, and on the west, along the shore of the gulf to the provinces of Mexico and their eastern boundaries; and in compliment to him, this immense region received the name of Louisiana, which was subsequently divided into lower and upper; the last, commonly and first called and better known as "Les Illinois," which name is yet retained by the flourishing State, whose extent is but a portion of the territory within its original boundary.

Illinois is an Indian term, and, like most of the aboriginal appellations, is beautifully expressive, signifying a man in the flower of his age, and doubtlessly will be considered as appropriately applied by all who have witnessed the beauty of that country, the fertility of its soil, and the luxuriance of its vegetation.

La Salle having visited his trading posts, left De Tonti commandant of Fort Saint Louis and general superintendent of all his affairs, and returned to Canada for supplies. The governor of Canada, Le Ferre de la Barré, had misrepresented him in his despatches to the king, and though the Count de Frontenac, at that time in Paris, had used all his influence to counteract the impression they were intended to create, La Salle deemed it necessary to cross the Atlantic to confute all accusation and explain his plans of colonization. He arrived at the close of the year 1683 at Paris, and was well received by the Marquis de Seignelay, the minister and son of Colbert, the great prime minister of the Grand Monarque. The energy La Salle had evinced, and the comprehensive views he entertained, secured to him and towards his schemes all suitable consideration. He was selected to put in execution the design of establishing a chain of forts and posts from the mouth of the Mississippi to Canada. He had proved that he possessed the administrative qualities that fitted to command; he was also courageous, confident, and self-reliant, characteristics which failed not to beget confidence and reliance in his followers. This last peculiarity of his temperament is always of importance to a leader, but has too often been the fount of great disasters ; continued success frequently causes a neglect of the suggestions of another qualification, with which it should always be accompanied. The stirring events of history detail many examples, and the pursuits and avocations of common life constantly present them ; it was on this ruin of myriads, this rock every where so prominent, that the ardent and adventurous La Salle was most miserably wrecked. Had he heeded the whispering of prudence he had avoided the error which led to the fatal end of the career which seemed to be entering the vista of a glorious future. On the 24th July, 1684, an expedition sailed from Rochelle consisting of four vessels : one, Le Joli, a thirty-six gun frigate, commanded by Monsieur de Beaujeau. There were twenty families on board, furnished by the government with every necessary to form a colony, artificers to erect fortifications, and soldiers to protect them. The evils of a mixed command were early apparent on the voyage. The naval commander was arrogant and self-willed, and was envious of the rising reputation of La Salle.

In the West Indies, one of their vessels containing their goods for trade and mechanics' tools was taken by the Spaniards. They remained there some weeks, losing some men by fevers and recruiting others, of whom a part had been buccaneers. Leaving San Domingo on the 25th November for the Mississippi, they arrived on the 10th January to where it was thought the proper longitude had been attained, and it was proposed to alter their course northwardly for the mouth of the river. La Salle, adhering to his own computation, which made a different allowance for set of current than those of others, persisted it should be continued westwardly. He afterwards admitted that he might be wrong, and requested Beaujeau to return: he refused, and after losing another vessel in a storm, landed La Salle and his party at a bay called by the French Saint Louis, and now known as Matagorda, in the present State of Texas, seven degrees west of, and by the coast line some eight hundred miles distant from the Mississippi. He said he had fulfilled his instructions by landing them on the shore of the gulf, and sailed in the Joli, leaving La Salle to find the river as he could. La Salle took formal possession of the country, hence it was always considered by the French as part of Louisiana and included in the territory under Jefferson's treaty. In Mr. Monroe's administration the Sabine was assigned as the boundary; but the people of the great valley were never satisfied until Texas was reannexed. Having built a fort for the security of the colonists, he penetrated the country in various directions, during his absence on one of which his last remaining vessel was lost, and his movements by water were closed. In March, 1687, being near the head waters of the Trinity River, he received a lamentable death from the hands of some of his own followers, who considered him the sole cause of all their calamities. He may have been truly so; but his horrible assassination may be marked as one of the numerous instances of the blindness of passion, for it must be admitted that he was the best fitted, by his previous experience, to rescue this party of newly arrived Europeans, lost in the wilds of America, from the perils of their situation. His murderers, quarrelling soon after, killed each other.

Some of this last party of La Salle returned to their companions at the Bay of Saint Louis, others remained with the Indians and assisted them in their war against the Spaniards. Seven determined to go to the Illinois, among whom were the brother and nephew of La Salle, Father Anastatius, and Monsieur Joutel, who, upon his arrival in France, published a narrative of their last voyage and wanderings through the wilds of Texas. They, with the loss of one of their number, arrived at Fort Saint Louis in September. For prudential reasons the fate of La Salle was kept secret for a time, both in Canada and France. The mouth of the river was found by Iberville in 1699. Shortly after the discovery of the Mississippi became known in Canada, La Salle's followers, who continued at Kaskaskia and Cahokia, were joined by parties of their friends from thence and from France; every year added to their number: their trail through the wilderness was distinct; along which the adventurous voyageurs first established their trading posts, and the Canadian government soon sent soldiers for their security: various forts were erected at the most commanding points, and hamlets and villages indicated the current of civilization.

The last fort on the line from Canada to the Mississippi was Fort Chartres; placed about a mile from the river, and built with all the attention requisite to the construction of a regularly fortified place of importance, and furnished with every convenience for the officers and garrison as well as magazines for munitions and stores; there was also within it swalls an entrance to a subterranean communication with the river. The French have always been remarkable for the care they bestowed in the construction of the fortifications in their colonies; the cost of this, which was built in 1720, has been stated to have been equal to eleven millions of francs; that at Louisbourg (considered the Dunkirk of America), which was taken by the Provincials under Colonel Pepperell and the English squadron under Commodore Warren in the year 1745, employed the French troops twenty-five years in its construction, and involved an outlay of thirty millions of livres.

The protection afforded by the erection of Fort Chartres was a great attracting cause of the several little towns and villages in its vicinity. St. Genevieve was one of the first on the west bank of the Mississippi that availed itself of the advantages it secured. The early settlers there could always be certain of the means of regular communication with their European friends, receive clerical ministration, and obtain medical assistance and such needful stores as their situation required.

Considering the spare accommodation, the great inconvenience and danger attending a sea voyage at that period, and the no less deterring difficulties then consequent to the long land travel; it is surprising such thriving industrious communities of civilized Europeans should at that early day be placed on this distant and secluded frontier. The emigration here was of a very superior character; mostly agriculturists from the vicinage of the city of Paris. They had heard of the surpassing fertility of the soil, and were aware of the facilities with which it could be obtained under an easy soccage tenure, and did not remain in Canada like their brethren from the maritime parts of western France, whose trading and commercial instincts and propensities stayed them on the borders of the St. Lawrence in facile communication with the ocean.

Early in the eighteenth century emigration received a great impulse from the stimulating excitement produced by one of those epidemics of enthusiastic delusion, which occasionally occur in the progress of time, something of which has been witnessed in our day. The "Mississippi scheme," one of the several gigantic plans of the confident visionary Law, which were to have enabled France and the French people to become the recipients of the wealth of the world, certainly was advantageous to the Illinois, however different it may have been to the great majority of the duped victims who held shares when the great bubble collapsed. Were it possible that any company could now obtain and exercise the privileges and monopolies Law possessed, it might be said of him as has been said of other projectors, that he only lived a century too soon. The settlers on the Illinois never had occasion to draw from distant points the articles of first necessity. These, from the first, their industry obtained from the teeming soil on which they had transplanted themselves, not only enough for themselves, but sufficient and to spare for all new comers. Not long after the establishment of New Orleans, during the war of 1744, these settlements, responsive to a demand from thence, in a short time furnished four or five thousand barrels of corn, flour, and other provision. Kaskaskia, the pioneer of the Illinois villages, for a long time maintained its supremacy; in 1721 there were 100 houses and a convent; and in its vicinage reductions of red men, the neophytes and catechumens of their beloved "long robes." It was afterwards of greater importance, but declined from various controlling causes, and it may be considered to have been almost totally destroyed by the great flood of 1844.

In 1762 D'Abadie the Governor-general of Louisiana granted to Pierre Ligueste Lacede and his associates, under the name of the "Louisiana Fur Company," the privilege of trading with the Indians on the Missouri and west of the Mississippi: the succeeding year he ascended the river to the Illinois with several companions, among the youngest of whom were the brothers Pierre and Auguste Chouteau, whose names have been identified with the growth and prosperity, not only of the great city Lacede founded, but of the noble and then unknown territory over the western plains. Every point considered as eligible was personally visited and carefully examined with a view to select one as most suitable for his purpose for a depot, not omitting St. Genevieve, which for many years had been of importance as the centring position of the fur, peltry, and lead trade of the region: he preferred an entirely new and unoccupied place, of which he took formal possession, as his intended principal trading post, on the fifteenth day of February, 1764; and that which is now the great inland mart of the great valley, on that day received from Lacede the name of the courageous soldier, wise king, and humble Christian, Saint Louis. At this period there occurred a political event of the first importance to "the Illinois:" The Treaty of Paris, under which Great Britain received from the French all their territory east of the Mississippi, with the exception of New Orleans; which city, with all their domain west of that river was ceded to Spain. Those of the inhabitants who were by the treaty under the jurisdiction of the English government, evinced great repugnance to dwell under the drapeau of the arrogant islanders; they crossed the river in great numbers, joining their relatives on the western bank, filling and extending their towns and villages, and forming new communities. The present villages of Carondelet and Florisant are of those thus founded. They did more; with their western brethren they set up a government of their own, the spontaneous act of all, and St. Ange De Bellerive was the first governor in America elevated by the living voice of the people, under no commission or charter from any foreign king or government, and without aid or hindrance from any previously contrived machinery. He had been the commandant of the French at Fort Chartres; he crossed the river in 1765; whereupon he was invested with civil and military command over the "Upper Louisiana," and this power he most beneficently exercised and held with a firm and able hand, though legally he had no right to its sway, save the acclaim of the people. He was "every inch a governor," and no act of his, will ever militate against the advocates of popular sovereignty. His name is in benediction; his very name,—if one who has scarce a pretension to the most imperfect knowledge of the elegant language in which it is written can be permitted to say,—"Saint Ange De Bellerive," may be rendered as having been, the Blessed Angel of the beautiful water-side. He, supported by the unanimous voice of his constituents, did and performed every act and deed deemed necessary or proper for the common weal of all, without fear, favor, or affection. His numerous grants of land, to their honor be it spoken, were afterwards confirmed by the Spaniards, and again reconfirmed by the United States commissioners, notwithstanding the efforts of the speculating land-sharks who sought to oppugn their validity. In 1768 a body of Spanish troops under Rious arrived at St. Louis with the claim of possession for his Catholic Majesty; it was peacefully admitted, but the authority of St. Ange continued with undiminished force until 1770. Mr. Chambers of the Missouri Republican, in his valuable Annual Review (1854), adverting hereto, says: "This anomaly may be explained by the condition of political affairs in New Orleans, it not being till 1769, after serious collisions, that under O'Reilly, the representative of the King of Spain, the transfer so unpalatable to the French was finally acquiesced in at the capital of the country." Pedro Piernas was the first lawful governor of Upper Louisiana; he took possession towards the end of 1770; the Spanish rule continued through Cruzat, De Leyba, Perex, Trudeau, and ended with Delassus in 1804. By the treaty of San Ildefonso in 1800, France again became possessed of the vast territory of Louisiana; and the sagacious Jefferson, by the treaty of 30th of April, 1803, added this empire to the domain of our Republic, at the insignificant cost of fifteen millions of dollars. Scarcely any act of our government has been fraught with greater beneficial results, both immediate and prospective; or met (in some sections of our country then influential) a more malign reception; the bitterest denunciators, the most active stirrers of strife were they, who claimed to be followers of the Prince of Peace, the political parsons then, as from the beginning, and now, the pests of the society that support them; they hesitated not to announce and denounce from their "sacred desks" the chief executive of their country as a perjured tributary of Antichrist—the man of sin—conveniently transferring for the time, their habitual appellation of the Pope, to the ruler of the French, and knowing, and caring not to know, that the spiritual supremacy of the Bishop of

Rome being not of the kingdoms of this world, was as effective in the depths of a French dungeon, as from the hills of his eternal city. Under Jefferson's treaty and a consequent act of Congress, Captain Amos Stoddard, on the 10th March 1804, as agent for the United States, received from Don Carlos Dehault Delassus, the Spanish Lieutenant-governor, the possession of Upper Louisiana, the keys of the government house, the public archives and property: the flag of Spain descended, and the ensign of our Union, amid salvos of artillery, waved free in the breeze over the *western* bank of the great river. At this period the inhabitants of the territory were nearly all of French lineage (there being then but two Anglo-American families in St. Louis); they, having again been, without any voice of their own, transferred as subjects to another system of government, were not without the natural feeling of apprehension which such a change must ever produce; but the conduct of the United States agents, and the character of the fast-coming new emigrants soon dissipated their anxiety. The first families arriving among them from the States were not the Bostonians of their tradition, being from Virginia, Maryland and Kentucky; whose social, frank and open manners most nearly resembled their own, so different from the arrogant English of the Canadas, and others with whom some among them had the unpleasant experience of previous intercourse: they rendered a cheerful fealty to that government whose institutions, in accordance to the legend of its national emblazonment, are so happily constituted to absorb and blend into one homogeneous people the varieties of different nations. Should any one be disposed to doubt this, let them, or any one of them, point to their exemplar of a community of more law-observing and law-abiding citizens than can be found among the old French villages within the bounds of the State of Missouri.

All Louisiana north of the thirty-third parallel was designated by Congress in 1804 as the District of Louisiana, and the executive power of the Territory of Indiana was extended over the new District, and accordingly was first exercised by Gen. William Henry Harrison, then governor. The following year the District was changed to the Territory of Louisiana. James Wilkinson became its governor, and with Return J. Meigs and J. B. C. Lucas, the judges of the Superior Court, were the Legislature of the Territory; this system, with occasional change of person, remained for some time. In 1812 it took the name of the Missouri Territory; there was a Governor and a Legislative Assembly, the upper branch consisting of nine councillors, selected by the governor from double that number, nominated to him by the lower branch, and was represented in Congress by a delegate. The first governor of the Missouri Territory was Merriwether Lewis, and Edward Hempstead the delegate.

By the act of the 6th March, 1820, the terms of which being accepted by the representatives of the people in convention held at St. Louis on the 19th of the following July, Missouri was admitted as one of the sovereign States of this Union. The first Legislature met at St. Louis in 1820; the seat of government was transferred to St. Charles, and remained there until its removal to the City of Jefferson, in 1826. Alexander McNair was the first governor of the *State* of Missouri.

From the first settlement of the French in "Les Illinois," to the period when their descendants became citizens of the different Republican States among which their great territory has been divided, there were but few incidents arising immediately among them of special notice. They pursued the even tenor of their peaceful way; instructed their children in the precepts of their religion, and by their example of the practice of them secured the continuance of their living faith; they mostly cultivated the ground of their common fields contiguous to their villages; their traders trafficked with the Indians, and procured for them from Canada and New Orleans the textile fabrics and such other articles of European manufacture as they desired: they had not much money among them, they needed but little; almost all the transactions of a business character were effected through the medium of "peltry-bons," and the bills payable in this pecunia, so nearly allied to the primitive origin of the word, were every where current, and were far better and more substantially based, than the greater portion of the pretty promises to pay, now so prevalent with all their incongruous superadveniences of mythological device, medallion heroes and statesmen, beautiful belles and ugly usurers. It has always been noted as worthy of remark, that the Indians better preserved the terms of amity with the French, than with any other European nation. With them they seldom had trouble; when it did arise, it was usually traceable to English incitement. Thus, the death of the famous Pontiac in 1769; who, being on a visit to St. Ange at St. Louis, accepted an invitation to an Indian feast near Cahokia, during which he was killed by a Kaskaskia Indian, instigated by a British trader. His body was taken to his French friends in St. Louis, and there by them honorably buried. The French were unsuccessful in their endeavor to avert the consequences of this murder from their neighbors; for the Ottawas, in revenge for the loss of their chief, nearly exterminated the Illinois nation. Again, in 1779, during our war of Independence, when France was our valued ally, runners brought intelligence that the British meditated an assault upon St. Louis. Heed was given to the information, and such additions made to their defence as was in their power. In May of the following year, fourteen hundred well armed savages and one hundred and forty British regulars arrived on the opposite side of the river, and lay in ambush unknown to the St. Louians; on the 26th of that month they crossed, and killing some fifteen or twenty whom they found in the common field outside of the stockade, they advanced upon the village; but though taken by surprise, the French rushed to their barriers and met the foe with such a manful and determined resistance, that all his efforts to carry them were ineffective; and after experiencing great loss, the allied savages retreated towards Lake Michigan, as stealthily as they came. This first attempt to pass a ligature around the great artery of the West was as unsuccessful as the later trial at New Orleans. Mr. Chambers states, "The particulars of this defence reflect very great credit on the villagers. They numbered only about one hundred and fifty males fit for service. At the commencement of the attack, the Spanish troops, whose proper business it was to lead in the defence, ran off and secreted themselves in a garret. Leyba, the Lieutenant-governor, acted in a manner to show that he had been in traitorous communication with the enemy."

While the undaunted villagers were pouring grape

from the cannon's mouth on the host of assailants, Leyba made his appearance 'trundled on a wheel-barrow,' and ordered the guns to be spiked. Before this, he had discouraged all rumors of the approaching invasion, imprisoning those who set them afloat, and had sold all the powder in the place, on which he could lay his hands. An account of his procedure was transmitted to Galvez, then Governor of Louisiana, who immediately superseded him. After all fair deductions, enough remains to show that Leyba was unworthy of the trust confided to him, and that the defenders of St. Louis deserve to be held in honorable remembrance for their bravery." It was an epoch whence other occurring matters in these peaceful communities were dated, as afterwards this year 1780 was generally spoken of as "*L'année du grand coup.*" There were some other periods during the continuance of the Spanish rule considered sufficiently out of the course of ordinary events as to obtain a general definitive; as 1785, "*L'année des grandes eaux,*" from an unprecedented rise of the river, and since only equalled by the devastating floods of 1844 and '52. 1788, "*L'année des dix bateaux,*" from the arrival at one time of a fleet of ten barges, who had associated for mutual protection against the river-pirates on their voyage from New Orleans. 1798, the arrival of galleys with Spanish troops as "*L'année des galeres.*" 1799, the thermometer indicating 32° below zero, was "*L'année du grand hiver.*" 1801, the remembered scourge of the small-pox, "*L'année de la Picotte.*"

St. Louis, though among the younger, has far outstripped and outgrown her sister villages in the matters of more material progress, but not in the sense of Pharaoh's dream as interpreted by the young Hebrew captive (no, not captive—Joseph was the captive of his brethren, but was the bargained, and sold, and money-purchased bondman of the Midianite merchant; and of Potiphar, the chamberlain of Pharaoh); some of them are yet flourishing "on the very bank of the river in green places." Of these St. Genevieve is not the least attractive; originally built upon the site of one long occupied by the Peoria Indians, and possessing all the advantages usually sought for in those days of primitive habits and moderate desires. The first buildings were erected close to the water-side, but in the memorable L'année des grandes eaux were swept away by the great Father of Waters, leaving the vestiges of that destructive inundation visible as late as 1832. Warned by this bitter experience, the inhabitants rebuilt their dwellings and business houses on a more elevated and pleasant situation: above their new town are several springs of extraordinary volume of water, the favored encamping ground of their long lingering red friends. The French and Spanish emigrants, the earliest pioneers in the exploration and settlement of our western wilderness, congregated in villages for greater security, and in accordance with their social instincts, as far as they could, they made their American homes to resemble those they had left in their father-lands. Unlike the Anglo-American, who, armed with axe and rifle, plunges into the primeval forest fearless and alone, building himself a little cabin and clearing a patch for the cultivation of the indispensable "soothing weed," is content to lead the life of a solitaire, until the tide of civilization invades his seclusion, and settles the waste places around him,—the natives of southern Europe, no less brave and adventurous, adhere to their innate and irradicable love of companionship, and with a facility of adaptation to new modes of life peculiar to themselves, cultivate every where the tastes, the habits, and social qualities, that distinguish them from all other people. It is owing to these characteristics, that the French especially have exhibited such a remarkable aptitude in contentedly and peacefully dwelling near and among our aboriginal tribes, and securing their faithful attachment, confidence, and affectionate esteem. They resided in villages and cultivated the earth, and pastured their cattle in common enclosures, the common property of all. These fields were divided into separate allotments, in which each proprietor planted and tended such products as he preferred; but if there was any difference of ownership or taste in the growth and culture of contiguous plants, when the harvest was gathered, it was freely offered to the enjoyment of all. Thus they peacefully and happily lived until some time after the appearance of the wonder which has contributed so much to the improvement of the West.

In 1817 the General Pike, a Louisville low-pressure steamboat, first startled the quiet waters of the Upper Mississippi, reaching St. Louis on the second day of August in that year, under the command of Captain Jacob Reed. Two years afterwards, the Independence, Captain Nelson, ascended the Missouri, demonstrating that even the current of that more turbulent stream could be overcome by the new giant motor. This many of the old voyageurs and others had doubted, but they now saw that the days of the slow-progressing keel-boat and barge were about to pass, and with them the occupation of their previous life. Nothing has contributed so much to effect the surprising change noticeable within the last thirty years, as the introduction of the bateau-à-vapeur, not only over the face of the country, but in the manners, pursuits and occupations of the whole western people. For a time, the villagers, wedded to their old customs, were content with the slow and toilsome progress of their keel-boat and barge. To the successful prosecution of voyages in such craft, the services of the patient, abstemious, and light-hearted voyageurs were, until their business was broken up by the general use of steam, deemed absolutely indispensable. They were so thoroughly acquainted with the great rivers of the West, knowing every highland and jutting promontory, every rock, sunken tree, and shifting sand-bar, and every cleft and cavern on their shores. No danger appalled or difficulty disheartened them. Always cheerful and alert, they lightened their labor at the oar, and enlivened the long dreary nights by song and dance, and traditional tales of love, or war or daring adventure, giving a romantic or historical interest to the wild and comparatively tenantless scenes along which they passed. But the keel-boat, the barge, and the lithe, athletic and joyous voyageurs, may be said to have disappeared, and with them the limited desires and few and simple wants, which for a long series of years they so abundantly supplied.

In 1817 St. Genevieve contained a goodly number of American families, and a much greater proportion of French; many of whom were descended from the best blood of France, and retained, in a remarkable degree, the refinement, the courtesy, and the ardent temperament which so pre-eminently distinguished their countrymen of the last century. To their hereditary gayety and inborn politeness, their close and frequent intercourse of late years with their American neighbors, have imparted not a little of the solidity and progressive energy which characterize the latter. Their manners and conversation, always sprightly and agreeable, rendered their society at home or abroad, universally and at all seasons, most attractive and acceptable. Those parents who possessed the time and means, gave to their children the best education the circumstances of place and period permitted; all, however, received moral and religious instruction from the faithful pastor of the church, and acquired, from the constant association of every class, an amenity of deportment more captivating than any learning without it,—a deference for the feelings and wishes of others, which never failed to secure it for themselves. No matter how poor or how ignorant they at first to some appeared to be, they were rich and instructed, possessing a grace so winning, an address so fascinating, a bearing so manly, that it levelled all distinctions of birth and education, and not to admire and respect them was an impossibility. The men of this interesting society were proverbial for their probity, for their gentleness and devotion as husbands, fathers and friends, while the women were no less remarkable for their warm and ingenuous affections, their purity and scrupulous neatness, their untiring attention to their household duties, and for all the little nameless offices of kindness, whose ministrations enter so largely into the sum of domestic felicity. Their many attractive little fêtes and observances cannot fail to make a favorable impression on a stranger. One, a custom common to all classes, so touching and beautiful, so instinct with gracious sentiment and genuine refinement, that the portraiture of excellent friends would be wanting in its crowning grace, and perhaps most characteristic trait, if it were omitted. The oldest male member of each family is looked up to by all who compose it, as its patriarch and head; and on the morning of every new year all its branches, young and old, gather around him, and each one kneeling in turn begs his blessing for the coming year. The venerable sire first extends his arms over them and says, in an affectingly solemn and affectionate voice, "My children, is there peace between you all?" If answered affirmatively, as it always is, he, placing his hand on the head of each, gives the much-valued blessing; this exquisite usage has the happiest effect in preventing and healing family feuds; for, if difficulties occur, all are interested in their disappearance, they must be reconciled before the year expires, else the erring parties would be deprived of the annual benediction so piously and so hopefully looked forward to by all, and the withholding of which is considered not merely a stigma, but one of the heaviest calamities that could befall them. Can the vapid morning receptions, or the glittering soirées of our eastern cities welcome the incoming of the new year with a more attractive beauty, or confer more enduring benefits? The people of this little community paid a more than Spartan reverence to old age, and it differed not whether it was arrayed in rags, or clothed in the costliest apparel. The silvery sheen of gray hairs seemed in their eyes as a halo of glory, and to claim for the form of feebleness and decrepitude they covered a sort of devotional respect, originating, not in the mere sympathy and compassion which helplessness seldom fails to awaken, but from a feeling, that, having reached the last resting-places of this imperfect existence and being purified from its stains, they were almost within the portals of the true and perfect life to come, and already appeared imbued with a portion of its unearthly and inconceivable purity and splendor. The mutual kind love and esteem subsisting between the master or mistress and their servants, are only surpassed by the relation of parents and children. The tender and faithful remembrance of those who have passed before them with the sign of faith to their peaceful rest, is a beautiful instance of the enduring affection, always observable among them.

Such were the people among whom Dr. Linn's lot in life was cast, and with whom himself and family long lived so happily, and who are left the beloved guardians of his mortal remains. At St. Genevieve is a convent founded in 1832, by a wealthy lady, a descendant of the last European governor of Upper Louisiana. Attached thereto, is an academy of great excellence, in charge of the Sisters, for the education of young ladies in the different branches of useful knowledge, and all the accomplishments usually deemed necessary to a female in polite society. The present Mother Superior is a jewel from the Emerald Isle of unusual intellect and administrative capacity, of great and varied attainments, and being specially educated herself for communicating knowledge to others, has with these advantages the natural tact so useful to a teacher; a commanding personal appearance and deportment, and the most attractive manners. Parents and pupils all speak the praise of these sisters. This is written by one who is a Methodist, and surely may be considered impartial, who had children to educate, and was as an anxious mother desirous to select the *best* school where the moral instruction, health and deportment of the pupils would receive the requisite attention, as well as learning and accomplishments. She knew of several, and could have had choice of any in the land; this she deemed the best, and although warned by some of her friends that the religion of her daughter would be interfered with, has had no reason to regret her choice, but on the contrary, is gratefully thankful. Her daughter received an excellent education, at the St. Genevieve convent, and soon after leaving that institution, became a member of the Methodist Church.

CHAPTER II.

On the first day of July, 1818, Dr. Linn was married to the only daughter of Mr. John Relfe, of Virginia, whose early death (at the age of 29) cut short a life which his attainments and acknowledged abilities promised to adorn and render useful to his country. His son, Dr. James Relfe, of Washington County, Missouri, was several years a representative in Congress from that State.

Providence, in depriving Mrs. Linn and her brother of a father in their early life, yet left them the inestimable blessing of a devoted and most intelligent mother, who was descended from an ancient family in Scotland, and had received from nature a character of singular firmness. Her personal beauty and highly cultivated mind led to eligible offers of a second marriage, which, though only twenty-seven years of age, she declined, and made the care and education of her children the sole object of her existence. Educated herself in the most intelligent circles of the day, and eminently pious, her capacity as a guide and instructress was equal to her anxiety as a mother. Many of her declining days were passed at the house of her son-in-law, in whose charitable ministrations to the sick and distressed she deeply sympathized. He constantly said that her religion and pure benevolence brought blessings upon the household and those around it.

Immediately after he established himself in St. Genevieve, Dr. Linn commenced the practice of his profession with the most unwearied devotion, and derived the greatest pleasure in witnessing the relief his rare medical skill gave to poor suffering humanity. He was no respector of persons in his practice; the poor and lowly received his unwearied attention with the same zeal that it was extended to the wealthy and aristocratic. The destitute widow and orphan, and all other indigent persons obtained his medicine and personal attention, knowing that they would never be required to pay for them. Dr. Linn had a large press in his house which was called "the closet for the poor," and which contained every thing necessary to add to the comfort of the sick who were unable to provide for themselves. One day, a wine merchant who lived near the doctor, said to Mrs. Linn, "Do your family use all the wine your husband sends for during the sickly season? I should think you would have enough to bathe in, but I believe every drop of it goes to the sick who are not able to procure it for themselves." The doctor had a very extensive practice in three counties, and was frequently called to St. Louis to visit the sick. He loved his profession and attached great responsibility to it. Night and day he would watch over his patients with intense solicitude, as long as his physical powers would permit, and not unfrequently did he need assistance on returning home, when exhausted from watching over and administering to the wants of the sick and dying.

When it became evident that the Asiatic cholera had taken its direction towards this side of the Atlantic, and while as yet all attention was absorbed in the fatality of its ravages in Europe, Dr. Linn opened a correspondence with medical men abroad, who were familiar with the symptoms it presented, the treatment and remedies most successfully used, and the theories held in relation to it. He received from various sources a mass of information in advance of its appearance here, and was thus prepared to use and disseminate such information, and to grapple with the terrible foe upon its advent and desolating march over our continent.

When the scourge at length reached the Atlantic cities, and it was impossible to doubt its malign presence in New York, Dr. Linn immediately published in the form of a circular, a history of the disease and its peculiar effects upon the human system, and he warned the people of Missouri and Illinois that it would ere long sweep like a desolating blast over their homes. He enjoined them to be prepared to resist its visit by observing the premonitory symptoms which he indicated as its attendants, and assured them that its inroads could be arrested and life saved.

The recipe he had received from foreign faculties was composed of ingredients so simple and accessible, that the poorest as well as those in the most secluded corners of the States could obtain and keep them ready for use. He also urged them to dispel their fears as far as practicable, as fear was a great predisposing cause of the cholera, by rapidly enervating the physical power.

Owing to these investigations and timely counsels, the strides of the pestilence were arrested on both sides of the Mississippi River, its fatal course controlled by the distant hand of medical science and the benevolent discernment of one of its votaries. The foresight which provided against its advent before it had left the shores of another hemisphere, elevates the skilful physician from the position of individual merit to the rank of philanthropist, whose unselfish toils ask to be repaid only by the benefit bestowed upon the human family. To the latest period of Dr. Linn's life he derived the most lively satisfaction from dwelling on the vast number of letters from different parts of Missouri and Illinois, which were addressed to him by persons pouring forth the deepest feelings of gratitude for the medical advice imparted to them through his timely warning. They did not hesitate to say that they believed the diffusion of this information was the cause of saving of the lives of hundreds of persons; for previous to its reception they were all paralyzed with horror at the approach of the disease; but when they saw those circulars from one who had attained so high a reputation as Dr. Linn, they became inspired with hope and courage.

It was a cold and very disagreeable morning in October, 1832, when a gentleman, a citizen of St. Genevieve, came riding rapidly to the door of Dr. Linn's house, and calling to him, said that a steamboat had left an unfortunate stranger very ill on the bank of the river, a little distance from town: that he appeared from his violent struggles to have the cramp, and that his cries for assistance were truly distressing. No person would approach him, for by doing so they thought it would seal their own doom, not doubting that he was a victim of the cholera. "Now, good Dr. Linn," the gentleman continued, "if you decline doing any thing for the stranger, no other person will venture to aid him, and it is dreadful to think of his dying on the cold, wet earth, deprived of assistance, and so many persons near him!" Without an instant's hesitation, the Doctor replied that he would take charge of the invalid; and looking with great affection on his wife and children, he said, "My dear wife, the time is at hand when it becomes necessary for you to take our children, and without delay hasten to the country, to avoid this strange and awful scourge which is about to visit us; my duty is to remain here and do all I can for the sick." Mrs. Linn, looking with affection on her noble and self-sacrificing husband, replied—"The time has indeed arrived when I too must do my duty, and that is to stay with my blessed husband and relieve him as far as it is in my power, in watching over and nursing the sick. Dr. Linn fondly embraced his wife, saying, "Such a determination is worthy of you, my beloved wife, and I should have expected it from you; now let us hasten to do something for the suffering stranger whom Providence has intrusted to our keeping." In vain, however, were all their efforts to get any person or any sort of conveyance to bring the sick man to their house. Such was the dreadful panic which had seized the inhabitants of the place (believing the cholera was as infectious as ever the plague had been), they could not think of Dr. Linn going near the diseased person, or that he should be brought to town. The Doctor finding all his servants had fled from home on hearing his intention, requested one of his students,

Mr. Wilkerson, to assist him, as he thought they together might be able to convey the patient in a blanket from the river to his house. While they went on this mission of mercy, Mrs. Linn commenced to prepare, in great haste, a room for her expected guest; but was interrupted by a number of persons collected around the house, who clamorously assured her that her husband would not be permitted to bring a person in their midst with the cholera, for contagion and death followed in its wake. Serious apprehensions entered her mind that they might molest the Doctor and his kind-hearted student; for she saw in the wild excitement of the panic-stricken people that they were not responsible for their acts. Her fears were increased when she saw one of her most intimate acquaintances with a torch in his hand, and heard him exclaim, "Mrs. Linn, let me see the Doctor turn the corner of that street, and I will apply this torch to his office* and burn it to its foundation." Another still more energetically called out, "Let us tear down the house and save our community from the pestilence." It was in vain she attempted to be heard, they were beyond the bounds of reason; their ears open to but one word, *cholera;* and that word closed all the avenues to charity, humanity and hospitality. While thus contesting the point, a little

* Rooms were prepared in Dr. Linn's office for the reception of those sick with the cholera.

colored messenger whom she had sent to inform her husband of the threats that had been made, returned in haste to inform his mistress that Dr. Linn and Mr. Wilkerson were approaching, bearing the sick to the house. This struck the crowd with panic, and as if by magic it broke and dispersed, scattering in every direction, terror giving speed to its retreat. When the Doctor arrived, not one remained to prevent his entrance to the house.

Life was not extinct in the unfortunate man, and he was soon made as comfortable as the case permitted; his first words to Mrs. Linn, who was standing near his couch, were uttered in a voice of agony: "Madam, if you wish God to bless you in your dying hour, pray give me something warm to drink." Mr. Hamlin (the name of the stranger) received all the attention that could be bestowed upon him, until death terminated his sufferings.

Three other victims of the cholera, left by steamers on the bank of the river, were taken in charge and nursed. During this time we all enjoyed perfect health. This circumstance, with the constant assurance of their kind physician, that the cholera was not infectious, dispelled the fears of the citizens of St. Genevieve, and they again became unwearied in kindness and attention to the sick and afflicted, hospitable and humane.

CHAPTER III

Dr. Linn was frequently urged by his friends to suffer his name to be used as a candidate for Congress. His popularity rendered his election certain. He declined, however, such friendly proposals, replying to them truly that he had no political aspirations. Soon after the lamented decease of the Hon. S. Pettis, a committee of gentlemen from St. Louis waited upon Dr. Linn, to request him to become a candidate for Congress as the successor of this gentleman. He again stated his unwillingness to enter into public life, and respectfully declined their friendly overtures. Once, and once only, he was prevailed upon to serve one session in the State Senate of Missouri, for the purpose of procuring the passage of a law beneficial to the southern part of the State.

In 1833, his reputation as a physician had become so extensive, and the demands on his time so constant, that his health became impaired from the fatigue he underwent. His friends and family became so much alarmed on his account, that they induced him to accept an appointment tendered to him by General Jackson, to act as one of three commissioners appointed to settle the old French land claims in Missouri. The change of occupation and relaxation from professional duties, it was trusted, would restore his health; and he consented to become a member of the Board.

The satisfaction he gave to all parties interested in these lands, by the mode in which his duties were discharged, added to the confidence of the public in his character, and enabled him, when in the Senate of the United States, to demonstrate the justice of the adjudication, and to procure from Congress an equitable law for the final adjustment of them all. Nevertheless, this new field of duties, instead of bringing the repose and change of life he so much needed, plunged him into the discharge of a more arduous and perilous professional life. His society was sought by all social circles with great eagerness. To the aged he was ever a most welcome guest; his animated conversation charmed them, and the enjoyment he received in hearing them relate events of bygone days, made them feel, as they expressed themselves, "young again." To those in the meridian of life his society possessed a general charm—his fine conversational powers, his winning manners, his versatility of talent, drawn from a mind that was a perfect storehouse of knowledge, could not be excelled by any one. By young persons his appearance was hailed with delight; his manly beauty, his graceful deportment, with his great desire to contribute every thing in his power to amuse or instruct them, made them anxious for his society. The Doctor's passionate attachment to children made their pure young hearts spring forth to meet his affectionate embrace wherever they beheld him. As it became necessary for him to live in St. Louis to attend to his duties as commissioner, he removed with his family to that city in June, 1833. A month after their departure from St. Genevieve, the cholera broke out in the most frightful form in St. Louis. Little could be done by the Board in a time of death and distress, and he devoted himself night and day to the victims of the pestilence. In the month of September his friends in St. Genevieve sent an express, entreating him to return to them, if it was only for a few days, informing him that many of his most valued friends had been swept from the world within a few days by the cholera, and that the deepest gloom hung over the village. They declared "that the united voice of every citizen implored their kind friend and successful physician to come and give them medical aid, that if mortal man could save them from the cholera he could." The Doctor was not proof to such an appeal: concealing from his family the cause of his departure, he went immediately to relieve his friends.

Many of the citizens when describing the effect of his arrival among them, said, "The very sight of Dr. Linn inspired hope and confidence, and they felt he was like an angel of mercy come to restore health and happiness to them, through the blessing of God." Taking little rest for twelve days and nights, the Doctor attended constantly to the sick and dying. At length he was seized with the cholera himself. Believing he would die, he despatched a faithful French servant, Antoine, for his wife. His greatest earthly hope was to see her before his death. In less time than the distance was ever travelled before, Antoine reached St. Louis, at eight o'clock in the morning. It required but a few moments for Mrs. Linn to take her departure to join her husband. As there was no steamboat to leave St. Louis for some hours, a friend brought an excellent horse and carriage to her, and offered to accompany her. Thanking him for his kindness, she preferred going with Antoine, as she knew she could accelerate the journey more with her servant than with any other person. Governor Dodge was at that time in the city, but unfortunately had walked out on business. As the exigency of her summons made every moment precious, she sent a messenger for him and hurried on her way. The road being better on the Illinois than the Missouri side of the river, they crossed the Mississippi at St. Louis and travelled at a very rapid rate; but night came on when they were still three miles from the ferry-house opposite St. Genevieve. A slow fine rain had been falling all day, and it now became so intensely dark that the nearest object could not be seen, and it was only by the flashes of lightning which now and then lit up the heavens, that they could see they were still in the road. At length Antoine told Mrs. Linn that there was a thick wood, more than a mile long, through which they must pass before they reached the ferry-house; that it was intersected with a great number of sloughs putting back from the river; that it was perilous to pursue the road in the darkness and storm, but that if she would permit him to turn back a little distance, he could find a road that led to a small village, where she could remain until daylight, and reach St. Genevieve early in the morning. Mrs. Linn implored him not to think of doing so, but to remember his promise to her husband to hasten her journey without any delay: that he must now keep on at all hazards, for she would not stop unless forced to do so until she was under the same roof with her husband. Antoine then gave her the reins and went in advance, feeling for the road through the woods a short distance at a time, and, as he found it, called to her and she drove up to him. In this manner, groping their way, Antoine in advance, they proceeded until they passed the woods, and reached the ferry-house.

Although saturated with the continued rain, and very much bruised by the limbs and low branches of the trees through which she had passed, Mrs. L. was so absorbed in agonizing apprehensions for her husband, that she was insensible to the injuries she had received and the discomfort of her person. On entering the ferry-house, a number of persons were found assembled in a large room,—many of them victims of the cholera—three were dying. Mrs. L. instantly requested the ferryman to take her across the Mississippi without delay. He pointed to the dreadful condition of his family, and told her it was utterly impossible to do so. He could not leave them, adding that the night was too dark and tempestuous to attempt crossing the river. In great distress she exclaimed, "Is there no one here who for the love of the Blessed Virgin will assist me over the river to my dying husband?" Immediately a fine-looking young girl rose from the bedside of one of the dying persons where she had been kneeling, and said, "Mrs. Linn, I will take you over with the assistance of Antoine, if you will go in a skiff." Her father, the ferryman, objected in the most positive terms to the attempt. The young woman remonstrated with him saying, "My father, do you not remember all that good Dr. Linn did for us when my mother died, and the great trouble he underwent when my brother James was so long sick, and that he never charged us for what he did? indeed I cannot refuse to take his wife to him when he may be dying." "Go, Margaret," said her father, "and may the saints protect you." Mrs. Linn, Margaret and Antoine, hastened to the river. The night continued intensely dark and the thunder rolled terrifically, but the rain had ceased, and flashes of lightning illuminated the water and the objects around them. They entered the skiff, and Margaret directed Antoine to take the steering oar while she used the paddles. At a short distance from the shore the waves filled the boat and it sank, fortunately in shallow water. They waded to the bank, Antoine dragging the skiff with him. Mrs. Linn persuaded him to empty the water, and prepare for another endeavor to cross the river. Margaret directing him to take the paddles, said she would manage the steering oar, and get safely across, although the wind was very high. Again they embarked in the skiff, and in a few moments were rapidly gliding over the water. As they approached the Missouri shore, they discovered that the skiff was leaking very fast. Margaret told Mrs. Linn that she would find a tin bucket under the seat, and that she must use it with all her strength in throwing the water out of the skiff, or it would sink and all would be lost. Mrs. Linn followed the instructions of the admirable girl, and the powerful use Antoine made of the paddles brought them safely to the shore. They had but abandoned the skiff an instant when it filled in deep water. Mrs. Linn urged Margaret to go with her into St. Genevieve and remain until daylight, but the kind-hearted girl replied, "Oh, I must return as soon as possible to my suffering family." Being near the house of a friend on the river bank, Mrs. Linn procured a good boat, and two stout men to take Margaret back to her father. She pressed her to receive money for the great services she had rendered, but the noble girl positively refused, and said, "that which she had done was for the sake of her religion and the debt of gratitude she owed Dr. Linn."

Mrs. Linn was repaid for the risks she had encountered by finding her husband still living, and that hopes were entertained of his recovery. Ill as he was, he was inexpressibly rejoiced to behold her, and prayed God to spare his life for the sake of his wife and children. Governor Dodge reached St. Genevieve the following morning, and told Mrs. Linn that he had frequently overtaken Indians running from him with all the fleetness for which they are remarkable, but he should never again try to overtake a wife flying to seek a sick husband. He had left St. Louis half an hour after her, and although mounted on a fine horse, had tried in vain to overtake her

CHAPTER IV.

The day before Dr. Linn was taken ill, his predecessor in the United Sates Senate, Col. Alexander Buckner, and his wife, both died of the cholera. Immediately numerous petitions were sent from different parts of Southern Missouri to Gov. Dunklin, urging him to select Dr. Linn to fill the vacancy occasioned by the death of Col. Buckner (in the U. S. Senate). A large number of Whigs signed these petitions, stating that they knew a *Democrat* must fill the office, and they preferred Dr. Linn to any other man of that party, as they knew he would attend to the business of his political opponents before Congress as faithfully as he would discharge his duty to his democratic constituents. Before Dr. Linn was sufficiently restored to health to leave the hospitable mansion of his friend, the Hon. John Scott, in St. Genevieve (where he had been attended with unwearied kindness by that gentleman and every member of his family), he received the appointment of U. S. Senator from Gov. Dunklin, which was confirmed by the unanimous vote of the Missouri Legislature, as soon as that body convened.

One of the agreeable anticipations he had indulged in taking his seat in the U. S. Senate was, the opportunity it would afford him to cultivate an intercourse with Gen. Jackson, who had been the hero of his heart's warmest admiration from his youth. He had frequently expressed the hope that Gen. Jackson would be elected to the presidency. In 1823, when Gen. Jackson was elected to the U. S. Senate from the State of Tennessee, Dr. Linn said at a large dinner party at the Hon. John Scott's, in St. Genevieve, where there were present several distinguished politicians, that he firmly believed the election of Gen. Jackson at that time to the Senate was the precursor of his being elected to the presidency in a few years. His friends laughed at his enthusiastic admiration of the Hero of New Orleans, and Judge Pope of Illinois remarked to him—"You never will be able to find seven votes in Missouri or Illinois that would sustain Gen. Jackson for that high station." Dr. Linn replied, that such was the confidence he had in the sound judgment of his countrymen, that he would be willing to pledge his life that before the expiration of ten years, no political men in either Missouri or Illinois would be sustained, who were not in favor of Gen. Jackson for the presidency. In five years the Doctor's prediction was verified.

Diffident of his powers in public debate, Dr. Linn rarely spoke in the Senate during the first few years he was a member of that body, but devoted his attention to the private claims of Missouri, in which he was very fortunate; for, of the number of bills he presented to the Senate for his constituents he never lost one.

He possessed the respect and esteem of every member of the Senate without regard to political opinions. The highly gifted and liberal senator, Mr. Crittenden, from his native State of Kentucky, was his warm friend, and said of him, that Dr. Linn possessed a high order of intellect; was resolute, courageous, and ardent in all his pursuits. A decided party man, he afterwards participated largely in the business of the Senate and the conflicts of its debates, but there was a kindness and benignity about him, that, like polished armor, turned aside all feeling of ill-will or animosity. He had political opponents in the Senate, but not an enemy.

The eloquent W. C. Preston, senator from South Carolina, once said to a gentleman in Philadelphia, "Dr. Linn is the only Democrat I should be distressed to hear had become a candidate for the Presidency; for, good Whig as I am, I could not bring myself to vote against such a pure and noble patriot as I know him to be, and one who loves his country with a zeal rarely equalled and never surpassed."

The great Western statesman, Mr. Clay, in a letter addressed to Mrs. Linn, expressing his grateful feelings for Dr. Linn's great kindness in his medical attention on his son, observed, "The greatest boon you can ask from Heaven, my dear madam, is that your son may resemble his father, who commands the admiration and gains the love of all that know him." If such were the sentiments of Dr. Linn's political opponents towards him during exciting times in the Senate, what may be imagined were the feelings of his own political friends, where not a cloud of political difference could cast a shadow over the warm sunshine of their friendship?

During the first session Dr. Linn was in the Senate, he became acquainted with our present Chief Magistrate, Gen. Pierce, then the much-admired, and youngest member in the House of Representatives. The Doctor deemed himself most fortunate in living in the same mess with Gen. Pierce, for whom he soon formed a warm friendship; he loved to dwell on the rare combinations in his friend's character—of the cool, discriminating judgment of the North, with the warm chivalry of Southern feeling. Little then could he imagine that the friend in whose society he spent so many happy hours, was to be the best friend of his bereaved family in adversity, when he slept in the

6

tomb—not only to aid his only son on the field of battle in a distant country, but to kindly extend his friendship to him from the highest station on earth.

When Gen. Pierce became a member of the U. S. Senate, the pleasure of Dr. Linn's intercourse with him was increased by forming the acquaintance of Mrs. Pierce, whose pure and lovely character made the Doctor esteem and admire her as one of the first ladies in our country, a model for her sex. Ardent in his feelings, the deep attachment he felt for some of the senators, with the kindest regard for all of them, appeared daily to increase until the time of his death—he felt, with all the sensibility of his noble nature, the kindness with which they had all treated him while discharging his senatorial duties. His absorbing love for Missouri had made him ask much for his gifted State, and, as all he required was reasonable, not a senator felt disposed to vote against him who was ever happy to have it in his power to do a favor for any one of them.

So fortunate was Dr. Linn in getting bills through the Senate for the benefit of Missouri, that one day, when in his usual happy manner he was presenting a number of bills to the Senate, his friend Mr. Buchanan remarked jestingly, "that it would save much time to the Senate, and great trouble to the Doctor in reading these bills, to put them in a pile and say, 'These bills are Dr. Linn's for the benefit of Missouri,' and thus let them pass as they are sure to do." This suggestion was in the same spirit of pleasantry seconded by Mr. Clay. There was one bill for the benefit of Missouri which Dr. Linn carried twice through the Senate, and was much grieved that the House of Representatives did not act on it—it was the appropriation which the Senate made to drain the swamp lands in the southern part of the State, which were so deleterious to the health of a large portion of the country during the warm season. To drain these swamps would not only be beneficial to the health of the inhabitants of the country, but land would be redeemed that would form many rich counties for the State.

At the time Dr. Linn took his seat in the U. S. Senate there was great excitement in the two political parties of our country. It was frequently the case that some of the distinguished statesmen of our nation rather avoided forming the acquaintance of new senators, because they were of different political opinions, while others took pleasure in cultivating an intercourse with those who possessed a similarity of taste and feeling with themselves, not permitting a difference of politics to mar the pleasure of social intercourse.

Dr. Linn had been in the Senate some time before any thing more than the common civilities of life had taken place between himself and Mr. Clay. At length a young son of Mr. Clay's came to visit his father at Washington City. A few days after his arrival he was taken very ill, and his life appeared in imminent danger. Many of Mr. Clay's personal friends who had received medical aid from Dr. Linn, urged Mr. C. to send for the Doctor to visit his son, expressing their confidence in his medical skill. Mr Clay said it was impossible for him to ask such a favor of the Doctor, as he was scarcely acquainted with him, and knew the Doctor would receive no remuneration for his professional services. Young Clay grew rapidly worse, and it was thought he could live but a few hours. His father, overcome with anxiety and the entreaties of his friends, addressed a note to Dr. Linn, soliciting him to come as "the Good Samaritan," and strive to save the precious life of his son. The Doctor immediately complied with the request. Mr. Clay meeting him at the door of the sick room, his countenance expressing the deepest anguish, accosted him with, "I thank you with all my heart, Doctor, for coming to see my son, but it is too late; I am confident his hours on earth are numbered; my dear boy must die." Dr. Linn tried to inspire hope in the heart of the parent, and after a close examination of the youth, who lay in a lethargic state which appeared to be the precursor of death, said, "Mr. Clay, trust your son to me; go to the Senate, and should my vote be wanted for Missouri, send for me; in the meanwhile I will stay with your son, using every effort with God's blessing, to save his life." In an instant of time how were the feelings of these two gentlemen changed towards each other! the cold frost of party feeling was swept off by the warm sunshine of the heart's best impulses, and they both felt how much pleasure was in store for them in a future friendly intercourse. Mr. Clay went to the Senate, leaving his son in charge of Dr Linn, by whose medical skill he was once more restored to health, and from that time forth the Doctor was the friend and medical adviser of Mr. Clay. The friendship of the latter continued towards his family as long as he lived.

A few years previous to Mr. Clay's death he visited St. Louis, and the morning after his arrival, in leaving his own church he observed Mrs. Linn returning from hers; coming up he accosted her, saying, "although it was the Sabbath he could not refrain from inquiring after her health." After entering her house his eye rested on the portrait of Dr. Linn, and he added, "I wished to talk to you of the light of other days, as this is the first time we have met since your great bereavement."

Dr. Linn's enthusiastic devotion to Missouri carried him far beyond political feeling: towards every son and daughter of that noble State he felt the strongest fraternal regard. He lived in the utmost harmony with his colleagues from his own State, highly respecting Col. Benton as a great statesman, and feeling the warmest attachment for the energetic and generous Gen. Ashley, who had for long years been on the most intimate terms of friendship with himself and many members of his family. The unwearied zeal with which Gen. Ashley served Missouri met a ready response in the ardent bosom of Dr. Linn; they both felt their State pride much gratified in seeing it so well represented in our national halls, and also in the salons of fashion by many of the most lovely and attractive ladies. The charming and intellectual Mrs. Ashley (now Mrs. Crittenden), the beautiful and attractive Mrs. Col. Stuart, and the lovely Mrs. Decansor, were greatly admired by Dr. Linn, as they were universally. Like himself, in their youth they had been transplanted from their dear native State, Kentucky, to the State of their adoption, Missouri.

It gave Dr. Linn great pleasure to meet in the Halls of Congress his gallant young friend, Geo. W. Jones, a delegate from Wisconsin Territory, who had been his devoted friend from his boyhood, and took great pleasure in spending much of his time with the Doctor, and frequently visiting his family, every member of which felt the warmest attachment for Gen. Jones.

It was with a feeling of parental pride and pleasure that the Doctor beheld the energy and devotion with which Gen. Jones served his constituents; and it was with lively satisfaction he heard the great Webster once say to Mrs. L., he "thought her young friend had done more to aid his constituents than had been accomplished by any other delegate." Although the general had no vote in Congress himself, he obtained an influence with those who had votes, which was of great advantage to the prosperity of Wisconsin.

When Dr. Linn first entered the Senate, Missouri had but four representatives; two in the Senate, and two in the House of Representatives. There were but few newspapers printed in the State, and general information was very far from being largely diffused among its rapidly increasing population. To obviate this want as much as possible, and to give pleasure to those that had reposed so much confidence in him, Dr. Linn, on coming to Washington, sent a great number of newspapers and public documents to his constituents: to obtain their names and places of residence, application was made to the sheriff of every county in the State, and a list of names being taken from the poll-tax books, the Doctor arranged them in a large book, so that all of the citizens of Missouri might receive some papers from him during the sessions of Congress. To meet this expense, he appropriated from three to five hundred dollars every session while he served in the U. S. Senate.

Not satisfied with serving Missouri in the Senate with all the energy of his noble heart, Dr. Linn did every thing in his power to develope the vast resources of his State. While the Northern and Eastern people of our country were amusing themselves at the *fable* (as they termed it) of an *iron mountain* in Missouri, he had a lump of iron, weighing two tons, taken from the mountain and sent to Paris, to be submitted to the inspection of men of science. They reported that it was the best of iron, and, for many purposes, far superior to any they had ever seen. In compliment to the Doctor, these gentlemen had a beautiful set of ornaments made from some of the iron, and sent as a present to Mrs. Linn.

The pure and very white sand which is found in great quantities near St. Genevieve, was first taken to Pittsburg by the Doctor to be tried in the Glass Works there, and was found to make the most beautiful glass. It is now used exclusively in the great manufactories of glass along the Ohio River.

As there were constant new discoveries of precious metals in the different mines in the southern part of Missouri, and the mode of mining was in a very imperfect state, Dr. Linn determined to visit the mines in Europe, and bring home with him men experienced in mining, who could instruct our own people, who, for want of information on the subject, had many difficulties to contend with, which retarded the prosperity of a country rich with a great variety of metals. Many a Missourian felt interested in the laudable motive which prompted Dr. Linn to visit Europe; and one accomplished gentleman, who is not only an honor to the American army, but whose pure and patriotic feelings induce him to aid his country in every way in his power, was so much pleased with the Doctor's design, that (aware of his limited means) he tendered him what money he could readily command, and his credit for any amount he might find necessary to carry out his plans on a large scale, as it would be of such great advantage to Missouri. This generous and patriotic individual was Col. A. D. Stewart, Paymaster U. S. Army.

That the Doctor was an observant traveller, the letter here published, addressed to his wife from London, will abundantly show; and it will probably be regretted by the reader that this is the only one from his pen it is in my power to present; others addressed to his family at various times from Washington, descriptive of men and society in that political centre of this great Republic, of fashionable life as he saw it, have unfortunately been lost. He was a discriminative observer of human character, and a great admirer of elegant simplicity, unpretending manners, and genuine goodness of heart; while no one held in greater dislike every thing like assumption, hauteur, pretence, affectation, and that bad taste which overloads with dress or ornament.

Though eminently social in his disposition, gifted with conversational powers in a high degree, and full of pleasantry and anecdote, which caused his society to be much sought, and insured him a warm and cordial welcome wherever he came, he had little taste for what is termed fashionable society in Washington, looking upon it as ostentatious, heartless, chilling, and unsatisfactory. It was in a small circle of select friends, and in the bosom of his own beloved family, that the subject of this memoir delighted to indulge in a free and easy social converse, and to give the reins to his scintillating wit and innocent mirth. For fashionable society he had no love; but for his friends the warmest affection, and this was ardently reciprocated. No one had warmer friends, no one was more truly esteemed and sincerely beloved.

The incident mentioned in the following letter in regard to the purchase of a shawl for Mrs. Linn, by direction of one to whom it had been in the power of the Doctor to show kindness and render professional service, will illustrate his power of winning the affections as well as the esteem of those with whom he was brought in close contact, as it was also illustrated in the incident related in regard to Mr. Clay's son. The whole secret of this power lay in the warm and generous feelings of his own guileless heart, the entire absence of all selfishness, and that overflowing goodness which ever prompted him to do all in his power to alleviate the sufferings and promote the happiness of those around him, thoughtless of himself. But though in rendering services to, and conferring benefits upon others, self never entered his mind, yet such goodness is like mercy :

> "It droppeth, as the gentle rain from heaven,
> Upon the place beneath: it is twice blessed :
> It blesseth him that gives, and him that takes."

It is a perpetual sunshine in the heart that beams forth through the countenance, and gives it that indescribable expression which makes even ugly features lovely and attractive.

The letter to which I have referred will show that Dr. Linn had an eye for the picturesque, and all the beauties of cultivated and of uncultivated nature, as well as a pen of most graphic power. With the aid of this we shall find the journey from Boulogne to Paris one of continual interest and pleasure.

LONDON, September 17, 1839.

MY BELOVED WIFE :

I have written you many, very many letters since my arrival in England, and hope most sincerely that they all may have reached you, as I flatter myself that they would prove a great source of consolation. Your truly affectionate and beautiful letters, four in number, have proved a blessing to me, and have been read over and over again, as proving that I still live fresh and green in the memory of my beloved wife and children; for to be embalmed in their affections, is the height of my earthly wishes and hopes.

I will commence where I left off in my longest letter. I took lodgings in a boarding-house kept by an Englishwoman on the plan of an American house. She is short, thick, fat, loquacious, obsequious to those above her, and a tyrant to those below; keen, sarcastic, unfeeling and avaricious,—these are her principal virtues. Her daughter, Miss F——, is about twenty-two years of age, above the ordinary stature, quite fat, or rather as a Frenchman would say, inclined to "*embonpoint*," with a tolerably handsome face, shaded very much by a profusion of dark brown curls of her own, or borrowed from the dead or bought from the living—cannot say which—she plays well on the piano and harp, and speaks the French remarkably well. She is certainly an accomplished woman, and would she permit common sense to have fair play, would be an interesting one. She assumes the delicate, sensitive, languishing, lacadaisical beauty. Her eyes are usually cast down, and have a half-sleepy and dreamy expression.

The living was only tolerable, for which I had to pay $20 per week, and for candles and servants besides. Will you believe it? my washing costs me from $5 to $7 per month. You can get nothing done here without paying well for it, for there seems to be an organized system of extortion upon strangers from one end of the island to another. Prices are extravagant for almost every thing but clothing, and to strangers there is very little difference between this and our own country.

Mr. Lamb soon changed his quarters, and it seemed from some cause or other that I should not go with him, for as Col. March of St. Louis soon after arrived and came to the same house, I concluded to remain, particularly as it was difficult, even in this great city, to better ourselves. Hotels and eating-houses are abundant, whilst boarding-houses are few in number, so that you are limited in choice.

There was only one Englishman in the mess—the remainder, perhaps twenty in number, were Americans, with and without families, and among the number was a Mrs. Hoffman from Baltimore. She was a delicate, sickly-looking little creature, with jet-black hair, eyebrows just *commingling*, just *dividing*; nose straight, but slightly turned up at the end, giving a piquant expression to the countenance—mouth small, beautifully shaped, and when sne smiled or laughed many dimples played about it—the lower lip *slightly pouting*; chin small and well turned; eyes large, black, brilliant and expressive; skin not fair but of a mellow, lustrous white, more deeply interesting to me than red and white. When I first saw her it was at the breakfast table; her head was inclined to one shoulder, when she turned it slightly and her eyes met mine—and such a look from those lovely eyes fringed with long, black, silken eyelashes as made me nearly start from my seat; it seemed as if my long-lost daughter had again returned to earth; but how much grown, and how little changed in face from the little girl we had parted with! it seemed as if the dead had arisen—my feelings can be better imagined than described. They stayed but a few days, and as sickness often confined her to the room I saw but little of her, but that little convinced me that she was as pure in morals and mind, as she was lovely in person; and though we may never meet again, the recollection of my first view of her beautiful face will always be pleasant and mournful to the soul.

You will doubtless remember a handsome young man by the name of Plitt, of Pennsylvania, who, as post-office agent visited our house in St. Genevieve, and perhaps called on us in Washington. He married a Miss Wager of Philadelphia, a tall, stout, well-made Dutch girl, with dark skin, noble Roman features, showy and dashing manners, very intelligent, and a heart beating with kindness and affection—she is an admirable lady, and one that you would love. I found them a truly admirable couple, and great source of enjoyment to me in this stranger land.

The next in order for the present was the Robinson family of New York, consisting of father, mother, and daughters. Mr. Robinson is a most excellent and amiable gentleman, who left his own dear America in search of health for himself, and pleasure for his family. He is about fifty-six years of age. Mrs. R. was a tall, graceful, dignified, intelligent, noble-looking lady, about forty-eight or fifty years of age. She was the life and soul of our society, and her lively sallies of wit and humor diffused warmth and sunshine wherever she went.

The eldest girl is dark-skinned like her mother, but has the high features of the father: she is in stature above the usual height, graceful and easy in her manners, though they might be considered by the world a *little* too cold and distant. Her eyes are very black, and the whole expression of her countenance pensive and pleasing. The second daughter is a tall, slender, graceful, blue-eyed, fair-skinned girl, of gay, sprightly manners, and cheerful disposition—always on the wing in search of pleasure, and always ready and willing to impart it to others; and pleasure they *all* had to overflowing, even to satiety; for Mrs. Robinson being second cousin to Sir George Rose, a distinguished baronet and an important member of Parliament, they were invited to a great many dinners, balls, parties, concerts, theatres, operas, &c., &c., &c.

They often remained out at night until three o'clock in the morning. This lasted about ten days after my arrival, when one morning at breakfast Mrs. Robinson complained of being very sick, and leaving the table, retired to her room. During the fore part of the day I often sent to know how she was, and her daughters uniformly answered to these inquiries that their mother was quite sick. I repeatedly offered my services; they were gently but firmly declined, and even an admission into her room to see how she was. In the course of the day I often met Mrs. Plitt, who uniformly expressed great uneasiness for Mrs. Robinson. Still she would neither see me nor send for another physician.

On pressing Mrs. Plitt to know what was the matter with Mrs. R., she informed me that it was almost incessant vomiting. Just after supper I told one of the girls that although her mother had persisted in refusing my services, I was determined to see her, *even* if I had to enter her room contrary to her wishes. She smiled at my earnestness, but whilst at tea she came and informed me that her mother was not only willing, but anxious to see me then, as she felt herself much worse. I found her laboring under the second stage of cholera. I prescribed the usual remedies, and most earnestly requested to be sent for in the night, in the event of the medicines producing no salutary effect. This was not done, for fear of giving trouble to me as a stranger upon whom they had no claims whatever. In the morning at nine o'clock I found her decidedly worse. I then informed Mr. Robinson of her critical situation, and desired that he would call in other medical aid; not that I had any difficulty in the treatment of her case; but that, being out of regular practice, I wished to avoid so responsible a trust; and, moreover, if the attack should end fatally, the family and friends would have good reason to congratulate themselves upon the reflection, melancholy as it was, that *they* had done all they could do to avert the arrow of the Grim Tyrant. He called in consultation Sir James Anderson, who coincided with me in opinion that she was in decided danger. Our efforts for forty-eight hours were vigorous and unceasing, but alas! unavailing. She died in the arms of her beloved husband, children and brother, and surrounded by a few friends from her native, but far distant country. And such a death—so triumphantly Christian! so calm, so self-possessed, that I would give all the glory and wealth of this world, if in my power, to die as she died. Such thrilling advice and admonition to husband, daughters and brother,—such heart-rending adieus I never heard in all this checkered life of mine, so full of melancholy and sorrowful recollections. She bade a most affectionate farewell to Mrs. Plitt, and, indeed, to all who had been near her person during her sickness; and when she called me to her bedside I sunk upon my knees, her glazed and sunken eyes were turned upon me, with her clay-cold hand in mine; she said she hoped that God would guard, guide, and keep near *Him* me and mine, for my kindness and attention to her in that, her last hour of life, suffering and trial. She prayed earnestly for forgiveness for past sins, and felt a lively and cheering conviction that they would be forgiven through the blood and intercession of Our Saviour, the Lord Jesus Christ. My heart felt much too big for my body, and many were the tears shed by me on this melancholy occasion.

She was placed in a leaden coffin enclosed in one of wood, and on the second day after her death conveyed to Kensall Cemetery, about three miles from London, on the road to Windsor Castle. Your imagination, my beloved wife, can scarcely picture to itself so sweet a spot, devoted to so sad a purpose—it is just out of the great Babel—just out of the verge of its sins and sorrows, and seems on the borders of the spirit-land. It contains about fifty or sixty acres of ground, enclosed by a high brick wall, immediately within which is a beautiful green hawthorn hedge. The whole lot is laid out in little plantations already occupied, or to be occupied by the last remains of poor mortality, until the angel of God shall sound his trump from on high, to call up by its thunders the quick and dead to stand before the everlasting throne. Around each *flourishing plantation* is a row of tombstones marking the *who* and the *when.* Between each tombstone are planted flowers, evergreens and rose-bushes—in every spot where grass grows it is cut down close to the earth—fit emblem of man's frail and mortal condition. The roads throughout the grounds are broad and neatly gravelled, and at regular distances the mournful cypress and other evergreens are planted, alternately with rose-bushes and other flowering shrubs; whilst at their feet bloom every variety of beautiful flower that Flora can offer to man. In the midst of all this display, which seems intended to take as much as possible from the *horrors* of the tomb, stands a neat, beautiful little chapel, of the Church of England, but at which ministers of other denominations officiate on such occasions.

Into this the body of Mrs. R. was conveyed on a dark, damp, gloomy English day, and set down half way between the door and altar. She was of the Anglican Church, consequently the officiating minister was of that persuasion. He read in a deep, solemn, and impressive voice, the service for the dead, which was responded to by the clerk; and now and then the trembling voice of a mourner might be heard mingling in the service, and echoed by the lofty walls and arches of the building. When the service was near the close, the coffin was seen to move by an invisible hand, and sink through the floor gradually and slowly. When it had nearly disappeared, the melancholy sounds were heard which struck a cold damp to the heart of each sorrowing friend, "dust to dust," and dust was scattered upon the coffin as it departed from our sight and sunk into the damp vaults below, there to remain until taken from thence, to be conveyed, according to her own request, to her beloved America. A few days after the interment, Mr. Robinson came to my room with tears in his eyes, and remarked that he had seen enough of me to know that he could not hope that I would accept any pecuniary compensation for my attentions to his wife, but he thanked me in the most kind and feeling terms for those attentions, and left my room for the country with his daughters, after a warm shake of the hand, and with professions of sincere regard.

After my pamphlet was finished with the map, having some leisure, I took a flying trip to Paris, the great seat of learning, science, and art. Mr. Plitt, wife and self, left London Bridge in the steamship Magnet for Boulogne in France. We had literally to weave our way through a forest of masts, or rather through a vast crowd of ships and watercraft of every size, sort, and description. We passed the Royal Docks of Deptford, Greenwich, Gravesend, Sheerness, the Nore, and turning the point to the south, on which stands a very lofty lighthouse, whose bright blaze is thrown far away upon the wide and stormy deep, to cheer the heart of the sailor when tempest-tost and seeking a safe haven for his little bark, we came broad out into the English Channel—night came on, and as we passed along the coast, the lights of Ramsgate, Margate, and the celebrated Dover, became visible along the English side, and Calais and Boulogne on the French.

We continued our course until twelve o'clock at night, when we entered the harbor of Boulogne at high tide. Our trunks were immediately taken possession of by the custom-house officers, whilst, after examining our passports, we were permitted to go to our hotel. Morning came with slow and measured steps to me after passing a sleepless night, and looking out, I found the harbor perfectly free from water, and all the shipping sticking bolt upright in the mud. I had forgotten that this harbor is *made* by the rise of the tide, which is very great at this point, and *unmade* by its retirement. After breakfast we took our departure in the cumbrous French diligence, and began our journey over the vine-covered hills and gay regions of France. A diligence, my dear Libby, is about three times as large as our stage coaches, and is divided into three compartments; and so lofty is it, that a ladder is used on which to mount on the top—the whole will contain fifteen or twenty persons.

We travelled day and night over this beautiful land; but still I find many objections to the country on the route from Boulogne to Paris—there is too great a scarcity of villages, towns and country-seats—and when you do find the latter, they are generally much out of order, and in the construction of the mansion house, and in the arrangement of the grounds, a want of taste is very manifest; indeed, it was only in dense forests which were like oases in a desert, whose umbrageous shade was too thick for even a straggling sunbeam to enter, that you found these manor-houses at all. As to the villages and towns, they all presented a most antiquated and worn-out appearance. Our own St. Genevieve is a *perfect beauty* to any of them, I assure you; and blessings on its simple and venerable head; the seat to me of youth's early and romantic dreams, of the joys and sorrows of manhood's maturer years, and holding at present all that my heart holds dear; wife, children and friends. Yes! it is a perfect *beauty spot to me*, and although I may travel to the uttermost ends of the earth, tread the palaces of kings, and stand unawed in the presence of princes, my heart will turn with fond affection to the home of my youth, and to the land that has so lavishly heaped honors upon me.

The large towns were Montreuil and Abbeville, both

walled and strongly fortified; but on entering their gates the same marks of age and decrepitude appear; narrow, dirty streets, crumbling walls and dilapidated ruins; but still much of animation is seen, and the music and dance of our French friends of St. Genevieve are almost seen and heard, for it was a festival day when we passed through, and all the young girls were dressed in white and walked the streets bareheaded, whilst the old folks had caps or *blue* handkerchiefs on theirs.

We passed Abbeville at nine o'clock at night, and not long after came upon the ground where was fought the celebrated battle of Cressy. Ages seemed to roll back to the period when this spot was the scene of a fierce and bloody conflict between nations hostile to each other almost from their origin. The shouts of victory are no longer heard, even to the ear of imagination, the shock of contending armies no longer seen, and nothing is left to tell the fate of the mighty dead but a few lines of history. As we passed along through the woods of Cressy the cold night winds swept mournfully through its venerable trees, resembling the fitful moans of departing spirits. Morning came, and the sun rose in beauty over the plains all glittering with dew; and his roseate beams were shed over tower and tree in glorious effulgence. This gave us an opportunity to examine the country with an inquisitive eye—here and there a small hamlet rising out of a clump of tall and graceful trees ; or now and then a more considerable village, partially hid by orchards, might be seen, and close by a huge windmill, whose enormous wings and arms are waving in endless rotation in the air. Almost every hill or eminence in France is crowned with one or more of these mills.

About nine o'clock in the morning we reached Beauvais, a large town, from which emigrated the ancestors of our friends, the St. Genevievans. On the approach to the place, its venerable, stately, and truly noble-looking Gothic cathedral first rose to view. Time with his effacing fingers has been at work; as yet he has only touched, not destroyed. I believe this church is the work of the twelfth or thirteenth century, and Beauvais is celebrated in history for one of the most affecting incidents ever recorded: it was besieged by a hostile army, and reduced to the last extremity; quarter was refused to the men, but leave given to the women to leave the town with as much as they could carry on their backs of their most valuable effects. Accordingly they were seen issuing from the gates of the town with their fathers, husbands and lovers on their backs. The church is one of the finest memorials of the age in which it was built now extant, and presents a grand and imposing appearance—but here again we have narrow, crooked, and dirty streets, with crumbling walls and decayed columns; sad remembrances of better days. We passed along these streets until the diligence stopped at apparently a decayed tavern, which no one under heaven—no, not even a Yankee, could guess capable of furnishing a breakfast for so many hungry and half-famished travellers; and yet it did: *and one of the very best*—first-rate coffee, bread and butter, stewed and fried chickens, fresh pork and broiled ham, boiled and fried eggs, excellent soup, and, indeed, every thing that could satisfy the appetite of a famished traveller. "Well done, Beauvais," cried I; "my friends of St. Genevieve preserve their love of good living, which doubtless their family acquired whilst residing here"—but stop—on looking out of the window, many signs over doors caught my eye on which were written J. B. Beauvais, "marchand," or Beauvais "Tient Auberge ici," or A. Beauvais, "Forgeron"—Ma parole, c'est vrai.

We left Beauvais in the finest humor, and as we slowly ascended the hill that overlooks the town I showered praises on it, on account of its name and the excellent cheer it had afforded us. It has perhaps a population of five thousand souls, and the country around fertile, well cultivated, and presented us with the first vineyard we had seen in France. We moved on slowly, and in the course of the day passed many such venerable-looking towns and villages, and in the evening arrived at Paris, and put up at the Hotel

Meurice, Rue Rivoli, near the Palace of the Tuileries.

Paris is beautifully situated on the Seine, in a lovely valley, overlooked by several heights, in the distance, such as Montmartre, and Mont St. Louis, on which is situated the celebrated burying-ground of Père la Chaise, where repose in eternal silence some of the most stupendous intellects that ever adorned the globe. The pensive man, as he wanders through these death paths, will experience sensations of melancholy mingled with delight, for here death seems to have existence in the quiet, and the perfume, and the beauty of nature. The sad cypress hangs over the passer-by, but roses and violets are at his feet; the monumental urn is before his eyes, but it is relieved by a thousand beautiful objects, in which art and affection have combined to honor the memory and decorate the mansions of the dead. The *lustres* of centuries have burned out, but their light still seems to stream through the mind. Here, as he wanders through the tombs, filled with a holy fervor before those which contain the ashes of the good, and over which myrtles and jessamines, planted by a sorrowing wife or pious child, spread their rich fragrance; or turns with pity for poor humanity from those pompous mansions of dust, in which lie the remains of men to whom wealth and power *alone* gave distinction in life, and procured for them a gilded sepulchre and a *lying monumental history*, he stops before the plain wooden tablet where the only sign of funereal greatness is the gilded cross ; but around which shrubs are smiling and flowers are bursting forth, whilst a sister, daughter or wife, may be seen sending forth a silent prayer to the ever-living God, to be merciful to the living and to the dead. Excuse me, dear wife, for thus often introducing you to the mansions of the dead; but if God in his mercies will spare me, my children shall have a tomb worthy of their beauty and angelic natures. Morning comes, and they are present to my mind, and as sleep falls upon me in the silent watches of the night, their visions pass before me as the images in a magic lantern.

But to go back a little—the country from Boulogne to Paris is gently rolling, but strangely destitute of houses, villages, and even trees, at least along the route ; and as you see no fences or hedges, it strongly reminded me of my own dear prairies adorned with their islands, clumps, and islets of trees. But still every inch of ground is highly cultivated, and the traveller is constantly asking himself the question, where do the people come from that perform all this labor? The secret is they reside in little villages off from the roadside, and go to their work like our good people in their big field. Occasionally we met a wagon or cart, in structure exactly like those of Vide Poche, and as to the plough and harness, they are exactly the same—even the names of their horses are alike, and you will hear them calling to " Dauphin and Libertin," to quicken their step.

As I had but a few days to stay in Paris, they were devoted to the paintings and statuary in the Louvre and Luxembourg, Jardin des Plantes, Hospital of the Invalides, Pantheon, Notre Dame, which is a vast and venerable Gothic pile, the palaces of St. Cloud and the glories of Versailles—the magnificence of which surpassed all that my imagination had conceived or pictured of oriental gorgeousness and splendor. In my opinion, it stands *alone and unrivalled;* and may it always so stand, whilst palaces are built by money wrung from the sweat of the people's brows.

The day after our arrival, Mr. and Mrs. Plitt urged me to go with them to a celebrated shawl merchant's, to aid in the selection of those elegant French shawls so much like the cashmere and almost as costly. She insisted on my making the choice, which I reluctantly did at 250 francs. On our return in the carriage she placed it in my hands, as a present to you from Mr. Robinson, with the letter from him to me, and which is sent with this. It would be difficult to portray my feelings at such delicacy of gratitude, as it was entirely unlooked-for.

Occasionally I attended to the debates in the House of Lords during the sitting of Parliament—but ghosts of Chatham, Burke, Fox and Pitt, what speaking! If the characters of these great men for eloquence could be torn up and divided among the speakers I heard in Parliament, broad as their mantles were, there would not be enough to hide the *nakedness* of their successors. Such stammering, repetition, and unfitness I never heard. Bad as the nonsense was, it was rendered infinitely worse by the delivery; and such speaking I assure you would soon deliver both Houses of Congress or any of our Legislatures.

I arrived here after the last drawing-room, and consequently could not be presented to the queen. But at all events I could not, or would not go to the expense of several hundred dollars to purchase a court dress, and I am rather too proud to *hire* one, which was sometimes the case here this season. Webster, I am told, went to the expense of a new suit. I have occasionally seen the queen on several public days, and think her rather pleasing in her appearance, and very much like Antoinette Roy, raised by old Madame Lecompte, though Antoinette is much the best looking of the two.

I will not attempt to describe to you the splendor, riches and beauty, of this great commercial metropolis of the world. The concentrated riches of the globe seem to be here—spacious parks dressed in the deepest green, and divided into beautiful parterres, rendered lovely as the eye could desire by evergreens and flowers—every where over the city open squares have been left, surrounded by elegant iron railings, and planted with shrubbery, where groups of children may be seen at play—these add greatly to the health and beauty of this noble city. Paris excels in its paintings, palaces and public buildings, London in every thing else.

Since my arrival, money affairs here have been in the worst possible condition—men looked into each others' faces with suspicion, and turned with disgust from every proposition relating to American property and security, and the recent protest in Paris of a million and a half of drafts drawn by the Bank of the United States, I fear will give the finishing blow to every thing American. Mr. Lamb and myself have done every thing that could be done to insure success, but I fear the result. We will continue our efforts up to the last moment.

I will return to Missouri to attend to my private affairs, as you suggest in your letter of the 3d of August (your last), and to take you on to Washington, and accordingly make your arrangements. I think I will place my boy at the college near St. Louis. Should I not succeed in getting money I shall be dreadfully harassed, but in no event will we be separated this winter.

* * * * * * *

* * * *

Present me to all my old friends—love to my children, and blessings upon your head.

Yours affectionately,

L. F. LINN.

MRS. E. A. LINN.

CHAPTER V.

FROM childhood Dr. Linn had serious feelings on the subject of religion; he daily read portions of the Bible, and took the most lively pleasure in having clergymen of every religious denomination make his house their home whenever they visited St. Genevieve; and in particular those self-sacrificing pioneers of religion, the Methodist clergy, who endured every sort of privation and suffering to preach the Gospel to the inhabitants scattered along the frontiers of our Western country. Those pure and holy men cheerfully did so much for the cause of our Blessed Redeemer, desiring nothing for themselves, that Dr. Linn and every member of his family deemed it a blessed and most delightful privilege to entertain them. The Doctor felt a decided preference for the Methodist Church, and united himself to it on the 5th day of April, 1839, at Wesley Chapel, in the City of Washington.

The winter previous he had been a constant attendant on the ministry of that good man, the eminently pious Mr. George Cookman, then chaplain to Congress, with whom he formed a warm personal friendship which was so soon to terminate painfully in the loss of the latter, who was a passenger on board the ill-fated steamer President.

In March, 1843, on his return home from Washington Dr. Linn, with his usual considerate kindness to others, relinquished a very comfortable state-room that had been engaged for him in a steamer, to an old gentleman who was in bad health, and took a room near the wheel-house which was very damp. In consequence of this, the Doctor took a violent cold: he, however, resisted all entreaties to take medicine, when he reached home, feeling confident he would soon be well. But in a few days he became very ill, and continued so for two weeks: he at that time informed his wife and children that he believed it impossible for him to live. This mournful presentiment was confirmed by both the attending physicians, and they frankly told the Doctor that they feared he had but a few hours to live.

He received this information with great calmness, and with the deepest tenderness bid his wife and children farewell, praying that they would meet him in Heaven. With hearts overwhelmed and ready to burst with agony, his wife and children clasped the hands of their dearest friend, when he suddenly exclaimed, " My sight is failing, my beloved wife, my darling children, I cannot see you." Mrs. Linn implored to know of the physicians if they had done all they could for the Doctor, they assured her they had ; " Then," she exclaimed, "I will do for him that which I have seen him do for others," and immediately ordered a quantity of turpentine to be heated, into which she dipped flannel, and with the assistance of others, commenced rubbing her husband's body so as to give him a bath of turpentine with much friction. In a few moments a profuse perspiration overspread his forehead, and he cried out, " My dear wife and children, I again see you. I am better, but greatly exhausted." He immediately dropped into a sweet sleep which continued for three hours and then awoke free from all pain. He requested his friends to retire to rest and leave him alone with his wife. Left together, they held such a sweet and holy conversation that the recollection of it will be a consolation to the lone widow's heart to the latest hour of her existence. Mrs. Linn, fearing that talking too much might injure her husband, besought him to try and compose himself and strive to rest ; she drew her chair near his bed, and placing her head on the pillow which supported his, holding one of his hands, said, " Let us both try to sleep, for my anxiety about you has been too great to permit me to take any rest for some time; but now, thank God, you are safe and I can sleep peacefully." They both sank into a deep slumber which continued a length of time, when the Doctor awoke with a violent start and exclaimed, "Dear wife, did you hear that?"

She assured him she had not heard any thing, and that all was quiet about them. "You are under a great mistake," he replied, "for I heard distinctly a voice say, *Prepare, Lewis F. Linn, for this year thy soul shall be required of thee.*" Mrs. Linn tried to convince her husband that he had been dreaming; but he insisted that it was not so, for the voice he heard was so loud as to awake him from a deep sleep. He requested her to look at her watch and see what hour it was, then to take his day-book and write in it the time and day of the month, for she would find before that time twelve months she would be a mourning widow.

To gratify the Doctor, she did as he desired; it was half-past one o'clock on the morning of the 28th of April, 1843.

He then requested her to summon all their family, and two visitors then staying with them, to his room, and especially to call her mother and send for Dr. Sargent. When all these friends were assembled around him, Dr. Linn told them what he had heard, and expressed his firm conviction that his life would terminate before the expiration of that year.

His manner was so calm and solemn when he gave his friends this information, that not one of them ventured to try and convince him that he had been disturbed by a painful dream, though such was their belief. He requested his friends to unite with him in prayer, and in a most powerful and thrilling manner he implored our Heavenly Father to have mercy on him, and in the blessed Redeemer's name to give him strength to prepare for eternity.

He expressed his belief that his severe illness had greatly increased the disease of his heart, and that he was liable to be called to depart at any time, without a moment's warning. He recovered his usual health in a little time, but still retained the impression that he should die soon, and commenced arranging his worldly affairs. He made many improvements on his place, and when his friends expressed their pleasure in seeing him do so (as it was an evidence that he did not intend to leave them to move to St. Louis, as they had long feared), the Doctor would smile sadly, and remark, that he was striving to make his home comfortable for his wife and children, for he knew that he would soon be taken from them. All who heard him make this observation listened with incredulous astonishment, as they saw him, to all appearance, in most perfect health; but his medical knowledge made him fully aware of the slight tenure by which he held life.

It had been some time since he had seen his very dear sister Mary and her family, and he determined to visit them in Wisconsin, and also his brother, Gov. Dodge, and his family, to whom he was tenderly attached: then to visit his friend, Gen. George W. Jones, who had ever been to him like a cherished younger brother. He anticipated lively pleasure in seeing all these dear and highly valued friends in their own homes, and his noble heart entered joyfully into this last visit to those to whom he was so devotedly attached.

On his return, although looking well, he complained frequently of a violent palpitation of the heart, and a difficulty of breathing; these painful sensations would not continue long, but they often recurred, and while they lasted were very distressing.

His business matters annoyed him greatly, as he was compelled to pay some heavy security debts for those in whom he had placed great confidence.

Only three weeks before his death, Dr. Linn called to see a lady for whom he felt a great friendship, (Mrs. Rousan, daughter of the Hon. John Scott of St. Genevieve,) and told her that he had a great favor to ask of her, which was, that should she hear of his sudden death, she would hasten to his wife and remain with her until her mother could arrive. Mrs. R. was disposed to smile at such a request, coming from one looking in such perfect health. The Doctor took her hand and said in an impressive manner, "I know my true situation; I may drop dead at any moment from this dreadful disease, and the better my health appears, the worse it is for me, for I am far too plethoric. My death will be an awful blow to my dear wife, who cannot believe that my life is in danger while I am looking in good health, and therefore I hope you will stay with her until her relations come to her." Mrs. R. gave the promise which she most faithfully kept.

The Doctor went to Mine Lamotte where he was detained by very harassing business for twelve days, and on his return appeared very nervous and excited about a paper he feared was lost, and which was of great pecuniary value to him. The morning after his return, he desired Mrs. Linn to accompany him to his office and assist him to look for the mislaid paper, and the greater portion of the day was spent in a vain search for it.

Mrs. Linn became alarmed at finding the Doctor's nervous agitation rapidly increase, and begged him to sit still while she continued the search. He replied that he should be compelled to do so, as he felt a violent vertigo in his head, which nearly made him blind. Mrs. L. continued searching, when suddenly her husband calling to her, observed, "There is a trunk under that table, in which, my dear wife, I have faithfully kept every line that you ever wrote me; I may have put the paper with your letters, and I will look there for it." He then stooped to draw out the trunk, when his head dropped on the arm of the chair, and a horrid spasm passed over his face. In an instant she was by his side supporting his head. The Doctor's countenance soon regained its wonted composure, and he sat up apparently unconscious that any thing painful had taken place, and inquired if the paper had been found. Mrs. L. implored him to go to bed immediately and send for a physician, as he was ill; he smiled and replied that he was in his usual health, and insisted on still continuing to search for the missing paper, which Mrs. L. was so fortunate as to find a few moments after.

Just at this time a young friend, now an eminent lawyer in the City of New Orleans, called to Mrs. Linn and requested her to come to him in her garden, and give him some of her beautiful autumnal flowers to send to N. O. on a steamer about leaving for that city; the Doctor accompanied her, and for some time the three walked in the garden enjoying a most cordial conversation—the last they were ever to have with each other in this world. For this young friend the Doctor and Mrs. L. entertained a warm, parental affection. They had watched him from infancy to the bright maturity of manhood, possessing endowments to command their admiration and win their love. The Doctor took great pleasure in conversing with and advising him in regard to his future course in life, and became warm and animated on the subject. Never, I am sure, will that young friend forget the eloquent and paternal solicitude which he manifested for his prosperity on that, the last evening that good man spent on earth.

The shades of night were closing around the three who continued to walk in the garden, unconscious of the lateness of the hour, when supper was announced. Mr. R., having an engagement, declined entering the house with Dr. and Mrs. Linn, who then approached the table to take the last supper that they were ever to enjoy on earth together. Before taking his seat at the table, the Doctor extended his arms over it, and made a beautiful prayer. His good old mother-in-law gazed on him with delight, and said, "My dear son, you look far more attractive and interesting than you did the evening you married my daughter, twenty-six years ago." The Doctor remarked, "You all keep me in such good humor with myself when I am at home, that I am induced to forget how heavily time has laid his hand upon my brow." After supper the Doctor continued in unusually fine spirits, and did not exhibit any ill-effects from the momentary spasm which had so greatly alarmed his wife. For more than an hour he entertained his family with his violin, upon which he played with exquisite taste. He held his daughter (twelve years of age) a long time in his arms seated on his knees, telling her if God spared his life how perfectly her education should be finished. He then had a long and most affectionate conversation with his son, expressing his conviction that he would die soon, and committing to his care his mother and sister, when they would have no other protector.

Mrs. Linn could not refrain from feeling the most painful anxiety in regard to her husband, although he looked so well, and urged him to retire to rest, but he declined doing so until twelve o'clock. He then requested her to read a chapter in the Bible, and some hymns, remarking that there were two of a number of hymns she had often read to him, which he would like to think would be sung at his funeral. Finding this observation greatly distressed his wife, he begged her to forget it, and said he would retire to rest. After praying, he requested her to lie down, and scarcely had she done so when he threw himself on the bed, looking very weary. His head resting on her bosom, in an instant he appeared to be in a heavy sleep. She did not move, fearing she might disturb him, but she felt too much concerned to sleep. Day began to dawn, and Mrs. Linn discovered that the window shutter near their bed had not been closed; fearing the light would awake her husband, she tried to rise as gently as possible to close it. With all her care she could not avoid making a little noise, and the Doctor awoke and asked her why she rose so early? When informed of the reason he said, "It is ever thus with you, my dear wife; I firmly believe that your sleepless vigilance and kind nursing have added many years to my life." He then inquired whether she felt well; if so, he requested her to write the letters he had mentioned to her, and after he had taken a little more sleep he would get up, sign the letters, and they would both leave home in the first steamer, on a visit to St. Louis. He desired her to bring a little table near his bed and write there, that he might feel that she was near him. Mrs. Linn was leaving the room to get her writing materials, when her husband called to her to come and place another pillow under his head, which felt as if it was pressed down by a great weight. While doing this, the Doctor threw his arms around his wife's neck and pressed her head upon his bosom, and while using some affectionate expression dropped into his last sleep. For some hours Mrs. Linn sat close to her husband's bed, writing and watching.

As she finished her letters, her son came into the room, and seeing how calmly his father appeared to rest, urged his mother to try and sleep herself, as she looked very weary. Not wishing to leave her husband, whom she expected to wake every moment and call for her, Mrs. L. thought she would rest a while on the back part of his bed. In passing round to do so, she stopped and looked at the Doctor, who appeared to be sleeping as sweetly as an infant. Suddenly a dark shadow passed over his face, which greatly alarmed her, and she called a servant. In an instant more the same dark and unearthly expression came over the face of Dr. Linn, and the cries of both Mrs. L. and the servant soon filled the room with anxious friends and several physicians. Every effort was made to restore the Doctor to life, but all in vain; he breathed for fifteen or twenty minutes after being bled, and expired without a struggle or a groan.

In moving him, the blood gushed from his eyes, nose and mouth; the fatal aneurism had burst in his noble heart, and his precious soul was in heaven,—2 O'CLOCK, OCTOBER 3D, 1843.

As soon as Dr. Linn's death was known, meetings were convened in every county in the State of Missouri for the purpose of paying tributes to the memory of their deeply-lamented and favorite statesman. Eloquent speeches were made on this mournful occasion, and from all these meetings letters of condolence were sent to his bereaved family.

Wisconsin and Iowa, then territories, claimed the privilege of mourning the death of Dr. Linn, as if he had been their own senator; he had served them so faithfully in the U. S. Senate, where they were too young to have a voice, that their citizens felt with the deepest gratitude all he had done in that body, for the prosperity of their respective territories; and on the assembling of their Legislatures, after pronouncing beautiful eulogies on Dr. Linn, passed unanimous resolutions in both their legislative bodies to wear mourning for him, and send letters of condolence to his widow and family. So great were the number of letters of condolence addressed to Dr. Linn's bereaved family, from every part of the United States upon the announcement of his death, as to form a large volume. Copies of some of them will serve to show what were the feelings of sympathy expressed in all.

The State of Missouri erected a splendid monument over the remains of their favorite statesman, Dr. Lewis F. Linn, by the unanimous vote of their Legislature.

Here rests the Remain
of
LEWIS F. LINN
The model Senator
of
Missouri

PUBLIC LIFE OF DR. LINN;

OR,

TEN YEARS' SERVICE IN THE UNITED STATES SENATE.

BY N. SARGENT.

ADVERTISEMENT.

I FEEL it due to myself to say, that, to prepare a notice of the Public Life of Dr. Linn, was an undertaking I should never have voluntarily, and at the suggestion of my own mind, assumed; and I have prepared the following at the request of his amiable relict, with a consciousness of my inability to do justice to the late Senator, and to meet the expectations of his numerous and warm-hearted friends.

It is to be regretted, that some one of those whose intimacy with Dr. L. would have enabled him to have written an account of his senatorial life more satisfactory to his friends, and with an ability that would have enhanced the value of the work, did not take upon himself to perform this duty.

There are those who had the privilege of an intimate and familiar personal intercourse with him for many years, who, of course, knew him far better than I did, and who could have enlivened the narrative of his public life with many interesting and characteristic anecdotes. It was not my lot to be upon intimate terms with him. Our personal acquaintance was but slight. I knew him only as a Senator; and considering that our acquaintance was so slight, and that we belonged to opposing political parties, it is not a little singular that the labor of preparing a notice of his public services should have devolved upon me. All I can say in regard to the manner in which this has been executed, is, that I have endeavored to do justice to Dr. Linn, and with that view, to make him speak for himself as often as possible, through the debates of the Senate in which he took part.

I am indebted solely to the public records of the country,—chiefly to the journal and debates of the Senate,—for the materials from which I have compiled this memoir. I had hoped to have obtained some anecdotes and incidents of an interesting character from the few personal friends of the Doctor who are still here, that would have broken the monotony of the narrative; but in this I have been disappointed.

From the only specimen of his epistolary talent that has not been lost,—his letter to Mrs. Linn, from London,—we cannot but regret that the numerous letters he must have written from Washington, in his playful moods, and when he felt keenly and spoke freely in regard to public men and measures, fashionable society, the gayeties, follies and frivolities of metropolitan life during the winter season, have been lost. The absence of such anecdotes and incidents, and also of his private letters, is thus accounted for. It is hoped, however, that the account of his ten years' service in the Senate will be found neither uninteresting nor unprofitable reading.

N. SARGENT.

Washington City, Oct., 1856.

PUBLIC LIFE OF DR. LINN;

OR,

TEN YEARS' SERVICE IN THE UNITED STATES SENATE.

CHAPTER I.

IT has already been mentioned that Doctor Linn was, in the autumn of 1833, appointed by the Governor of the State of Missouri, a Senator of the United States, to fill the vacancy which had been created by the death of Alexander Buckner. He accepted the unsought appointment with that distrust of his own merits and ability to discharge the arduous duties acceptably to the people of his State, which often marks talent of a high order and great capacity for usefulness in public station.

Upon entering that august body he deported himself with a modest reserve most creditable to him, and commendable as an example to others of less ability than fell to his lot; yet this diffidence in his own powers, and that sense of propriety which prompted him to allow more experienced senators to take the lead in the business and debates of the Senate, did not prevent him from giving his unremitting attention to whatever affected the interests of the State he in part represented, nor from bringing forward measures calculated to promote her welfare and that of her citizens.

Seldom has the Senate of the United States contained a greater number of men distinguished for talent and eloquence, and eminent for public services, than belonged to that body at the time Dr. Linn entered it; and becoming a member for the first time of any legislative body, it cannot be matter of surprise that he should at least not seek to attract attention by occupying much time or taking a prominent part in debate. Nor did he consider this necessary to the interests of his State, since his colleague, Colonel Benton, was already numbered among the oldest senators, and one of the most prominent in all important debates.

The following gentlemen constituted the Senate at the commencement of the session of 1833–4, on the first session of the 23d Congress, the time Dr. Linn entered it, to wit:

Maine—Peleg Sprague, Ether Shepley.
New Hampshire—Samuel Bell, Isaac Hill.

Massachusetts—Nathaniel Silsbee, Daniel Webster.
Rhode Island—Ashur Robbins, Nehemiah R. Knight.
Connecticut—Gideon Tómlinson, Nathan Smith.
Vermont—Samuel Prentiss, Benjamin Swift.
New York—Silas Wright, N. P. Tallmadge.
New Jersey—T. Frelinghuysen, Samuel L. Southard.
Pennsylvania—William Wilkins, Samuel McKean.
Delaware—John M. Clayton, Arnold Naudain.
Maryland—Ezekiel F. Chambers, Joseph Kent.
Virginia—Wm. C. Rives,* John Tyler.
North Carolina—Bedford Brown, Willie P. Mangum.
South Carolina—John C. Calhoun, Wm. C. Preston.
Georgia—John Forsyth, John P. King.
Kentucky—George M. Bibb, Henry Clay.
Tennessee—Felix Grundy, Hugh Lawson White.
Ohio—Thomas Ewing, Thomas Morris.
Louisiana—G. A. Waggaman, Alex. Porter
Indiana—Wm. Hendricks, John Tipton.
Mississippi—Geo. Poindexter, John Black.
Illinois—Elias K. Kane, John M. Robinson.
Alabama—Wm. R. King, Gabriel Moore.
Missouri—Thos. H. Benton, Lewis F. Linn.

This was the first session of Congress held after the election of General Jackson for a second term, and was as remarkable for the exciting topics introduced and

* In consequence of a series of resolutions adopted by the Legislature of Virginia, expressing views and sentiments different from those held by Mr. Rives, and instructing her senators to support measures which he could not conscientiously support, he resigned his seat early in the session, and was succeeded by Benjamin Watkins Leigh, a man of great eloquence and distinguished ability.

made the subjects of heated political discussion, as it was for the amount of talent and the number of distinguished men it contained.

The bill to recharter the Bank of the United States, passed by the preceding Congress, had been vetoed by President Jackson in 1832, and the public deposits or government funds had been removed from the bank shortly preceding the commencement of this session. Upon these subjects the country had been, and now continued to be, greatly agitated, and political feeling probably never ran higher. Every man in the community became to a certain extent a politician, and thousands of wealthy business-men—merchants, manufacturers, artisans, mechanics and professional men, who never before interested themselves in political affairs,—now took an active part in the disturbing questions of the day. From every quarter—State Legislatures, county conventions, cities, towns, various mercantile and mechanical associations, from citizens of every class, profession and employment—came pouring in resolutions, memorials and petitions, condemnatory of the removal of the deposits from the United States Bank, and depicting in glowing language the stagnation in business, and the general derangement and distress it had occasioned. These were mostly sent to the Senate, and when presented, were made the occasion for an eloquent speech or speeches by the senator to whom they had been intrusted, and not unfrequently by Mr. Clay, Mr. Webster, Mr. Calhoun, Mr. Ewing, Mr Clayton, and other distinguished senators, opposed to the administration, and by Mr. Wright of N. Y., Mr. Forsyth, Mr. Grundy, Mr. Benton, and others in reply and in defence of the President.

Early in the session Mr. Clay introduced resolutions condemnatory of the President for dismissing the Secretary of the Treasury (Mr. Duane), because he would not remove the money of the United States in deposit with the Bank of the United States in conformity with the President's desire, and appointing his successor (Mr. Taney) to effect such removal, and declaring that in so doing, the President had "assumed the exercise of a power over the Treasury of the United States, not granted to him by the constitution and laws, and dangerous to the liberties of the people."

These resolutions were the subject of a very able, but very heated and acrimonious debate, which lasted until the 28th of March, when they were modified by the mover, and that relating to the President passed in the following words:

"*Resolved*, That the President, in the late executive proceedings in relation to the public revenue, has assumed upon himself authority and power not conferred by the constitution and laws, but in derogation of both."

In opening the debate upon his resolutions in an elaborate, highly-wrought and powerful speech, on the 26th of Dec., 1833, Mr. Clay commenced by saying, "We are in the midst of a revolution hitherto bloodless, but rapidly tending towards a total change of the pure republican character of the government, and to the concentration of all power in the hands of one man. The powers of Congress are paralyzed, except when exerted in conformity with his will, by frequent and an extraordinary exercise of the executive veto, not anticipated by the founders of the constitution, and not practised by any of the predecessors of the present Chief Mgistrate."

In addressing the Senate upon this subject in one of his thrilling speeches, Mr. Calhoun said, alluding to the entrance of Cæsar, sword in hand, into the treasury of Rome: "They [the Administration] have entered the treasury, not sword in hand, as public plunderers, but with the false keys of sophistry, as pilferers, under the silence of midnight. The motive and the object are the same, varied in like manner by circumstances and character. 'With money I will get men, and with men money,' was the maxim of the Roman plunderer. With money we will get partisans, with partisans votes, and with votes money, is the maxim of our public pilferers. With men and money, Cæsar struck down Roman liberty at the fatal battle of Philippi, never to rise again; from which disastrous hour all the powers of the Roman republic were consolidated in the person of Cæsar, and perpetuated in his line. With money and corrupt partisans a great effort is now making to choke and stifle the voice of American liberty, through all its natural organs: by corrupting the press; by overawing the other departments; and, finally, by setting up a new and polluted organ, composed of office-holders and corrupt partisans, under the name of a national convention, which, counterfeiting the voice of the people, will, if not restrained, in their name dictate the succession; when the deed will be done, the revolution be completed, and all the powers of our republic, in like manner, be consolidated in the President, and perpetuated by his dictation."

In closing this celebrated speech, Mr. Calhoun gave utterance to the following impassioned and impressive language:

"We have arrived at a fearful crisis; things cannot long remain as they are. It behooves all who love their country, who have affection for their offspring, or who have any stake in our institutions, to pause and reflect. Confidence is daily withdrawing from the General Government. Alienation is hourly going on. These will necessarily create a state of things inimical to the existence of our institutions, and, if not speedily arrested, convulsions must follow, and then comes dissolution or despotism, when a thick cloud will be thrown over the cause of liberty, and the future prospects of our country."

In opening his speech, Mr. Ewing said: "The sudden alarm in all quarters of the country, occasioned by the removal of the public funds, the magnitude of the calamity which it has brought upon the people, and the just apprehension of still greater evils which are to follow in its train, give to the subject a grave and absorbing interest."

These extracts will suffice to show the temper of the times and the inflammatory character of party politics at the period when Dr. Linn first became a member of the United States Senate. Of the debates which took place during this session, he was a silent but not an indifferent listener. Ardent and sincere in all his opinions and sentiments; entering, as he was accustomed to do, with his whole soul into whatever interested him, and being a warm personal as well as political friend of General Jackson, whose measures he approved, and whom he believed to be a bold, upright, and patriotic Chief Magistrate, though his modesty and distrust of his own powers of debate deterred him from entering the arena where so many, and such celebrated champions were contending with keen weapons and bright and polished armor, yet he failed not to sustain the President by his votes and by his sympathy and encouragement, which the latter by no means undervalued.

The war carried on during this session by the Whigs against the Administration, and the Administration against the Whigs, may well be styled, from the character of the leaders and champions on both sides, "the war of the Titans, or Giants." Truly, when we behold the number of able, eloquent, and distinguished statesmen who were then arrayed against each other in the Senate, we may exclaim, "There were giants in those days." But those giants have passed way; the noise and din of their battle has ceased, and many of them have been called to a higher sphere of action, where the wicked cease from troubling, and the weary are at rest.

Having devoted himself heretofore most assiduously to the studies and arduous duties of a profession which required him to give attention to the constitutions and diseases of the human body rather than to those of the body politic—unaccustomed to the duties of a legislator and to grappling with the knotty questions and nice distinctions of law, and never having made the great science of jurisprudence a study, he was now placed in a field of action not only new to him, but for which his previous studies and occupation in life had not altogether prepared him. No one knew this better than himself; no one saw as he did the necessity of familiarizing himself with those great and general principles of constitutional, international and municipal law, which form the basis of our free institutions, and guaranty to us a degree of civil liberty which falls to the lot of no other people. With senators and members of the House of Representatives of the United States, generally, who are mostly lawyers, these leading principles of law are familiar acquaintances and of frequent reference; they have been with them subjects of study and of daily forensic discussion before judicial tribunals; not so with those of other professions and occupations, and they must therefore feel less at home amid such discussions, and more reluctant to take part in the debates of the body of which they are members, especially if, as was the case with Dr. L., they had never taken part in the discussions of political questions before the people in popular assemblies, and upon what is technically called "the stump," where, according to the practice in some States, mind grapples with mind, logic with logic, and all the powers of the speaker are tasked, called forth, exercised and improved.

But though Dr. Linn did not venture into the arena of debate amidst the Titans of the Senate, he was not unmindful of the interests of the State which he represented and her citizens, but exerted himself to obtain appropriations for the improvement of the harbor of St. Louis and of the Mississippi river.

Singularly but characteristically it appears, in examining his "record," that the first time he stood prominently forward in the Senate, was to act the part of a mediator or peacemaker.

Mr. Calhoun had made an elaborate speech upon the dangerous abuse of Executive Patronage. Mr. Benton replied, commenting upon the report of the committee, of which Mr. Calhoun was chairman, and who reported the bill under consideration, "with great warmth and severity." Mr. B. read from the report the following: "It is to convert the entire body of those in office into corrupt and supple instruments of power, and to raise up a host of hungry, greedy, and subservient partisans, ready for every service, however base and corrupt." Mr. B. remarked, "corrupt and supple instruments of power," and the gentleman has done me the honor to identify me with them, 'as base and corrupt.' * * * It is not necessary that I should repel the accusation, for the whole people of the United States will drive it back upon him as a bold and direct attack upon truth!" Mr. B. was here called to order by Mr. Poindexter, and the objectionable words "a direct attack upon truth" taken down.

A debate ensued upon the question whether the

words were a breach of order, during a part of which much excitement prevailed in the Senate.

The Vice President, Mr. Van Buren, decided that the words did not charge the senator from South Carolina with falsehood, and were therefore not of a personal character; from which decision an appeal was taken. After several senators had spoken eloquently and warmly on the subject, Mr. Linn rose to express his deep regret that any thing should have arisen to disturb the harmony of debate. For the honorable Senator from South Carolina he entertained the utmost respect, and for his honorable colleague, whom he had known so many years, he felt the warmest friendship. He regretted the unpleasant occurrence of that morning, though he was bound to say it was not an unusual one. He felt convinced that the Senate had been often out of order, in the course of debate, and the friends of the administration frequently had to bear much from gentlemen on the other side.

This was undoubtedly true. It was true that great latitude had been allowed in the debates of the Senate. Political feeling ran high throughout the country; the most intense acrimony characterized the political conflicts of the two parties into which the country was divided, and every where the war between them was a "war to the knife, and the knife to the hilt." No quarter was asked, none expected, and none given. It was not strange then that the feeling which animated the masses of the people should find its way into the bosoms of senators, and an outlet in language, which, if kept within the bounds of senatorial decorum, was not the less provoking and irritating to those to whom it was applied.

The decision of the President of the Senate was reversed, and without retracting any thing Mr. Benton was permitted to proceed with his remarks.

At the close of this session, the second of the twenty-third Congress, 1834–5, another subject was introduced which produced much feeling and called forth a very heated debate. A misunderstanding had sprung up between the governments of France and the United States in regard to the payment of indemnity for spoliations by the former to the latter. The amount due had been settled by treaty or convention, but the King of the French, Louis Philippe, had refused or unreasonably neglected to pay over the stipulated amount. Under these circumstances the President of the United States, Gen. Jackson, never disposed to be trifled with nor to permit his country to be, was strongly inclined to resort to coercive measures. An amendment was therefore adopted in the House of Representatives to the Fortification Bill on the last day of the session, appropriating $3,000,000, to be expended in whole or in part, under the direction of the President of the

United States, for the military and naval service, including fortifications and ordnance, and increase of the navy: Provided, such expenditures should be rendered necessary for the defence of the country prior to the next meeting of Congress.

This amendment, which was intended to enable the President, in case of a rupture with France, "to secure the safety of the country until the assembling of Congress," was earnestly and warmly opposed. In favor of the appropriation it was urged that it was well known that "there was a peculiar crisis in our foreign relations, and it was now too late to go into the detail of legislation."

Dr. Linn advocated the appropriation, and declared that he should vote for it, although it was an extraordinary one, because he thought it necessary under the present state of affairs. He could not believe that this Chief Magistrate or any other who might preside over the destinies of this people, would make a wrong or improper application of their funds.

The amendment failed to pass the Senate and therefore fell to the ground; but it was the subject of very acrimonious discussion subsequently in the public press, and served to add intensity to the already embittered feeling between the two great parties.

But though the amendment failed, it is proper to add that the high tone and firm stand taken by the

President, soon brought about an amicable adjustment of the misunderstanding by the payment, in gold, of the amount due from France to our citizens, which was all the President had desired or asked.

It was in connection with this affair that the President made the celebrated and patriotic declaration that "THE GOVERNMENT OF THE UNITED STATES WOULD DEMAND NOTHING BUT WHAT WAS RIGHT, AND WOULD SUBMIT TO NOTHING THAT WAS WRONG." A sentiment worthy of WASHINGTON himself, and which ought to be inscribed in letters of gold upon the front of the Executive Mansion, and over the seats of the presiding officers of both Houses of Congress.

Dr. Linn had now been two terms, or during one Congress, in the Senate, and had become known to the members generally; and with acquaintance grew esteem. From an examination of some of his private correspondence, it is seen that he had already won the friendship of many distinguished members of the body of which he was a member, to whom he was, personally, an entire stranger when he entered it; nor was this friendship in any instance interrupted so long as he and they lived; on the contrary, it became more and more ardent, and each was more and more esteemed by the other. Such, indeed, were the warm and affectionate disposition, the kindly social feeling, the agreeable conversation and the genial temper of the Doctor, that those who had once come in close and social contact with him, could scarcely prevent his taking captive their willing hearts, and loving him for his many noble qualities. He was the soul of honor, and his sense of what was due to others as well as to himself, of the most delicate kind; yet not such as to prompt him to be on the watch for personal affronts and neglects; far from it; for while he had a just appreciation of himself, his modesty would not permit him to doubt that he received from others all the respect that was justly his due. While no one had a higher reputation for chivalrous bravery and a readiness to resent any intended affront, yet no one had a more ardent love for peace, or a greater desire to live on terms, not only of amity, but of cordiality with all with whom he was brought in association; and no one was more ready to act the part of a peacemaker, and heal misunderstandings between others.

It was the esteem which Dr. Linn won from his brother senators by these generous, amiable, and manly qualities, and the rule he invariably observed, never to throw any obstacle in the way of any bill or measure in which other senators took an interest, unless compelled to oppose it by a sense of public duty, that enabled him to carry so many of his own through the Senate, and render such important services to his immediate constituents, and to the people of the West generally. In this respect, no one could be more fortunate and successful; indeed, it came to be considered that almost, as a matter of course, whatever bill or measure Dr. Linn introduced, would find favor with the Senate, and be sure to be passed. Such is the power of courtesy, kindliness, and condescension in a grave, dignified, deliberative body; but, where the human heart beats with the same impulses, is subject to the same passions, and influenced by the same motives as subject, influence, and control men in a less elevated sphere of life.

CHAPTER II.

FROM the commencement of the 24th Congress, Dr. Linn began to take a more active part in the business before the Senate. Nothing in which his own State and constituents were interested, or that concerned that portion of the country then denominated "the far West," or that which lies west of the Mississippi river, escaped his notice. Identified, as he was, in interest and association with this interesting section of the Union, his home from youth to manhood, containing all that he most loved and cherished, his wife, children and friends, no wonder he looked upon it with fond affection, and to whatever affected its interests, prosperity, security, and happiness, with filial attention and dutiful devotion.

The settling the Missouri land claims, or claims to lands in Missouri and Arkansas, under Spanish and French grants, by a law of Congress, was one of the important subjects which engaged his attention, and by which he rendered a very essential service to a large class of worthy citizens. A Board of Commissioners had been appointed under the acts of July 9th, 1832, and March 2d, 1833, for the purpose of receiving testimony in support of these claims, and of reporting thereon to the government, with a view to determine what claims were valid and what were otherwise. Dr. Linn had been a member of this Board, and the bill referred to was brought in for the purpose of confirming the decisions the Board had made, so that the inquietude of the claimants might be removed, and their titles established by law. Aided by his advocacy, and the lucid and satisfactory explanations of the whole subject he was able to give, the bill passed the Senate.

Another subject to which Dr. Linn gave much attention, was the putting of the Western country in a state of defence against the large bodies of Indians that had been congregated west of Missouri and those occupying the country north. Addressing the Senate on this subject on one occasion when Mr. Clay's land bill was under consideration, "he implored senators to look at the great western frontier, from the Falls of St. Anthony to the Gulf of Mexico, and the examination he was sure would produce feelings of sympathy for the situation of the people of Louisiana, Arkansas, Missouri, and Wisconsin. The existence of the numerous tribes of Indians claiming to be independent within the

States, had shaken the Union to its centre, and at one time appeared to threaten a dissolution of the confederacy. To get rid of this embarrassing subject, and to save the Indians from destruction, their removal to the west bank of the Mississippi was determined on by the General Government, and following out this line of policy, tribe after tribe has been located, until the aggregate amount has become alarming to contemplate. These Indians were placed there for the benefit of the old States respectively. Have we not, then, the right, asked Mr. L., to demand from the justice of Congress all the means necessary for our defence and protection? War, he said, was at all times terrible; but a war with Indians doubly so. They are our hereditary enemies, and we may expect combinations among them. A genius of the commanding character of Tecumseh, possessing a mind to concoct and a hand to execute, could form combinations among the discordant elements that would set our whole border in a blaze. From the moment the foot of the first white man touched the soil of this continent, a system of injustice and aggression commenced towards the Indians, which has been persevered in and perfected, until they find themselves on the confines of the great western plains, far from their homes and the graves of their fathers. Their hatred, therefore, is natural. But the laws governing population can no more be stayed than the tides of the ocean.

Cain slew Abel, and the farmer will ever possess power over the hunter or herdsman. The Indians are therefore a doomed race; treat them with all the kindness and humanity in your power, and to this melancholy complexion it must come at last. * * * * * *

"But he found himself, he remarked, wandering from the subject that had induced him to obtrude himself on the notice of the Senate. He rose merely to state, that for months previous to the celebrated Black Hawk having crossed the Mississippi to commence the war, which afterwards raged, he had despatched emissaries to every tribe from the Mississippi to the Sabine, with a view to form combinations, and holding out inducements to the different tribes, to make a simultaneous attack on the whole line of frontier. From information imparted to him, and which came from a reliable source, he felt justified in asserting, that if Black Hawk had gained a decisive battle, such an assault would have been made, the consequences of which would harrow up every feeling of the soul.

"Mr. L. looked upon such combinations among the Indians, as he had spoken of, more than probable, and should that happen, and the thirst for plunder and revenge urge them on, they would burn, plunder, murder and destroy; and if, at length, they met an overpowering force, they would fly to the boundless plains behind them, where they could sustain themselves on the countless herds of buffalo that roam over these plains, until such period as they might think proper to renew the attack. Nothing, at some future day, will prevent this state of things, he said, but the presence of a force sufficiently great to overawe the disaffected, and restrain the unruly. The presence of such a force is due to them from humanity, and to us (he spoke for the people of the West) from justice."

It must be recollected, that this view of the impending dangers to the people of the West from a terrible Indian war, was presented twenty years ago; and though no such apprehensions can now be entertained from the same cause, yet that the dangers thus glowingly depicted at that time were imaginary and unfounded, no one at all conversant with Indian and frontier affairs will pretend. The danger of such combinations as Dr. Linn spoke of among the western tribes of Indians, from St. Anthony's Falls, or from our extreme northern boundary, to Texas, was perceived by the government, and provided against by raising and stationing one or two regiments of dragoons on the western border, and directing them to penetrate the Indian territories occasionally, and let the savages see that they were watched, and a force was ready to meet them whenever they should assume any hostile attitude. Even within a year or two the Government have found it necessary to greatly increase the military force stationed along the base of the Rocky Mountains and in the western forts generally, to curb the western tribes of Indians, and to punish their hostile acts, which has been done by General Harney.

On a subsequent occasion, Mr. Benton, from the Committee on Military Affairs, reported, with amendments, the bill from the House of Representatives, to authorize the President of the United States to accept the services of volunteers for the defence of the frontiers, and moved that the Senate proceed to the consideration of the bill.

Opposition being made, Mr. Linn sustained the motion of his colleague. He said, he could consider nothing more worthy of their immediate attention than the protection of our frontiers, threatened, as they now had good reason to apprehend, with the greatest dangers. He asked the Senate to look at the frontier from north to south, and they would see a vast column of Indians, the base of which rested on Texas, now fighting for independence, and against which the Mexicans were waging a war of extermination. No senator, he said, could turn his eye from this examination, without being convinced that a train of the most inflammable materials is laid around our borders, ready at any moment to have a spark applied, and light up the flame of war—of all others the most appalling."

At a later period of the session, the Senate, on motion of Mr. Benton, took up the bill to increase the military peace establishment of the United States. Mr. B. having explained and advocated the bill, Mr. Clay opposed it, and moved to strike out the first section, which would be killing it, should his motion be adopted.

Mr. Linn then came to the aid of his colleague, and opposed Mr. Clay's motion, urging, in the main, arguments, the substance of which has already been given. It would be a humane policy, he said, to the frontier States, to have such a force as would prevent the possibility of an Indian outbreak. He spoke of the warlike character of the Indians, the feelings of hatred and revenge they must necessarily indulge against the whites, and the facilities they had for forming combinations, which demonstrated the necessity of having a sufficient force to overawe them.

After further debate, in which Mr. L. replied to Mr. Crittenden, the bill was passed by the Senate by more than three to one.

It was at this session that a law was passed, annexing to Missouri what is called "the Platte country," now the most wealthy and densely settled part of the State, except St. Louis city and county. Dr. Linn took a deep interest in this measure, and exerted himself to procure the passage of the act. The territory gained thereby is a most valuable acquisition to the

State. By this addition, the western boundary was extended to, and is now the Missouri river. One of the objections to this measure was, that it would annex a large tract of country, over which, by the Missouri Compromise, slavery could not be extended, to a State in which slavery existed, and by whose laws, authorizing the holding of slaves, it would thereafter be governed. The subject was referred to the Committee on the Judiciary, then composed of the following distinguished gentlemen, all of whom, save one, are now living: to wit, John M. Clayton, James Buchanan, Benjamin Watkins Leigh, William C. Preston, and John J. Crittenden.*

The committee were fully aware that the annexation of this country to the State of Missouri, by extending her western boundary to the Missouri river, would be a breach of the Missouri Compromise; nevertheless, as it was situated, it had become a den of thieves, robbers, and outlaws, subject to no law and the jurisdiction of no State. It was then Indian territory, but filled with that infamous population which

* Since this was written Mr. Clayton has passed away; and it is no disparagement to others to say, that, as a statesman of broad, comprehensive, and national views; of a strong and highly cultivated intellect, and well stored mind; of ardent and patriotic devotion to his country, and zeal in promoting all her great interests, protecting her honor, and so elevating her character that she might be a light and a guide to, and command the respect and admiration of, all civilized nations, he has left no superior. Mr. Buchanan is now President elect of the United States.

delights to escape from the restraints which law imposes, to some place where they can give loose to all the evil passions and propensities of their degraded natures. To break up this nest of outlaws, who demoralized the Indian population, and committed all sorts of depredations upon the people of Missouri, was considered a greater good than the breach of the Missouri Compromise was an evil, and the committee therefore reported unanimously in favor of the measure; nor did it meet with any serious opposition in the Senate. The bill became a law on the 7th June, 1836.

During the first session of the 24th Congress, a large number of petitions for the abolition of slavery in the District of Columbia were sent to the Senate and House of Representatives from various parts of the country. The people of the North had become much excited on the subject, and in regard to slavery generally. Agitators were among them; meetings were gotten up, and resolutions of the most intemperate character adopted and published; these were scattered abroad like so many fire-brands, for the purpose of spreading the flame of excitement and agitation. The most incendiary publications were thrown in great profusion from abolition presses, and the mails were made the vehicle of scattering these among the people of the South, and of getting them into the hands of such blacks, bond or free, as could read. Calculated, and probably intended, to excite discontent among the slaves, if not to incite and encourage them to insurrection against their owners, the people of the slave States naturally became indignant and alarmed at this insidious and unjustifiable interference in their affairs, and the attempt to bring about a state of things in those States, at which humanity must shudder with horror.

To such an extent had this system of agitation been carried, and so inflamed had become the public mind in all parts of the country in consequence, that the President, General Jackson, deemed it proper to make it one of the topics of his annual message. In speaking of the affairs of the General Post Office, he said:

"I must also invite your attention to the painful excitement produced in the South, by attempts to circulate through the mails inflammatory appeals, addressed to the passions of the slaves, in prints, and in various sorts of publications, calculated to stimulate them to insurrection, and to produce all the horrors of a servile war. There is, doubtless, no respectable portion of our countrymen who can be so far misled, as to feel any other sentiment than that of indignant regret at conduct so destructive of the harmony and of the peace of the country, and so repugnant to the principles of our national compact, and to the dictates of humanity and religion. Our happiness and prosperity essentially depend upon peace within our borders—and peace depends upon the maintenance, in good faith, of those compromises of the constitution upon which the Union is founded. It is fortunate for the country that the good sense, the generous feeling, and the deep-rooted attachment of the people of the non-slaveholding States, to the Union, and to their fellow-citizens of the same blood in the South, have given so strong and impressive a tone to the sentiment entertained against the proceedings of the misguided persons who have engaged in these unconstitutional and wicked attempts, and especially against the emissaries from foreign parts who have dared to interfere in this matter, as to authorize the hope that those attempts will no longer be persisted in."

Early in the session, Mr. Calhoun moved that so much of the President's message as relates to the transmission of incendiary publications by the United States mail be referred to a special committee. This was agreed to, and Dr. Linn was placed upon this committee, which made a report, and introduced a bill to prohibit the circulation of such publications through the U. S. mail.

This subject, and that of receiving petitions for abolishing slavery in the District of Columbia, which came pouring in in great numbers, became prominent topics of debate during the session, and of the most heated and inflammatory speeches ever listened to in the Senate. One mode of treating these petitions, proposed, was to receive them, and silently refer them to the Committee on the District of Columbia, or, without debate, lay them on the table. Mr. Calhoun, however, objected to their being received at all, and upon this question arose a protracted discussion. The temper and spirit of this debate may be inferred from the following remarks of Mr. Preston, of S. C.

Mr. P. said: "When I consider the extraordinary excitement which has been produced throughout the country; the combustible material, in the shape of incendiary pamphlets, which has been accumulated and spread abroad; the vast multitudes which have assembled; the apostles who have addressed them; their acts and their menaces; though I am but little disposed to allude to them, yet a regard to the honor and interests of the South calls upon me to do so, and that, too, in language which she has a right to expect and demand.

"Sir, the Southern mind has already been filled with agitation and alarm. Their property, their domestic relations, their altars, their lives, are in danger; and, as if this were not sufficient, we have now these agitators and incendiaries calling upon Congress to act upon the slaveholding States, either directly or indirectly, through the medium of this District. And are we, sir, to sit still and see it? Are we to behold our rights and privileges trampled upon? All upon which the permanence and security of our prosperity depend, is assailed by these blood-thirsty fanatics, and Government called upon to participate in the wanton and malicious movement, without lifting a hand, without raising a voice, without acting as a due regard to the honor, dignity, and happiness of our constituents calls upon us to act?"

This exciting subject was disposed of in the Senate by coming to an understanding that all petitions should be received and laid upon the table, there to remain; which was much the wisest course, and least likely to produce and foster excitement either at the North or at the South. It was yielding to the petitioners the naked right to petition, but laying their petitions quietly on the table was saying to them that it was useless to send their inflammatory memorials to that body.

In the House, however, a more impolitic and unwise course was pursued. The subject was there referred to a special committee, who reported, among other resolutions, the following, which was adopted, and out of which grew the famous 21st rule, to wit:

"*Resolved*, That all petitions, memorials, resolutions, propositions, or papers, relating in any way, or to any extent whatever, to the subject of slavery, or the abolition of slavery, shall, without being either printed or referred, be laid upon the table, and that no further action whatever shall be had thereon."

That the adoption of this rule by the House, instead of pursuing the practice of the Senate, was the cause of the very great increase in the number of petitions of this kind presented, and of increased agitation at the North, no one, it is presumed, now doubts. Dr. Linn was in favor of the course adopted by the Senate, rightly judging what the effect of the other would be. The subject coming up again at the subsequent session, he took occasion briefly to express his views thereon.

A memorial from the grand jury of Washington County, D. C., having been presented, protesting against the interference of citizens from distant States in respect to the abolition of slavery in the District of Columbia, a motion was made that it be laid on the table and printed. Mr. Calhoun then moved to print an extra number of copies.

In making this motion, Mr. Calhoun said it was a most important paper, and there was one part of it at which he most heartily rejoiced. It took the true position—that abolition petitions should not be received. He further expressed himself very earnestly and warmly upon this subject in advocating the motion to print an extra number.

"Mr. Linn said he should be pleased to know whether any practical benefits were likely to grow out of circulating, by order of the Senate, copies of the document now proposed to be printed. What, he asked, was the proper remedy for the evil of which the people of the District of Columbia complained, and concerning which they had directed the attention of Congress? Was their property in danger? Were the laws insufficient to protect their slaves? If so, let us then march directly up to the subject, and enact such as will afford ample security. For measures of a practical nature, he would give his vote with a great deal of pleasure. He said, he was well aware that questions of this kind came up here, and incidentally impressed persons at a distance with the idea that Congress wished to deprive them of the right to petition. Nothing, in his opinion, was more erroneous. Refuse to receive and hear an abolition petition, and you render the abolitionist a thousand times more active and industrious in propagating their doctrines, and more successful in enlisting the sympathies in their favor of those who believed in the inherent right of the people to assemble and petition for a redress of grievances. He never had voted, and never would vote, for the printing and disseminating an abolition memorial; nor would he lend his aid for the printing of this document in favor of slavery.

"On the great question of slavery, the constitution and laws would find ample support in the good sense of the great body of the American people. He gave it as his opinion, that to insure tranquillity was to let this exciting topic alone."

The wisdom of this remark, and the correctness of the views taken by Dr. L., have now been fully proved. So long as the 21st rule existed in the House, the people of the North never ceased to pour in their abolition petitions; hundreds, and perhaps thousands of them, having been offered by Mr. John Q. Adams, more with the view to vindicate or claim *the right of petition*, than with any desire that the prayer of the petitioners should be granted. But scarcely had this rule been abrogated, as it was at the first session of the 29th Congress, than these petitions almost wholly ceased; and we now hear no more of them, though there are probably some of them occasionally presented and laid quietly on the table.

In the discharge of his public duties, no senator could be more constant in his attendance, observant of what was going on, watchful of the interests of the people of his own State, and efficient in promoting them. Whatever concerned Missouri, or the people of Iowa, or Wisconsin, had a peculiar interest for Dr. Linn; and the more deeply it concerned these, the more ardently did he embrace and labor to accomplish the object proposed. Among the subjects which seemed most to occupy his thoughts at this period, were the obtaining of grants of public lands for various purposes for his State, and the protection of the western and northern frontiers against the hostilities of the Indians, to which the people of Missouri and Iowa were at that time so much exposed. The Black Hawk war had shown what murders and depredations the Indians, if united in large bodies and led on by a warrior of genius and influence, might commit before a sufficient force to repel them could be got together and brought against them; and he constantly, therefore, advocated the increase of the army, or the raising of some regiments of dragoons to be stationed along the frontier, to scour the country, overawe the savages, and prevent them from committing outrages upon the whites.

At the second session of the 24th Congress, Mr. Benton, chairman of the Military Committee, brought in a bill to increase the military establishment of the United States. It being warmly opposed, chiefly by Mr. Calhoun and Mr. Crittenden, Mr. Linn took part in the debate in aid of his colleague. After several days had been spent in dicussing the bill,

"Mr. Linn rose, and said, that it was now the settled policy of the Government to remove those remnants of Indian tribes who yet retained some territory within the States, from the positions they occupied, and to give them in exchange a territory west of the Mississippi; thereby at once protecting the Indians from the encroachments and depredations of a surrounding white population, and enabling the State Governments to exercise uninterrupted jurisdiction over the entire extent of their own territory. It was a noble policy, characterized alike by wisdom and humanity. It had originated in the cabinet of which the Senator from South Carolina had been at the time a distinguished member, and it would stand in the history of the country a glorious and enduring monument of the enlightened views and enlarged benevolence of its authors. The process had commenced, and the plan was in the course of execution by the present administration, notwithstanding many obstacles. The Indians had been removed from many of the States, and collected in their respective tribes on our Western frontier. Now, Mr. L. would ask the Senator from South Carolina, and all those other senators who represented States that had formerly been burdened with an Indian population, whether they were not under the most solemn obligations of justice to the States of Missouri, Louisiana, and Arkansas, and Territory of Wisconsin, in whose immediate vicinity this large body of Indians had been assembled, to protect her people from the Indians, and to protect the several Indian tribes from each other? Now, what course of policy was it necessary to pursue, iu order to effectually accomplish this end? Having removed these people from their native haunts, and brought them together under new circumstances, the

Government was obviously under obligations to extend to them, so far as it should be in their power, the blessings of government, religion, and civilization; and for this purpose the great and efficient means must be, to break up the war spirit amongst themselves. Unless that spirit could be put down, these warlike tribes would in a little time destroy each other, or cause aggression upon us. For this purpose, it was indispensable that we should have at our disposal, and ready for action, a respectable military force. Successive Secretaries of War, and among them the late Secretary Cass, than whom no man was better acquainted with the Indian habits and character, had estimated the force requisite for this object, at 7,000 men. General Jessup, in a communication made by him to the Government, had made the same estimate, and all the Indian agents who had been consulted, concurred in the same opinion. The present acting Secretary of War fully agreed in it. They all agreed in opinion, that a permanent military force must be established on that frontier. When not engaged in military duty, they might be employed in constructing military roads and fortifications. Forts must be established at short distances from each other, and garrisoned by a standing body of troops, whilst cavalry should be employed to move from point to point. To hope for any thing like permanent peace among a large body of Indians, under any other circumstances, was idle. The very nature of the Indian was war; it was the element in which he moved; and he must see a force actually present, and sufficient to control him, or this warlike propensity could never be repressed. It was utterly vain to represent to these people the power of the United States Government. Nothing of the kind made any impression on the Indian mind, unless accompanied by a visible demonstration of military force.

"The Senator from Kentucky (Mr. Crittenden) had observed that the militia of the Union could defend themselves. It was unqestionably true; but Mr. L. contended that this Government had no right to place the people of the country in such a condition that they must take up arms to defend themselves. It was unjust. No one knew better than the gentleman, at what cost the dark and bloody soil of Kentucky had been conquered and maintained against a savage foe. Its soil had been fattened by the best blood of this land—blood which might all have been spared, if the Government had been in circumstances to afford to those hardy settlers the protection of a regular military force, but which was denied them in consequence of revolutionary struggles. Mr. L. did not want to see such scenes enacted in Missouri. No doubt the people of Missouri could subdue any Indian force which should invade their soil, but it was not their place to do it.

They ought not to be compelled to work out their own safety.

"Mr. L. spoke of the Black Hawk war and its cause; also of some of the incidents attending it, as illustrating Indian warfare and Indian character, and asked if the Indian character and habits had changed? Not at all. They were the same ferocious and bloodthirsty people they had ever been. No doubt the people of Missouri, after a bloody struggle, from time to time renewed, might subdue them. But he repeated the assertion, that the Government had no right to compel them into any such contest. It was the act of the Government which had congregated these Indian tribes on the frontiers of that State, and it was unjust to leave the inhabitants exposed to have their houses burnt, their farms laid waste, and their wives and children tomahawked before their eyes."

In the progress of this debate, Dr. Linn understood some senators, Mr. Calhoun especially, to have made charges against the people of Missouri, of having plundered and oppressed the Indians on their border. The least intimation of any thing of this kind, the slightest imputation cast upon the people of his State—a State which he loved and served with filial affection and devotedness,—was sufficient to rouse all his feelings, and call forth all his ability to repel the charges, and defend the fair fame of the State whose honor and interest had been in part intrusted by her to his safe-keeping. He was not the man to sit silent when even there was the least whisper of dishonor connected with the name of Missouri. *Sans peur, sans reproche* himself, with an honor as spotless as that of a Chevalier Bayard, of an Admirable Crichton, he felt with the keenness of a noble son, the least imputation cast upon the State of which he was himself an integral part, and to which he owed willing allegiance. As the debate was about to close, and the question to be taken on the passage of the bill,

Mr. Linn rose to reply to these charges. He said he had resided permanently for twenty-six years in the State of Missouri, and knew that the charge was wholly unfounded. There was not a man in Missouri or Wisconsin, who did not possess too much sense to plunder Indians. The people of Missouri had never robbed or trampled on these natives of the forest. They had been represented as a poor, spiritless, downtrodden race, ignorant of their own rights, and continually imposed upon by the whites. Nothing could be more opposite to the truth. No people were keener-sighted, or more fully awake to their rights and interests. No one could have personal intercourse with them, and not discover that they were shrewd in an unusual degree. The Black Hawk war was to be traced entirely to the fraud practised by that chief in the execution of the treaty. He had openly insulted General Gaines, and threatened his soldiers, and the General, to comply with the general peace-policy of the Government, bought him off. But he returned again the next year. Mr. L. claimed from this Government protection for his constituents. It was in vain for gentlemen to declare there was no danger, when 150,000 Indians had been collected on their frontier, and who were in reach, and might be in communication with 150,000 more, inhabiting the vast prairies of the West. Mr. L. here quoted:

"'On these extensive plains, a new state of things was likely to grow up. It is to be feared that a great part will form a lawless interval between the abodes of civilized man, like the wastes of the ocean and the deserts of Arabia; and, like them, be subject to the depredations of the marauder. Here may spring up new and mongrel races, like new formations in geology, the amalgamation of the "debris" and abrasions of former races, civilized and savage; the remains of broken and almost extinguished tribes; the descendants of wandering hunters and trappers; of fugitives from the Spanish and American frontiers; of adventurers and desperadoes of every class and country, yearly ejected from the bosom of society into the wilderness. We are contributing incessantly to swell its singular and heterogeneous cloud of wild population, that is to hang about our frontier, by the transfer of whole tribes of savages from the east of the Mississippi to the great wastes of the far West. Many of these bear with them the smart of real or fancied injuries; many consider themselves expatriated beings, wrongfully exiled from their hereditary homes and the sepulchres of their fathers, and cherish a deep and abiding animosity against the race that has dispossessed them. Some may gradually become pastoral hordes, like those rude and migratory people (half shepherd, half warrior) who, with their flocks and herds, roam the plains of Upper Asia; but others, it is to be apprehended, will become predatory bands, mounted on fleet steeds of the prairies, with the open plains for their marauding grounds, and the mountains for their retreats and lurking-places. Here they may resemble those great hordes of the North, "Gog and Magog, with their bands," that haunted the gloomy imaginations of the Prophets. "A great company and mighty host, all riding upon horses, and warring upon those nations which were at rest, and dwelt peaceably, and had gotten cattle and goods."'

The way to prevent the existence of this state of things, Mr. L. said, was to civilize the Indians. This was a noble design, and, properly pursued, would succeed; but never, until the warlike habits of the Indians were broken, and they were converted into agriculturists. So long as they should be left unawed by a military force, and at liberty to butcher each other, the benevolent design intended in their removal could never be acomplished.

"Mr. L. said he had travelled through the Indian settlements near Fort Leavenworth, and he had found fields cultivated, houses built, school-houses erected, workshops opened, the loom going, young Indian boys, from sixteen to eighteen years old, learning the mechanic arts, and some of them as good workmen as could be found any where. Here the Indians were perfectly peaceable; and, beholding the controlling force in their presence, had abandoned their warlike habits, and were beginning to cultivate the arts of peace. Let but this system be carried out, and the same results would follow throughout the Indian country. Was it not worth an experiment? Did we not owe it to these people thus to secure to them a fair start in the course of civilization? This once secured, their progress would afterwards be certain. Only keep down the tomahawk for a few years, and interest and experience would convince these people of the advantages of peace and civilization. But leave them to their own savage nation, refuse to the white settlers any military defence, and these Indians, whenever their resentments should be awakened, could at any time make an irruption into our settlements, burn, scalp, slay and butcher, without mercy, and then retreat to their swamps and deserts before any force could be collected to resist them. It required no spirit of prophecy to foretell, with great certainty, the recurrence of scenes of this character on our frontiers, if the Government should neglect to erect forts, and, after they were erected, should be unable or unwilling to garrison them. And when the blood of helpless women and children had thus been shed, would not those senators feel bitter remorse, who, by opposing a measure so necessary and so salutary as that now before the Senate, had, to a certain extent, made themselves sharers in that blood?

"Mr. L. had repeatedly heard it said, that Missouri would find ample compensation, in the vast expenditure of public money on her borders, for the evils that might grow out of the congregation of such fiery and discordant tribes of Indians on her borders. She wanted wealth from no such sources. The God of nature had been most bountiful to her; and all her population earnestly desired, was to be left in peace to cultivate the blessings so lavishly showered upon them. Washed on the east by 'the Father of Waters,' some of whose tributaries inosculate with the silver lakes of the north; divided into nearly equal parts by the mighty Missouri river, whose sources lie hid in the recesses and caves of the Rocky Mountains, where silence loves to keep her long millennium of unbroken repose ; a rich virgin soil, mountains pregnant with mineral wealth; extensive plains and noble forests—much reason has she for rejoicing, but let her rejoice with modesty."

Mr. Calhoun remarked, that the Senator from Missouri had represented the Indians in his neighborhood as far advanced in civilization, yet was demanding troops to protect his constituents against their ravages.

Mr. Linn explained: "What he had said about advanced civilization, referred not to the body of Indians on the frontiers generally, but to those only who were in the vicinity of Fort Leavenworth ; and his argument had been, that, if similar forts should be distributed at short distances along our frontier, the same effects might be hoped for on a wider scale."

The bill then passed the Senate, 26 to 13.

No one will doubt that Dr. Linn looked forward with fearful apprehension to the consequences that might result from the gathering together of such great numbers of Indians upon the western borders of Missouri, and their banding, as he was fearful they would, with the ferocious and warlike tribes of the plains and the Rocky Mountains. His fears have not been fully realized, fortunately; but the Government has prevented their being so, at least in part, by keeping an active and vigilant military force in the plains, and establishing and garrisoning forts in the heart of the Indian country. The acquisition of California and New Mexico, and the rapid increase of the emigrants to these countries as well as to Oregon; the increase also of the trade to Santa Fé, New Mexico, as well as the hostile demonstrations of some of the Indians, and the murders and depredations continually committed by others, rendered such a measure indispensable to the safety of persons and the protection of property on the frontiers and in the Indian country. But in spite of this military force, many murders have been annually committed, and much property stolen and destroyed. A continued war has existed with some of these fierce and warlike tribes occupying a part of Texas, New Mexico, and Utah, and the hostile demonstrations of other more northern tribes has rendered it necessary for the Government to throw at once and with all speed, an effective force into their country, and to attack and disperse them.

But for these vigorous measures, the necessity of which was eloquently and forcibly urged by Dr. Linn, no one can doubt but that all the horrors of an Indian war, and an Indian raid upon the unprotected white settlements exposed to their incursions, so graphically and truthfully depicted by him, would have been realized. Well he knew, that nothing but force and fear would restrain them from indulging their natural bloodthirsty disposition; and that, to produce fear, the force must be present or visible, and be sufficient to inspire them with awe. He knew the Indian character most thoroughly; and that he could never be civilized, so long as he was permitted to carry and use his tomahawk and rifle; that he could never be Christianized until he had become domiciled, and had learned to depend upon the earth for his sustenance, rather than upon robbery and the chase. The only mode of civilizing savages is by teaching them to cultivate the earth; to raise flocks and herds, and to confine themselves to the spot they cultivate, instead of roaming about. And it is the veriest waste of effort, time, and expense, to attempt to Christianize them, until they have acquired agricultural habits. The hunter has no Sabbath, and no church, save that not made with hands, and covered by the canopy of heaven. He may have renounced his false gods, and professed his belief in the true God and His Son Jesus Christ, and may have done so sincerely; but let him go afterwards into the woods or prairies to hunt, and meet with bad luck, and he will at once attribute it to the anger of his object of worship, whatever that be, and will take such means as his ignorance and superstition prompt, to appease the anger of his god and propitiate his favor. What then becomes of his Christianity? It is gone. Should it chance, then, that this son of the forest, immediately after, or during the day, was lucky enough to discover and capture a deer, buffalo, moose, elk, or other game, would he not attribute his change of fortune to his having discarded his new religion, and sacrificed to the spirit to which he and his fathers had always paid homage? Undoubtedly such would be his conclusion.

The condition of the Indian population in the vicinity of Fort Leavenworth, as described by Dr. Linn, is the condition in which they are almost invariably found when compelled to rely upon the productions of the earth for subsistence, are prevented from leading a roaming, vagabond life, are taught how to cultivate the soil, furnished at first with agricultural implements, and have with them white men to teach them various mechanic arts, and to make and repair their agricultural tools. Without this aid, instruction, and encouragement, they are unable to surmount the first difficulties of their new mode of life; become discouraged and disheartened; will not apply themselves to labor, resort to drink, petty thefts, and vagabondism, and drag out a miserable existence, constantly diminishing in numbers, until what was once a powerful, warlike tribe, terrible in its numbers and ferociousness, is dwindled down to half a dozen families of miserable, ragged, half-starved, wandering beggars and pilferers, more like gypsies in their appearance and habits, than the well-formed, dauntless, bloodthirtsy red men with whom our ancestors had so often to grapple in deadly conflict, from whom these miserable remnants descended. If our Government would prevent the red men from being swept away entirely, and becoming an extinct race, it must be by teaching them the arts of civilization, and compelling them to draw their subsistence from the bosom of mother earth. They must be taught to depend upon the products of their own labor, and to respect the property of others; to learn the law of *meum* and *tuum*, the foundation of all civilization. Wherever this has been done under the auspices of the Federal Government, it has been attended with the most gratifying results. By no other process or system can the red man be civilized, and saved from the doom that seems to threaten him.

With this, the 24th Congress, closed the eight years' administration of Gen. Jackson, of whom Dr. Linn was a most ardent and devoted personal and political friend. Warm in his temperament, sincere in his attachments, giving his whole heart where he gave his confidence, brave and chivalrous himself, and an admirer of heroic courage and noble daring in others, it is not surprising that Dr. Linn should have felt that almost filial attachment and veneration for the Hero and the Chief Magistrate, which all knew him to feel, and which the latter so warmly reciprocated. In his speech on the bill to indemnify General Jackson for the fine imposed upon him at New Orleans in 1815, made several years after this, he gave utterance to his feelings towards him in the following language: "I would have avoided," he said, "if possible, saying any thing in reference to the deeds of General Jackson; neither do I wish to point the Senate to the halo with which those deeds have surrounded his venerable head, and illuminated his country. My voice will not be heard in utterance of his praise, to induce senators to support the bill which they are now considering. Nor is it necessary; for even those who have opposed obstacles to its passage, have admitted his just claim to honor and fame, and the gratitude of his countrymen. His actions proclaim for themselves their enduring fame; gratitude has stamped them upon our memories; and the true and steady hand of History will grave them deeply upon her imperishable tablets. His good name cannot *now* be sullied; it is placed in the scroll which contains the list of those whom freemen and patriots delight to honor. His reputation, like a star, far above the clouds of detraction which float around our censorious world, will shine with brighter radiance as the flight of time shall hallow his memory. * * * * His country has manifested its confidence in his uprightness, by bestowing upon him the highest office in the gift of the people—and that confidence they have never had cause to repent. His history should become familiar to the youth of our land; it furnishes one of the best examples by which to shape their course as citizens of the Republic; and presents, in the most prominent manner, that great reward which is extended to honesty of purpose, disinterested love of country, and persevering efforts to promote its welfare—a reward greater than that which has ever been given by any other country to any man for like virtues."

The esteem in which Dr. Linn was held by General Jackson, will be seen by his letters both to the Doctor and to Mrs. Linn, given in a subsequent part of this volume. Love and esteem were never unreciprocated by him, but ever touched a responsive chord in his warm and manly heart. They parted at Washington, on General Jackson's leaving that city for the Hermitage, never to meet again.

CHAPTER III.

ON the 4th of March, 1837, General Jackson bade adieu to public life, and was succeeded in the Presidential office, which he had filled for eight years,—the last who held the office for two terms,—by Mr. Van Buren. The commencement of Mr. Van Buren's term was signalized by an extraordinary revulsion in the monetary affairs of the country. On the 7th of May, the Banks in Philadelphia stopped specie payments, and the moneyed institutions in almost all parts of the country immediately followed their example. A universal alarm was felt; a commercial crisis of a most serious character followed, and deranged and depressed all kinds of business for an unusual period. Such was the condition of the country, that the President deemed it advisable to call an extra session of Congress in September; but this seemed rather to increase the general "hard times," instead of relieving them. Mr. Linn took a lively interest in all these public matters, but as he did not participate prominently in the debates which took place at the extra and subsequent session, I deem it proper to pass these over without entering into a circumstantial account of them. Other subjects not of a party character, chiefly occupied his attention; and among these was the introduction and promotion of the growth of tropical and fibrous plants in Florida. His friend, Dr. Perrine, who had been U. S. Consul at Campeachy, where he had had favorable opportunities of becoming acquainted with the nature, value, mode of cultivation, &c., of the plants proposed to be introduced into Florida, had devoted himself zealously to this subject, and had become persuaded that he might render his country an important service by introducing and cultivating these plants in the United States; he had also induced Dr. Linn to lend his aid in accomplishing the important and patriotic object, convinced, as the latter was, that the plan was eminently practical, and that results of the most important and beneficial character would follow its execution.

Accordingly, Dr. Linn introduced a bill at the second session of the 25th Congress, "to encourage the introduction and promote the cultivation and growth of tropical plants," and in a few days thereafter he made a report upon the subject, which attracted much attention, especially at the South. The report was founded upon a memorial presented to the Senate by

Dr. Perrine, which was referred to the Committee on Agriculture. The committee, through Dr. Linn, say that, "In obedience to the Treasury Circular of the 6th of September, 1827, Dr. Henry Perrine appears to be the only American Consul who has perseveringly devoted his head, heart and hands to the subject of introducing tropical plants in the United States; and his voluminous manuscripts alone exhibit a great amount of labor and research which promise to be highly beneficial to our common country. The memorialist founds his hopes of final success for the immediate propagation, and subsequent cultivation of tropical plants in Florida, on four leading facts: 1. Many valuable vegetables of the tropics do actually propagate themselves in the worst soils and situations, in the sun and in the shade of every tropical region, where a single plant arrives by accident or design. 2. For other profitable plants of the tropics which require human skill or care, moisture is equivalent to manure, for tropical cultivation essentially consists in appropriate irrigation. 3. A tropical climate extends into Southern Florida, so peculiarly favorable to human health and vegetable growth, that the fertility and benignity of its atmosphere will counterbalance the sterility and malignity of its soil. 4. The inundated marshes and miry swamps of the interior of Southern Florida are more elevated than the arid sands and untillable rocks on the coast; and hence the same canals which may drain the former will irrigate the latter, and afford the appropriate proportion of moisture for both. The memorialist founds his hopes of success for the *gradual acclimation* of many profitable plants of the tropics, throughout at least all our southern and southwestern States, on, 1st, the general history of all tropical plants, whose cultivation has been gradually extended towards the poles; 2d, the particular history of our great staples of the south and southwest, viz., tropical rice, tobacco, cotton, and sugar; and 3d, the important fact that kindred species of many profitable plants, which will be still more important objects of *agriculture*, are indigenous to our worst soils between the Potomac and the Mississippi, viz., of Agava and Yucca. * * * * In relation to the immediate propagation of tropical plants in tropical Florida, on the most arid, the most humid, and hitherto most worthless soils, the committee expressed their conviction and belief from the facts and statements presented to them: and they further expressed their confidence in the possibility of acclimating at least the fibrous-leaved plants, whose foliaceous fibres are superior substitutes for flax and hemp. "Hitherto," say the committee, "Southern Florida has been considered so sickly and so sterile, as to be unworthy the expense and trouble of surveying and of sale; and even now it is seriously contended that this section of the territory is uninhabitable by the white man, and should therefore be abandoned to the savages and runaway negroes from the neighboring States. * * * * * * But if the suggestions of the memorialist, and if his experiments should be successful, the arid sands and arid rocks, and mangrove thickets of the coast, the miry marshes, pestilential swamps, and impenetrable morasses of the interior, may all, ultimately, be covered by a dense population of small cultivators and of family manufacturers; and tropical Florida will thus form a well-garrisoned bulwark against invasion in every shape and shade. * * * * * By the introduction of such new staples as can be propagated on the worst soils of the old States more profitably than their old staples can be cultivated on the best soils of the new States, emigration from the South will be prevented, and even the ruined fields and barren wastes will become covered with a dense population of small cultivators; and that rural population may be tripled by the employment of new staples in the really domestic manufactures of their farms, families, and females. At all events, the numerous small cultivators of the South would thus be enabled to furnish the cheapest possible new materials for the numerous small manufacturers of the North, and would hence create, mutually, a profitable and harmonious dependence on each other, of the great pacific masses of population in both sections of the Union. With these views of the national importance of the enterprise of Dr. Perrine, the committee determined to report a bill of such a character as would, in their opinion, offer barely a sufficient inducement for him to undertake the experiment proposed by him, of introducing certain fibrous plants into Florida, and attempting their cultivation.

"In other countries," the committee remark, "an undertaking of such magnitude is the especial duty of the Government; but in the United States, we are indebted to individual zeal and perseverance for the origin and prosecution of the grandest plans of national utility."

"From the specimens of fibrous-leaved plants and foliaceous fibres submitted to the committee," they expressed their confident belief, that "if they could be propagated in Southern Florida, of which they had no reasonable doubt, they will form highly important additions to the agriculture, manufactures, and commerce of the Union."

This report was accompanied by a large mass of manuscripts prepared by Dr. Perrine, giving the history, mode of cultivation, botanical character, the kinds of soil, climate, &c., &c., necessary for the growth and successful propagation of the various kinds of plants proposed to be introduced into Southern Florida, which information the Doctor had spent many laborious years in acquiring, and which was not likely to be underrated by Dr. Linn. If Dr. Perrine's hopes were well founded, and not too sanguine, if his plan could be carried into practical operation, a service would be rendered to his country of incalculable value. Doctor Linn saw this, and could perceive no insurmountable obstacle in the way of the realization of Dr. P.'s most sanguine hopes. He himself was moved by an ardent and patriotic desire to secure so great a benefit to his country, to add new and valuable staples to her productions, to increase her domestic manufactures, and to convert arid sands and rocks, miry swamps and quagmires, drowned lands, and almost impenetrable morasses, into fruitful, healthful, smiling fields and densely settled plantations.

The object was worthy the attention, ambition, and labor of a patriot statesman: it was to make a thousand blades of grass grow where none grew before; to convert sterility into productiveness; a desolate waste into blooming fields, and pestilential swamps into healthful habitations. What higher or more noble motive could actuate or stimulate a patriotic heart? What American will not deeply lament that, after spending years of toil, anxiety, apprehension and suspense, in endeavoring to attain his great object, and wish of his heart, Dr. Perrine shonld have fallen a victim to savage ferocity, as he was about to prove the feasibility of his undertaking and the justness of his conclusions. But the importance of his life and labors could not stay the hand of the murderous savage, and he was cut down by those who regard neither age, sex nor condition. The Indians saw in him only an intruder into their country; they looked upon him as one of the nation with whom they were at war, and whose blood it delighted them to shed. With these feelings of hatred and revenge, the bullet was sped, and his earthly labors were closed.

Dr. Perrine having been thus cut off in the midst of his career of usefulness, and when, as he confidently believed, he was about to reap the reward of his many years of toil, anxiety, and perseverance, and enjoy the fruition of his hopes, there was no one to carry on his great work, which was therefore arrested at the point to which he had brought it. He had commenced the cultivation of some of the plants he designed to introduce into Florida, and to cultivate, but they were left unattended to or cared for; one of them at least, however, the *Agave Americana,* found a genial soil and climate, in which it now grows with great vigor and luxuriance, and may some day become a source of agricultural and manufacturing profit to the people of that section; indeed, it would be so now but that, on account of the great cheapness of labor in Venezuela and other tropical American countries from whence the plant was brought by Dr. Perrine, it can be raised and manufactured into sissal hemp at a less cost than it can be at this time in Florida.

There were those who doubted the feasibility of successfully transferring the plants proposed to be introduced and cultivated in Florida by Dr. Perrine, and of making them profitable productions. Dr. P., however, had confidence in the undertaking, and saw in its success a valuable acquisition to the agricultural and manufacturing resources of his country. Should the experiment succeed, he would have rendered his country a most important and lasting service, that of turning arid sands and rocks, and pestilential fens and morasses, into blooming, healthful, and profitable fields. But suppose the experiment should fail? he alone would suffer pecuniarily; he alone would feel the mortification attendant upon the disappointment; the country would have suffered no detriment. He possessed, however, that ardent, sanguine temperament, that confidence in his own judgment, and that perseverance in whatever he undertook, which were calculated to insure success, and without which no great enterprise, no important national work was ever achieved. In Dr. Linn, he found a genial spirit, and a friend who warmly sympathized with him, became convinced of the feasibility of his enterprise, and lent him his aid in every possible way he could, to enable him to accomplish his patriotic purpose.

Like Dr. Perrine's undertaking, the introduction and cultivation of cotton, sugar, wheat, and various other valuable plants, not indigenous to the country, was an experiment; so also was the introduction and growth of the silkworm, and the production of silk, from China or the East Indies, first into Italy, and subsequently into France and other European countries. It is the enterprising and sanguiue spirits of the country, like Dr. Perrine, who take the lead in making such experiments, and who, in case of success, become public benefactors; who confer immense and perpetual benefits and blessings upon their country, without the sacrifice of human hecatombs, and the drenching her soil in the blood of her own or any other people; and in view of this, we may well say, that peace has her victories and triumphs as well as war. Had Dr. Perrine's life been spared to carry forward his experiment to a successful issue, as we can hardly doubt would have been the result of his labors, it is not easy to estimate the benefits that would have accrued to the southern portion of Florida, and the addition that would have been made to our staple productions and profitable industrial pursuits.

Dr. Linn heard with deep and sincere regret of the fate that had befallen his friend, and put a stop to the enterprise in which he felt so lively an interest; but he was not destined long to survive him, and was, like his friend, destined to fall in the midst of his usefulness, and in the prime of manhood.

One great object Dr. Linn hoped would be accomplished by promoting the enterprise of Dr. Perrine, was the draining of the fens, swamps, and morasses of Florida, and converting them from pestilential, uninhabitable regions, into the smiling and healthful abodes of a numerous and industrious population. The same desire to confer blessings and benefits upon his fellow-citizens, prompted him to make an early proposition, that the Federal Government should convey the lands in Missouri and Arkansas, entirely and partially covered every year with water to such an extent as to render them not only untillable in their present condition, but wholly uninhabitable on account of their pestilential character, to those States, upon condition of their being drained, and rendered capable of being cultivated.

Dr. Linn, in pursuance of notice given, introduced, on leave, on the 21st of Feb., 1838, a bill to encourage and promote the introduction and cultivation of tropical plants in Florida, of which I have spoken, and on the same day he proposed that the Committee on Public Lands be instructed to report a bill granting to the States all the unsurveyed lands within their limits covered with water.

It was well known, he said, that large portions of land in some of the States were at times covered with water to an immense extent, which the Government officers had reported as not worth the cost of survey. If these lands were ceded to the States in which they lie, it might be attended with the most beneficial results. Those inundated lands were a curse to the States; they were the very hot-beds of disease, generating that dreadful malaria so fatal in its influence upon the surrounding country. If all such were given to the States, at least such as were deemed unworthy the cost of survey, they might be reclaimed, so as to prevent the ill effects usually arising from them.

Upon some objection being made to this proposition, Dr. Linn further and warmly advocated it as wise and salutary. The lands might be drained and improved by the States, or by individuals or companies under State regulations, but they never would be, so long as they belonged to the General Government; and as they were returned by the officers of the United States not worth the cost of surveying them, Congress, in giving them to the States in which they lie, would be bestowing very little indeed.

The subject having been laid on the table, nothing resulted from Dr. L.'s proposition at this time. But the minds of senators had been called to it; a commencement had been made, the seed had been dropped, and ere long it was destined to spring up and bear fruit. A few years after, but not while Dr. L. was living, a bill passed both Houses, and became a law, by which the drowned, inundated, or swamp lands were ceded to the States respectively in which they were situated; a measure which, though somewhat abused, has been and is likely to be productive of incalculable benefit to these States. Though Dr. Linn did not live to accomplish this benevolent and wise measure, yet he is entitled to honor and praise for having brought it forward and advocated its adoption from those States in which these lands are situated.

The subject of the purchase of Mount Vernon having been much discussed within a few years past, and being one that now occupies the public mind, and will continue to do so, probably, until the property shall come into possession of the United States, or the State of Virginia, it is due to the memory of Dr. Linn to note that, on the 4th of January, 1838, he offered a resolution in the Senate, which was adopted, "that the Committee on Public Lands inquire into the expediency of purchasing the Mount Vernon property, now belonging to the family of President Washington, for the Government of the United States."

Dr. Linn was desirous of seeing the consecrated spot, where rested all that was mortal of the illustrious Father of his Country,—of him whose fame is imperishable,—in the possession of that country in whose glorious diadem the name of WASHINGTON is the brightest star. He was anxious that MOUNT VERNON should become the Mecca of the Western world, and that it should be improved, beautified, and adorned in a manner befitting the resting-place of the most illustrious man the world had produced. He considered the fame of the great men and eminent patriots to whom we are indebted for our national existence, for the freedom and independence which they won and bequeathed to us, for the noble constitution, which, amidst trying difficulties, they formed, adopted, and established, as the choicest and most hallowed property of the nation; and in proportion as we venerate the mighty spirits who have passed away, leaving to us the great benefits of their wisdom and patriotic labors, and cherish, and teach our children to cherish and revere their memories, in that proportion shall we love our country, and value the inestimable birthright privileges and blessings for which we are indebted to them.

It was for this reason that he desired to make Mount Vernon,—hallowed as the residence and as the depository of the remains of GEORGE WASHINGTON,—the place of resort of all who should be in its vicinity. That the dwelling should be preserved as it was, in all its unpretending simplicity, when occupied by him to whom the great and the good of the whole civilized world paid the homage of their profound respect and admiration, and when it received the most illustrious as its guests.

If the purchase, adornment, and sanctification of the home of WASHINGTON could more largely infuse into the hearts of the American people the great principles which guided his action in public and private life; if it could be the means of inducing them to study more carefully and profoundly the maxims and precepts which he taught them, the example he set them, the great legacy of wisdom and advice he left them in his Farewell Address, if it could cause them to "lay up his words in their hearts, and in their souls, and bind them for a sign upon their hands, and teach them to their children, speaking of them when sitting in their houses, and when walking by the way, when lying down and when rising up—to write them upon the door-posts of their houses and upon their gates,"* and inspire them with a more animating veneration for his character, wisdom, and example,—if, in short, it could convert that dead reverence which all *profess* to feel for his great, noble, and patriotic traits of character, into a living, active, abiding, and animating feeling, no amount of money, however great, would be ill-spent thereon.

But while all pay lip-homage to the wisdom and

* Deuteronomy xi. 18, 19, 20.

patriotism of the Father of his Country, how few public men are animated by his desire to promote the welfare of his country, regardless of his own private interests, and follow in the paths which he labored so anxiously and earnestly to make smooth and plain for all who should come after him.

CHAPTER IV.

One of the subjects which Dr. Linn took an early, deep and lively interest in, was the exclusion of the British from Oregon, and its exclusive occupation by the United States. He had a high appreciation of that country, in an agricultural and commercial point of view, and being well satisfied of the soundness of the title of the United States, was unwilling she should be even partially dispossessed of it, or share her possession with a country having no title there whatever.

On the 7th of February, 1838, Mr. Linn, on leave, introduced a bill authorizing the occupation of the Columbia or Oregon river, [establishing a territory north of latitude 42 degrees, and west of the Rocky Mountains, to be called the Oregon Territory; authorizing the establishment of a fort on that river, and the occupation of the country by the military force of the United States; establishing a port of entry, and requiring that the country should then be held subject to the revenue laws of the United States; with an appropriation of $50,000.]

The bill having been read twice, Mr. Linn moved to refer it to the Committee on Military Affairs. He expressed his regret that some other senator had not moved in this matter; he had failed in his endeavor to that effect, and had in consequence now presented the subject himself as one of great importance. There was reason to apprehend, that if this Territory should be neglected, in the course of five years it would pass from our possession.

Mr. Clay, of Ky., said he thought the Senator and the committee would do well to make inquiries as to the stipulations of the present treaty with Great Britain, and whether we could occupy this country now without giving cause of offence. The country had been taken possession of by Great Britain, in contravention of the treaty of Ghent. There was a clause in that treaty, or rather a word, which was intended to cover this identical case, connected with the Oregon, and which covered no other case. It was founded on these circumstances: a settlement had been made on the Oregon by Mr. Astor, and the establishment was called Astoria. During the war, it was taken possession of by a British armed vessel. In the stipulation of mutual surrender by the two countries of places taken during the war, Mr. C. had introduced the word "*pos-*

session," as descriptive of the hold which we had on the Oregon country prior to the war. Mr. C. hoped the treaty would be examined before any decisive step should be taken on the subject.

Mr. Linn said he was aware of that provision, and it was his intention that the inquiry should be made. He designed to get all the information he could on the subject, and lay it before the committee or the Senate, that the Senate might make such modifications of the bill as they should think proper. He desired the bill to be made as perfect as it could be.

Mr. Lyon, of Michigan, said he knew one of his constituents who was desirous of going west of the Rocky Mountains, for the purpose of settling and carrying on a farm there.

Mr. Buchanan said, he was very glad the Senator from Missouri had moved in this business; and he had done himself injustice, when he said it might have been moved more appropriately by another person. The time had come when we ought to assert our right to the Oregon country, or abandon it for ever. We know, by information received from an agent of the Government, that the Hudson Bay Company are establishing forts in that quarter, cutting down the timber, and conveying it to market, and acquiring the allegiance of the Indian tribes; and while they had been thus proceeding, we had patiently looked on during a long period of years. Our right ought to be now asserted; but it should be done in a prudent and delicate manner. We were obliged by the treaty to give a year's notice. The time had arrived to settle the question, and there were too many such questions unsettled with the British Government already. While we should be careful to violate no treaty stipulations, we ought promptly to assert our right to this country.

Mr. BENTON urged the propriety of having this subject referred to a select committee, of which his colleague should be the chairman; he knew of no one better qualified.

Mr. LINN, after some demurring, assented, withdrew his motion of reference to the Military Committee, and the subject was referred to a select committee of five, consisting of Mr. Linn, Mr. Preston, Mr. Walker, Mr. Pierce, and Mr. Wall.

Shortly after, with the view to obtain all the information upon this subject within his reach, Mr. Linn submitted a resolution, which was adopted, that the Secretary of War be requested to send to the Senate all the information in the possession of this Department which may relate to the Oregon Territory; and also that he cause to be made for the use of the Senate, a map embracing recent discoveries of all the country claimed by the United States in the western slope of the Rocky Mountains, to the Pacific Ocean.

Having taken the lead in this important matter, and being placed at the head of the select committee to whom the subject was referred, Dr. Linn set himself to work to obtain all the information in his power, and to embody it in a report to the Senate. The preparation of this report required some months, and it was presented to the Senate on the 6th of June; and as it was a work of much labor, and embodies much interesting information in regard to that country, I have deemed it proper to make some extracts from it, which will be found not without interest at the present day, as it is mostly historical.

EXTRACTS FROM DR. LINN'S REPORT.

"The attention of the Government has been, on several occasions, called to this important subject [the occupation of the Oregon Territory] by bills and resolutions, through able and elaborate reports from committees of Congress, and in various executive communications. We will not ascend higher in the legislative history of this Territory than the last annual message of President Monroe, in which he says: 'In looking to the interests which the United States have on the Pacific Ocean, and on the western coast of this continent, the propriety of establishing a military post at the mouth of the Columbia river, or at some other point in that quarter within our acknowledged limits, is submitted to the consideration of Congress. Our commerce and fisheries on that sea, and along that coast, have much increased, and are increasing. It is thought that a military post, to which our ships of war might resort, would afford protection to every interest, and have a tendency to conciliate the tribes of the north-west, with whom our trade is extensive. It is thought, also, that by the establishment of such a post, the intercourse between our Western States and territories and the Pacific, and our trade with the tribes residing in the interior, on each side of the Rocky Mountains, would be essentially protected. To carry this object into effect, the appropriation of an adequate sum to authorize the employment of a frigate, with an officer of the corps of engineers to explore the mouth of the Columbia river, and the coast contiguous thereto, to enable the Executive to make such establishment at the most suitable point, is recommended to Congress.'

"Such were the views of an enlightened statesman and patriot. The administration which succeeded, took up this matter, and it became the subject of negotiation between the Government of Great Britain and the United States, in which nothing was done definitively to settle the claims of the parties. This correspondence was marked by great ability.

"The lapse of time and the progress of events in that quarter of the continent which are unfriendly to the interests of the United States, require, in the opinion of your committee, action on the part of this Government, as prompt and decided as may be consistent with the peace and good understanding which now exist, and we sincerely hope will ever continue to exist, between England and the United States, who have so many reasons to wish its continuance.

"President Jackson, aware of the importance of this country to our best interests, employed a special agent to proceed to the territory in question, who was charged with the duty of examining into its political, physical, and geographical condition."

The committee then gave the instructions which Mr. Slocum, the special agent, received from Mr. Forsyth, Secretary of State, and mention that he, on the 1st of June, 1836, proceeded to comply with these instructions. They then state the title of the United States to this country.

"The validity of the title of the United States to the territory on the northwest coast, between the latitude of 42° to 49°, is not questioned by any power except Great Britain. The 3d article of the treaty of Washington, of 22d February, 1819, between the United States and Spain, established their mutual boundary line on the parallel of 42° ; and from the Rocky Mountains to the Pacific Ocean, Spain made a formal and full relinquishment of all claim north of that line. The southernmost point to which Russia claims on that coast was fixed by her treaty with Great Britain of February, 1825, at 54° 40′. By the provisions of these two treaties, the space between the Spanish boundary north, at 42°, and the Russian boundary south, at 54° 40′, is *entirely* unclaimed except by the United States and Great Britain. The respective claims of these two powers have been, from time to time, the subject of negotiation and provisonal arrangement by treaty ; having in view the *temporary* protection of the interests of the parties, while the final adjustment of their rights is left open to future arrangements. These temporary arrangements, by the convention of 1825, are *mutually* obligatory, until either of the parties who may desire a change shall have given to the other one year's notice.

"The treaty of Ghent contains no *specific* allusion to the possession of the United States on the northwest coast ; but under the claim of the treaty, article 1st, which provides that all territory, places, and possessions *whatever*, taken by either party from the other during the war, &c., shall be restored without delay, the United States settlement at the mouth of the Columbia river, called Astoria, was included, and subsequently formally restored to an authorized agent of the United States; by which act the Oregon Territory for the first time became the subject of negotiation between the two governments.

"By the convention with Great Britain of 1818, it was stipulated that, east of the Stony Mountains, and west of the lakes, the northern boundary of the United States and the southern boundary of Great Britain, should be the 49th parallel of latitude; but in regard to the territory west of the Stony Mountains, and on the northwest coast, it was stipulated that any country which may be claimed by either party, shall, with its harbors, bays, rivers, &c., be *free and open for the term of ten years* to the vessels, citizens, &c., of the two powers; it being well understood that this agreement is not to be construed to the prejudice of any claim which either of the high contracting parties may have to any part of the said country, the only object being to prevent disputes and differences arising among themselves.

"When, in 1823, negotiations were opened for the continuance of the temporary convention of 1818, the question in regard to the title and boundaries of the mouth of the Columbia began to be considered of much importance in our relations with Great Britain. Although, previous to this time, there had been some diplomatic conversation on the subject, there had been no formal, written negotiation, until 1823, when Mr. Adams, as Secretary of State, gave instructions to Mr. Rush, the United States minister to England, to urge the settlement of our territorial limits west of the Stony Mountains. Mr. Rush was instructed to suggest the parallel of 51° as the southern boundary of Great Britain. But if the line already settled at 49° latitude to the Stony Mountains should be earnestly insisted on by Great Britain, 'we will consent to carry it in continuance on the same parallel west to the Pacific Ocean.' To the propositions of Mr. Rush, made in pursuance of these instructions, the British commissioners answered by controverting all the facts and principles on which the United States rested, and they declared that Great Britain considered the whole of the unoccupied parts of America as open to her future settlement, in the manner as heretofore, and they included in this description the unoccupied territory between the 42d and 51st degrees of north latitude. Great Britain would not relinquish the principle of colonization on that coast. She insisted on the principles established against Spain in the Nootka Sound controversy; besides, the commissioners contended that Great Britain had a paramount title by discovery and occupancy. The negotiation terminated in the convention of 1827, by which that of 1818 was indefinitely extended, with permission to either party to abrogate it upon twelve months' notice. This convention fixes the actual existing relations between Great Britain and the United States on the subject of the northwest territory.

"What little consequence Great Britain attached to her claim of right to colonize, and how little she relied on it for any permanent purpose, is shown by the fact, that during the progress of the negotiation, she proposed, in a formal *projet* submitted by her commissioners, to fix the dividing line definitively on the 49th parallel of north latitude, until that parallel strikes the northwesternmost branch of the Columbia river; thence down the middle of that river to the Pacific Ocean. And at the moment that this pretension of a right of colonization was urged upon our commissioners, it was *abandoned* by the Britith Ambassador at St. Petersburg, who, in February, 1825, concluded a treaty, relinquishing to Russia all claim of whatever nature, north of 54° 40′. Indeed, it was obvious that, whether the results of the Nootka Sound controversy, in 1790, had been wrung by Great Britain from the weakness of Spain, or had been yielded by her justice, that neither Russia nor the United States could acquiesce in a principle which would leave their valuable possessions on the northwest coast perpetually open to the capricious inroads of other powers. The pretension of an unoccupied coast in 1825, was not the less monstrous than that of Russia to a closed sea in that region, which disturbed the gravity of the diplomatic corps in 1820. The British nogotiators of all times declined the responsibility of starting this pretension in writing, and having, since the negotiation, in which it was verbally urged against us, abandoned it in regard to Russia, and as, in its nature, its existence is terminated by the lapse of time and the progress of events, it may *now* be considered *obsolete*.

* * * * * * * * *

"Certainly, if mere discovery of the coast could give title, that of Spain would be entirely incontrovertible; and this Government, having succeeded to her rights, the question would be at an end. Balboa discovered the western shore of America in September, 1513, and 'advancing up to his middle in the waves, with his buckler and sword in hand, took possession of that ocean in the name of the king, his master, and vowed to defend it with his arms against all his enemies.' Cortez discovered California in 1526, up to about parallel 30°. In 1543, Cubrillo explored the coast from that point up to 42°. In 1592, John de Fuca discovered the strait which bears his name, in latitude 48°. But the principle implied in the declaration of the British commissioners is unquestionably correct, viz., that discovery, accompanied with subsequent and efficient acts of sovereignty or settlement, are necessary to give title. Now there is no pretence that Great Britain has a title thus acquired; and all that is left is to ascertain whether the United States can establish such a one in herself.

"Not to dwell on the reported settlement by Hendricks, in 1785, in May, 1792, Captain Robert Gray, in the ship Columbia, from Boston, sailing under the flag of the United States, saw and entered into the land, which had a very good appearance of a harbor; and which was, in fact, the mouth of a very large river, then seen for the first time by a citizen of a civilized nation.

"Captain Gray entered the river, named it Columbia, and named the capes on either side; continuing to explore it from the 7th to the 21st of May. Having fixed its latitude, and distinctly marked the topography of the neighborhood, and the bearings of the various headlands around the bay, he returned to the United States, and announced his important discovery. Thus was the Columbia discovered by the United States, from the sea. In the year 1803, an exploring expedition was fitted out by this Government, to penetrate, over land, into the region west of the Rocky or Stony Mountains, as far as the mouth of the Columbia river. Every body knows the signal success of this admirably conducted enterprise, which opened to the world the vast regions of the Upper Missouri and Rocky Mountains, and added to geography the magnificent valley of the Columbia. Ten years before, Mackenzie had penetrated to the Western Ocean, but his route did not touch any of the waters of this grand basin, being several degrees north of it. And thus this great discovery, both from the interior and the coast, belongs to the United States. The exploring expedition of Lewis and Clarke following up the discovery of the Columbia river, by Captain Gray, is in itself an important circumstance in our title. It was notice to the world of claim, and that solemn act of possession was followed up by a settlement and occupation, made by that enterprising and intelligent merchant, John Jacob Astor, under the countenance and patronage of this Government. This settlement and occupation continued to the late war with Great Britain, and by the treaty of Ghent was restored to us formally, after its conquest from the United States during that war. Thus it will be seen that our title has the requisites prescribed by Great Britain herself. With this is combined the current title of Spain, which was derived also from discovery, settlement, &c., and which, by the treaty of 1819, was transferred to the United States. The extent of the territory on the northwest coast, which is properly embraced within our limits, is to be ascertained by the application of the two recognized principles to the established facts of the case. 1st. That the discovery and occupation of the mouth of a river gives title to the region watered by it and its tributaries, as in the case of the Hudson, James, Mississippi rivers, &c. 2d. That the discovery and settlement of a new country by a civilized power, gives title half way to the settlement of the nearest civilized power. The boundary between them is a medium line. Either of these principles will carry our line as far as 49°.

"Its occupation by our Government would secure a vast Indian and fur trade; its forests of gigantic timber, extended plains, rich alluvions, where animals and vegetables assume their brightest forms, would open a direct trade with California, China, Japan, and the Sandwich and Oriental Islands generally; it would secure its prodigious fisheries of sturgeon, anchovies, and salmon; for Lewis and Clarke say, 'that the multitudes of salmon in the Oregon are inconceivable, and they ascend to its very sources, to the very ridge of the dividing mountains; the water is so clear, that they may be seen at the depths of fifteen or twenty feet; at certain seasons of the year they float in such quantities down the stream, and are drifted ashore, that the Indians have only to collect, split them open, and dry them.' It would doubtless secure, beyond the danger of interruption, constant intercourse and trade between the valley of the Mississippi and the Oregon.

"But, to waive these advantages, the importance to

the United States, in a commercial point of view, of possessing *some* harbor on the northwest coast of America, will be seen at once, when it is recollected that upwards of $12,000,000 worth of property is afloat in the Pacific Ocean, in the whale trade alone, and which gives employment to 8,000 seamen. These whalers must have some place or places at which to refit after their long voyages. These vessels *now* resort to the Sandwich Islands; but it is to be remembered, that colonial restrictions may be enforced in time of peace, and in time of war this valuable and important branch of trade might fall an easy prey to a foreign power, for want of a port to give it shelter. It is the duty of a wise government to provide against such contingencies. The bay of St. Francis, into which is discharged the fine river Sacramento, is one of the noblest harbors on the continent, and capable of containing the whole mercantile navy of the world. But this magnificent harbor, unfortunately, is not within the jurisdiction of the United States, but belongs to Mexico."

Dr. Linn little dreamed then that this magnificent harbor would so soon fall into our hands, and did not live to see it.

After quoting from the reports of Mr. Slocum and Mr Baylies, Dr. Linn proceeds:

"The day is not far distant, when, by the opening of a direct communication between the Atlantic and the Pacific Oceans, across the Isthmus of Darien, the whole trade of the eastern hemisphere will be changed. The policy of Great Britain is, therefore, to possess the strongest points of control on this grand thoroughfare of commerce, as well as over every other commercial thoroughfare of the world. One of these points she already possesses in Jamaica, and the Sandwich Islands is to be, nay, is, the other point of her grasping ambition. These islands lie on that parallel of latitude which vessels seek in the passage to China, Manilla, and Batavia, from the west coast of America, in order to get the force of the trade-winds which are strongest between 18° and 24° of north latitude. They lie as directly in the route to China as the Cape of Good Hope for ships from the eastward. They would, therefore, become of immense value as a commercial depot, and in time of war they would, in a military point of view, be as important as the Mauritius in the Indian Ocean. It may be assumed, then, that these islands will fall into the hands of the British Government; for when has she neglected her foreign policy? Look at her possessions in the East—Malta, Gibraltar, the key to the commerce of the Mediterranean,—St. Helena, Ascension, Cape of Good Hope, the Mauritius, Singapore, (which effectually commands the Straits of Malacca,) the Benin Islands, lying off the coast of Japan; and she only lacks the Sandwich Islands and the beautiful river of Columbia, and the territory watered by its numerous tributaries, to command, by her mighty means, the commerce of the whole world."

Dr. Linn's apprehensions in regard to Great Britain acquiring the Sandwich Islands, though by no means then unreasonable, would now be groundless; since the United States, jealous of her, and she, jealous of us, have come to an understanding to let those islands remain as they now are, and that neither Government shall interfere with them.

As to the prediction that "the day is not far distant, when, by the opening a direct communication between the Atlantic and Pacific Oceans, across the Isthmus of Darien, the whole trade of the eastern hemisphere will be changed," it is now in process of fulfilment, and this route is now becoming the great thoroughfare of commerce. But the fulfilment of this prediction has been greatly hastened by the annexation of California to the United States, and the accidental discovery of the immensely rich gold mines of that country, which for a time set the world agog, and sent hundreds of thousands of emigrants to settle that far off land. Dr. Linn proceeds:

"Independent of the importance, in a commercial point of view, of this territory to the United States, it assumes vast importance when we come to consider the influence it is to have, in the hands of the British, over the fierce and warlike tribes of Indians on the north, and from our western frontier to the Pacific Ocean." He then quotes freely from Mr. Slocum's report, showing what the Hudson's Bay Company had done, and the influence they had acquired over the Indians of the Northwestern tribes. The farm of this company at Vancouver, contained about 3000 acres of land, fenced and under cultivation, employing generally one hundred men, chiefly Canadians and half breed Iroquois. The mechanics were Europeans.

"At first sight," continues Dr. Linn, "it would be reasonable to suppose that the rugged and stern Rocky Mountains, whose summits are covered with snow, and ascend *far* beyond the region of perpetual congelation, would constitute an everlasting barrier to the passage of hostile armies between the valley of the Mississippi and that of the Columbia; for all the journals and narratives of the early explorers of this gloomy region, are replete with the sufferings and privations of those who made the passage. The accounts given us by Lewis and Clarke, Andrew Henry, Wilson P. Hunt, Ramsay Crooks, and many others, seemed to have placed this beyond the possibility of a doubt. But of this we shall see. One of its loftiest peaks has been mounted by a traveller after incessant toil. The prospect presenting itself and the feelings of the beholder, are given in the gorgeous language of Irving:

"'Here a scene burst upon the view of Captain Bonneville, that for a time astonished and overwhelmed him with its immensity. He stood, in fact, upon that dividing ridge, which Indians regard as the crest of the world; and on each side of which the landscape declines to the two cardinal oceans of the world. Whichever way he turned his eye, he was confused by the vastness and variety of objects. Beneath him the Rocky Mountains seemed to open rugged defiles and foaming torrents; while, *beyond* their savage precincts, the eye was lost in an almost immeasurable landscape, stretching on every side into dim and hazy distance like the expanse of a summer sea. Whichever way he looked he beheld vast plains glimmering with reflected sunshine; mighty streams wandering on their shining course towards either ocean, and snowy mountains, chain *beyond* chain, and peak *beyond* peak, they melted like clouds into the horizon. For a time the Indian fable seemed to be realized. He had obtained that height from which the Black Foot warrior, after death, catches a view of the land of souls, and beholds the happy hunting-grounds spread out before him, brightening with the abodes of free and generous spirits.' This line of continuous mountains, when viewed at a distance, every where seems impassable: the mind shrinks or recoils from such frowning and forbidding obstacles. But within ten or fifteen years, passes of such gentle slope have been discovered that loaded wagons easily traverse them.

"From the valley of the River Platte, General Ashley passed to the opposite valleys of waters that fall into the Great Bear Lake.

"The waters of this great internal sea are much more brackish than that of the ocean. He descended, in canoes, one of the rivers that disembogued into it, which was 150 miles in length; and on coasting the lake, he found it 100 miles long, and from 60 to 80 wide. Since then, the passage of the Rocky Mountains has become an affair of ordinary occurrence, and even performed by delicate females.

* * * * * * * * *

"A vast chain of mountains commences at the southern extremity of the American continent, which ranges along the borders of the Pacific Ocean, and after *threading* the Isthmus of Darien, passes, with various altitudes through Guatemala, Mexico and its provinces, California, Oregon, and finally disappears in the Arctic region. The northern portion is called the Rocky or Stony Mountains, which rise in abrupt ruggedness on the side of the great North American plains, and apparently formed at a remote period in the history of the world, on its eastern face, the walls to a vast internal sea, the bed of which was the valley of the Mississippi; whilst from its western flanks the descent is in regular terraces to the ocean. The northern extremity of this great spine of the world, gives origin to some of the noblest rivers of the globe, the Missouri, Saskatchawine, Peace, Columbia, &c.

* * * * * * * * *

"Navigators, early as well as recent, portray the country in glowing language, and dwell with delight on the lovely variety of hill and dale, fertility of soil, noble forests, amenity of landscape, pure limpid streams flowing through the land; but above all, they dwell with the greatest satisfaction on the soft climate of this delightful coast. Cook, Dixon, Portlock, Vancouver, Langsdorf, Kotzebue, and many others, unite in the same opinion as to the benignity of the climate, which varies widely from that on the opposite coast of the Atlantic Ocean, where, in the winter and spring seasons, in the same parallels of latitude, storm, hail, snow, and sleet hold sullen sway.

* * * * * * * * *

"Mr. Prevost says that, 'the climate to the southward of 53°, assumes a mildness unknown in the same latitude on the eastern side of the continent. Without digressing to speculate upon the cause, I will merely state that such is particularly the fact in 46° 16′, the site of Fort Gregory. The mercury during the winter seldom descends below the freezing point; when it does so, it is rarely stationary for any number of days, and the severity of the season is more determined by the quantity of water than by its congelation. The rains usually commence with November, and continue to fall partially until the latter end of March or the beginning of April. A benign spring succeeds, and when the summer heats obtain, they are so tempered with showers as seldom to suspend vegetation. I found it luxuriant on my arrival, (October 1, 1818,) and during a fortnight's stay, experienced no change of weather to retard its course.'

* * * * * * * * *

"In conclusion, the committee would remark, that the title of the United States to the Territory of Oregon is, in their opinion, beyond doubt; that its possession is important in our commercial and Indian relations; that it is in danger of being lost by delay, and so viewing it, they hope the Executive will take steps to bring the controversy on this subject with England to a speedy termination. In the mean time, they have reported a bill, authorizing the President to employ in that quarter such portions of the army and navy of the United States as he may deem necessary for the protection of the persons and property of those who may reside in that country."

The reports of travellers and navigators in regard to the fertility of the soil and the beauty of the climate of distant and newly discovered lands, are proverbial, and a little of the color of the rose may have been thrown into their accounts of the Columbia or Oregon country, which was transferred to Dr. Linn's report. But the real value of the country in a commercial and political point of view, was by no means over-estimated. Dr. Linn saw this with the eye of a statesman; he saw that if the United States government did not act promptly in the matter, England, pursuing with steady perseverance her policy of grasping important positions in every quarter of the globe, would secure this country to herself, and would, in that case, exercise a controlling and dangerous influence over all the fierce tribes of Indians in the northwest and in the Rocky Mountains, whom she could at any time incite to commit depredations upon the people living along our western and northwestern borders. He saw, too, that the great fur trade of the Rocky Mountains and northwest, so profitable to those engaged in it, and the means by which a very great influence was exercised over the Indians, would be taken wholly from us, and monopolized by the British Hudson's Bay Company, which had already established forts and trading posts in various parts of it, and had large establishments on the Columbia river, Puget's Sound, &c.

But though he pressed this subject upon the attention of the Senate with zeal and earnestness, Dr. L. was unable to procure the passage of his bill at this time. It was not his nature, however, to give up the ship because he could not immediately command success, and he therefore continued his exertions in this cause session after session, and Congress after Congress.

Early in the next session, on the 11th Dec., 1838, he introduced a bill to authorize the occupation of the Columbia or Oregon Territory, which was read twice and referred to a special committee consisting of *Mr. Linn*, chairman, *Mr. Calhoun*, *Mr. Clay* of Ky., *Mr. Walker* and *Mr. Pierce.*

On the 28th of January, 1839, he presented the following memorial from the citizens of the Oregon Territory, which was ordered to be printed.

To the honorable the Senate and House of Representatives of the United States of America.

The undersigned, settlers south of the Columbia river, beg leave to represent to your honorable body, that our settlement, begun in the year eighteen hundred and thirty-two, has hitherto prospered beyond the most sanguine expectations of its first projectors. The products of our fields have amply justified the most flattering descriptions of the fertility of the soil, while the facilities which it affords for rearing cattle, are, perhaps, exceeded by no country in North America. The people of the United States, we believe, are not generally apprised of the extent of valuable country west of the Rocky Mountains. A large portion of the territory from the Columbia river south, to the boundary line between the United States and the Mexican Republic, and extending from the coast of the Pacific about two hundred and fifty or three hundred miles to the interior, is either well supplied with timber, or adapted to pasturage or agriculture. The fertile valleys of the Wallamette and Umpqua are varied with prairies and woodland, and intersected by abundant lateral streams, presenting facilities for machinery. Perhaps no country of the same latitude is favored with a climate so mild. The winter rains, it is true, are an objection; but they are generally preferred to the snows and intense cold which prevail in the northern parts of the United States. The ground is seldom covered with snow, nor does it ever remain but a few hours.

We need hardly allude to the commerical advantages of the territory. Its happy position for trade with China, India, and the western coasts of America, will be readily recognised. The growing importance, however, of the islands of the Pacific is not so generally known and appreciated. As these islands progress in civilization, their demand for the produce of more northern climates will increase. Nor can any country supply them with beef, flour, &c., on terms so advantageous as this. A very successful effort has been recently made at the Sandwich Islands in the cultivation of coffee and the sugar cane. A colony here will, in time, thence easily derive these articles and other tropical products in exchange for the produce of their own labor.

We have thus briefly alluded to the natural resources of the country, and to its external relations. They are, in our opinion, strong inducements for the government of the United States to take formal and speedy possession. We urge this step as promising to the general interests of the nation. But the advantages it may confer upon us, and the evils it may avert from our posterity, are incalculable.

Our social intercourse has thus far been prosecuted with reference to the feelings of honor, to the feeling of dependence on the Hudson's Bay Company, and to their moral influence. Under this state of things we have thus far prospered, but we cannot hope that it will continue. The agriculture and other resources of the country cannot fail to induce emigration and commerce. As our settlement begins to draw its supplies through other channels, the feeling of dependence upon the Hudson's Bay Company, to which we have alluded as one of the safeguards of our social intercourse, will begin to diminish. We are anxious when we imagine what will be, what must be, the condition of so mixed a community, free from all legal restraint, and superior to that moral influence which has hitherto been the pledge of our safety.

Our interests are identified with those of the country of our adoption. We flatter ourselves that we are the germ of a great State, and are anxious to give an early tone to the moral and intellectual character of its citizens. We are fully aware, too, that the destinies of our posterity will be intimately affected by the character of those who emigrate to the country. The territory must populate. The Congress of the United States must say by whom. The natural resources of the country, with a well-judged civil code, will invite a good community. But a good community will hardly emigrate to a country which promises no protection for life or property. Inquiries have already been submitted to some of us for information of the country. In return we can only speak of a country highly favored of nature. We can boast of no civil code. We can promise no protection but the ulterior resort of self-defence. By whom, then, shall our country be populated? By the reckless and unprincipled adventurer! not by the hardy and enterprising pioneer of the West. By the Botany Bay refugee, by the renegade of civilization from the Rocky Mountains, by the profligate deserted seaman from Polynesia, and the unprincipled sharpers from South America. Well we are assured that it will cost the government of the United States more to reduce elements so discordant to social order than to promote our permanent peace and prosperity by a timely action of Congress. Nor can we suppose that so vicious a population could be relied on in case of a rupture between the United States and any other power.

Our intercourse with the natives among us, guided much by the same influence which has promoted harmony among ourselves, has been generally pacific. But the same causes which will interrupt harmony among ourselves, will also interrupt our friendly relations with the natives. It is, therefore, of primary importance both to them and us, that the government should take energetic measures to secure the execution of all laws affecting Indian trade and the intercourse of white men and Indians. We have thus briefly shown that the security of our persons and our property, the hopes and destinies of our children, are involved in the objects of our petition. We do not presume to suggest the manner in which the country should be occupied by the government, nor the extent to which our settlement should be encouraged. We confide in the wisdom of our national legislators; and leave the subject to their candid deliberations, and your petitioners will ever pray.

(Signed) J. S. Whitcomb, and 35 others, March 16, 1838.

Upon the motion of Dr. Linn the memorial was ordered to be printed.

On the 22d of February the bill to provide for the protection of the citizens of the United States residing in the Oregon Territory, or trading on the Columbia river, was taken up, and Mr. Linn addressed the Senate in its support.

Mr. Linn said he thought it time the government of the United States stretched forth its protecting arm to such of its citizens as now resided in the Oregon Territory, and asserted our title to that country. That the title of the United States was clear and indisputable he had not the shadow of a doubt; this had been so often and so clearly demonstrated that he should not now detain the Senate by any remarks upon the subject.

By the convention of 1818, between the United States and Great Britain, indefinitely continued by that of 1828, it was agreed that both countries should have concurrent possession and jurisdiction of the Oregon Territory. But this convention has been, and now is, a nullity to us; for Great Britain, through the medium of the Hudson's Bay Company, has built and armed several forts in advantageous positions in that country, equipped ships, erected houses and improved farms; and has opened a trade with all the tribes of Indians on the western slope of the Rocky Mountains as far south as the Gulf of California. Their hunters and trappers have penetrated all the valleys and glens of the Rocky Mountains, scattering arms and munitions of war, and fomenting discontent against the United States in the bosoms of those Indian tribes. They have driven our people from the Indian trade, which yielded seven or eight hundred thousand dollars per annum, and even pushed their operations east of the Rocky Mountains to the great Mississippi valley.

To all these aggressions we have tamely submitted, and still tamely submit, though he hoped the extreme point of forbearance would soon be reached, and our government would assert and maintain its rights.

The haughty, grasping, unjust spirit of Great Britain was ever manifest; she had ruined or driven us from our fur trade, which she now monopolizes, and seems disposed to appropriate the splendid pine forests of Maine to her own use. This grasping spirit must be checked.

As regards this bill, Mr. L. said he should make no motion; leaving it in the hands of the Senate, as many esteemed friends around and near him seemed to think that, at this critical juncture, its passage might be misconstrued. But he pledged himself not to permit our claims to this territory to slumber.

On motion of Mr. Wright the bill was committed to the Committee on Foreign Relations; and on motion of Mr. Tallmadge, 5000 extra copies were ordered to be printed.

At this time there was a controversy between the

United States and Great Britain in regard to the North-eastern Boundary between the two countries; great excitement prevailed among the people of Maine, and troops had been, or were soon after, called out by the Governor of that State and marched to the territory in dispute, to defend it against British aggression, both parties claiming jurisdiction over it, and were undertaking to enforce their own laws upon the people. This was the "critical juncture" to which Dr. Linn alluded, and which induced him to refrain from pressing the bill at this session.

On the 8th of January, 1841, Dr. Linn again brought the subject of Oregon before the Senate, by moving a joint resolution of which he had given previous notice, to authorize the adoption of measures for the occupation and settlement of the territory, and for extending certain portions of the laws of the United States over the same.

Mr. LINN said that when his bill was up at the last session for discussion, both political friends and opponents pressed him to forbear urging it during the negotiations with the British government for the adjustment of another question, from a fear of embarrassing its settlement. Though this was not at the time convincing to him, it was sufficient that it was the advice of gentlemen of experience, and he had acted in accordance with it. But he now desired that measures should be speedily adopted to secure our rights in that territory. If his memory served him correctly, England, pending the negotiations at Ghent, had been willing to purchase the territory; he did not mean to say there was any formal offer made, but, finding that no such arrangement could be entered into, she had progressed step by step in her encroachments, until she now presented a bold claim where she had not a shadow of right; and such he believed would be the case as long as she was allowed to occupy any portion of the territory. Great Britain had extended her possessions gradually from the extreme branch of the Columbia River to the Pacific Ocean.

On the 18th December, 1839, Dr. Linn called the attention of the Senate to the subject by submitting a series of resolutions which were referred to a select committee, from which, on the 31st of March following, 1840, he reported a substitute which asserted the title of the United States, authorized the President to take such measures as might be necessary to protect the persons and property of citizens of the United States resident therein, and to erect a line of military posts from Fort Leavenworth to the Rocky Mountains for the protection of Indian traders. It provided also, that when the boundaries should be settled, one thousand acres of land shall be granted to each white male inhabitant of eighteen years of age; and for the appointment of an Indian agent for that territory.

On the 28th of April he introduced, on leave, a bill to extend a portion of the laws of the United States over the Territory of Oregon; and on his motion, May 24th, his Oregon resolutions were made the special order of the day for that day two weeks; but it does not appear that the day ever arrived, as nothing further is recorded as having been done during that session. Why it was so is not now easy to say, but Dr. Linn found the task he had undertaken in regard to Oregon a Sisyphean labor; a toil every session to be renewed, and never ended; nor was the accomplishment of the object at which he aimed, destined to cheer his spirits, gladden his heart, or reward him for his unremitting toil.

By a letter he had recently received, he learned that the Hudson's Bay Company was introducing emigrants from England and other parts by the way of Cape Horn; they brought shepherds and placed them on farms; they had erected forts on the Territory of Oregon, and had pushed their establishments on the south to California, and on the east to the Rocky Mountains; and by an act of Parliament, a portion of the criminal law of Great Britain was extended up to the very confines of Missouri and Arkansas. Now, if we have a just right to that territory, he was not the man to say it should be abandoned to any power on earth; he was for claiming and exercising our rights, and excluding those who were so insidiously, perseveringly, and audaciously endeavoring to gain possession of a country to which they had not the least pretence of a claim.

The joint resolution having been twice read, was referred to a select committee of five, to wit: Mr. Linn, Mr. Walker, Mr. Preston, Mr. Pierce, and Mr. Sevier: from which committee Mr. Linn reported the resolution without amendment to the Senate on the 14th of January.

But it does not appear that the subject came up for consideration during this, the short session of Congress, it being probably prevented by the usual press of the ordinary business of legislation. Dr. Linn had pledged himself, however, and had thus far proved faithful to his pledge, not to let the subject sleep, and our just claims to the country to be rendered nugatory by neglect; and he was not the man to give up the pursuit of a just and national cause, so long as there was a possibility of attaining his object.

Again, at the extra session of Congress, August 2d, 1841, Dr. Linn brought the subject before the Senate, by submitting a resolution that the President of the United States be requested to give the notice to the British Government which the convention of 1827 between the two governments requires, in order to put an end to the treaty for the joint occupation of the Territory of Oregon west of the Rocky Mountains, and which territory is now possessed and used by the Hudson's Bay Company, to the ruin of the American Indian and fur trade in that quarter, and conflicting with our inland commerce with the internal provinces of Mexico.

Subsequently the resolution came up, when, upon the motion of Mr. Morehead of Ky., and by the acquiescence of the mover, it was so amended as to direct the Committee on Foreign Relations " to inquire into the expediency of requesting the President," &c., in which form it was adopted. But it does not appear that the committee to whom the subject was referred ever made any report.

Early in the next session, Dec. 16th, 1841, Dr. Linn again moved in the matter, by introducing a bill to authorize the adoption of measures for the occupation and settlement of the Territory of Oregon, for extending certain portions of the laws of the United States over the same, and for other purposes, which was referred to a select committee; and on the 4th of January, submitted a resolution similar to that which he offered on the 2d of August preceding, mentioned above. These, the bill and resolution, came up for discussion on several occasions during the session, when, on the 31st of August ('42), Mr. Linn addressed the Senate in support of his bill concerning the occupation of the Oregon Territory.

Remarks of Mr. Linn of Missouri, in Senate of the United States, August 31*st,* 1842, *concerning the occupation of the Oregon Territory.*

Mr. LINN said that he was instructed by the Select Committee on the Territory of Oregon, to ask to be discharged from the further consideration of the memorials which he held in his hand; and, before putting the question, he asked the attention of the Senate to a few remarks, which he felt it was his imperative duty to make upon this interesting subject of the Territory of Oregon. Besides this bundle of memorials praying Congress to take steps to assert our title to the Territory, and to enact measures to encourage emigration, he said the Legislatures of two or three States had passed resolutions asking Congress to assert our rights to the country we claimed on the western ocean, and to take such other steps as the urgency of the case seemed to demand.

He had also in his possession hundreds upon hundreds of letters from every quarter of the Union, making anxious inquiries as to what was doing, and what was likely to be done by Congress, relative to this long-agitated and long-deferred question. It was due to his correspondents, his constituents, and to the country generally, to let them know the present posture of this business here. You will recollect, Mr. President, that at a very early day in this session, I asked leave of the Senate to introduce a bill to authorize the adoption of measures for the occupation and settlement of the Territory of Oregon; for extending certain portions of the laws of the United States over the same, and for other purposes.

The preamble of the bill reads thus:

"Whereas, the title of the United States to the Territory of Oregon is certain, and will not be abandoned."

This declaration was important to the citizens of the United States who reside in the Territory—now amounting to fifteen hundred or two thousand persons. To many on the road to the Territory, and to thousands who were preparing to move to that region, it was an assurance that, although upon the verge, the extremest verge of this Republic, the Government of the United States would not abandon them to any foreign power.

The next paragraph of the bill authorized the President of the United States "to cause to be erected at suitable places and distances, a line of military posts from some point on the Missouri River into the best pass for entering the valley of the Oregon; and, also, at or near the mouth of the Columbia River."

The establishment of such a line of posts had been

thought of by himself for several years past—had been recommended by Mr. Poinsett; by the President of the United States in his message at the opening of the present session; and also by the Secretary of War. The necessity of the establishment of a military post at the mouth of the Columbia would arrest the attention of the most casual observer. It was important as a nucleus around which our infant colonies could be firmly established; but, above all, as a naval station, where our vast commerce in the Pacific ocean could take shelter in time of war, and refit in time of peace.

The line of military posts from the Missouri River to the Rocky Mountains would serve a triple purpose—protection to the frontiers of Missouri and Arkansas; protection to the Mexican trade and the fur trade; and afford assistance to emigrants on their route to the Territory of Oregon.

For the purpose of ascertaining the best points for these posts, Lieutenant Frémont had been despatched by the War Department early in the summer, whose return is not expected before the month of November next. From the known abilities of this gentleman, we expect much valuable and interesting information relating to the valley of the river Platte; which river empties into the Missouri River, and whose sources almost interlock with the branches of the Columbia River, in the great southern passes of the Rocky Mountains.

The next paragraph of this bill provides "that six hundred and forty acres of land shall be granted to every white male inhabitant of said Territory, of the age of eighteen years and upwards, who shall cultivate and use the same for five consecutive years, or to his heir or heirs-at-law, if such there be."

This, Mr. Linn said, would be nothing more than a mere liberal donation to the early pioneers of the desert. It was the principle upon which France and Spain, and, indeed, every other European nation who had made settlements upon this continent, had proceeded. It was upon this foundation the "Old Thirteen" had been built up, and upon which policy they were enabled to contend successfully with the mightiest power in the world.

With such examples before us, surely we shall not pursue a less liberal course than that of our forefathers. Emigrants may, therefore, reasonably expect that, whatever bill may pass, this provision, or some one like it, will be preserved in it.

The next provides "that the President is hereby authorized and required to appoint two additional Indian Agents, with a salary of fifteen hundred dollars each, whose duty it shall be (under his direction and control) to superintend the interests of the United States with any or every Indian tribe west of any agency now established by law."

Hitherto, the British Government—or rather its agents, the Hudson's Bay Company—have had unlimited control over the Territory and its resources—have erected forts at the most important points—established trading-posts over the Territory—built trading-vessels—traded in lumber with the Sandwich Islands—in provisions with the Russians of the north—trapped the mountain's streams for their beaver—swept the coast of the valuable sea-otter—established valuable salmon fisheries on the Columbia—and exercised exclusive dominion over all the tribes of Indians west of the Rocky Mountains. It was time the people of the United States should participate in these advantages. It was time they should have agents, thus qualified, to give the government geographical, mineralogical, and all other information touching the Territory and its natural resources; and link, by the ties of treaties, all the tribes of Indians west of the Rocky Mountains with the government of the United States.

Mr. L. said at this moment he could do nothing more than just touch upon the various features of the bill.

The next section of the bill will speak for itself.

In the numerous communications which he had received from various individuals, all speak of the importance of military protection, but dwell with earnestness upon the absolute necessity of extending some portions of the laws of the United States over the Territory.

In the opinion of the committee, it was thought that the second, third, and fourth sections of the bill would be the most effective in the present condition of things, that could be devised; which are as follows:

"SEC. 2. That the civil and criminal jurisdiction of the supreme court and district courts of the Territory of Iowa be, and the same is hereby extended over that part of the Indian territories lying west of the present limits of the said Territory of Iowa, and south of the forty-ninth degree of north latitude, and east of the Rocky Mountains, and north of the boundary line between the United States and the Republic of Texas, not included within the limits of any State; and also over the Indian territories comprising the Rocky Mountains, and the country between them and the Pacific Ocean, south of fifty-four degrees and forty minutes of north latitude, and north of the forty-second degree of north latitude; and justices of the peace may be appointed for the said territory, in the same manner and with the same powers as are now provided by law in relation to the Territory of Iowa: *Provided*, that any subject of the government of Great Britain, who shall have been arrested under the provisions of this act for any crime alleged to have been committed within the territory westward of the Stony or Rocky Mountains, while the same remained free and open to the vessels, citizens, and subjects of the United States and of Great

Britain, pursuant to stipulations between the two powers, shall be delivered up, on proof of his being such British subject, to the nearest or most convenient authorities, having cognizance of such offence by the laws of Great Britain, for the purpose of being prosecuted and tried according to such laws.

"SEC. 3. *And be it further enacted*, that two associate judges of the supreme court of the Territory of Iowa, in addition to the number now authorized by law, shall be appointed in the same manner, hold their offices by the same tenure and for the same time, receive the same compensation, and possess all the powers and authority confirmed by law upon the associate judges of the said territory; and two judicial districts shall be organized by the said supreme court, in addition to the existing number in reference to the jurisdiction conferred by this act; and district courts shall be held in the said districts by one of the judges of the supreme court at such times and places as the said court shall direct; and the said district courts shall possess all the powers and authority invested in the present district courts of the said territory, and may, in like manner, appoint their own clerks.

"SEC. 4. *And be it further enacted*, that any justice of the peace, appointed in and for the territories described in the first section of this act, shall have power to cause all offenders against the laws of the United

States to be arrested by such persons as they shall appoint for that purpose, and to commit such offenders to safe custody for trial, in the same cases and in the manner provided by law in relation to the territories of the United States or any of them; and to cause the offenders so committed to be conveyed to the place appointed for the holding of a district court for the said Territory of Iowa, nearest and most convenient to the place of such commitment, there to be detained for trial by such persons as shall be authorized for that purpose by any judge of the supreme court, or any justice of the peace of the said territory; or where such offenders are British subjects, to cause them to be delivered to the nearest or most convenient British authorities as hereinbefore provided; and the expenses of such commitment, removal and detention, shall be paid in the same manner, as is provided by law in respect to the fees of the marshal of the said territory."

The committee unanimously instructed their chairman to report this bill back to the Senate with the recommendation that it pass. It was then placed in its order upon the calendar; but before it came up for consideration as a special order, Lord Ashburton arrived from England to enter upon a negotiation touching all points of dispute between the two countries—boundaries as well as others; Oregon as well as Maine.

In that posture of affairs, it was considered on all

hands indelicate (not to say unwise) to press the bill to a decision whilst these negotiations were pending. They are now over, and a treaty is published to the world, between the United States and Great Britain; in which it seems that the question of the Oregon Territory has been deferred to some more remote or auspicious period for an ultimate decision. He said he was confident that there were majorities in both branches of Congress in favor of this bill; and he felt equally certain that it would have passed this session but for the arrival of Lord Ashburton, and the pendency of the negotiations which terminated a short period since. He should deem it his imperative duty at an early day of the coming session to bring in the same bill, and press it to a final decision. That the decision would be favorable, he did not entertain the slightest doubt; and he took great pleasure in making that opinion public (as far as his opinion was of any weight), for the satisfaction of all those who may take an interest in the occupation of this new and beautiful country, the germ of future States, to be settled by the Anglo-Amercan race, and which will extend our limits from the Atlantic to the Pacific Ocean.

Again Mr. Linn was urged by friends not to press the consideration of this bill upon the Senate at this session, on account of the negotiations that were then pending between Great Britain and the United States, Lord Ashburton then being in Washington as a special minister extraordinary from that government to ours; and again he yielded to their urgent solicitations against his own anxious desire that some measure should be adopted by Congress to assert and preserve our rights, and protect our people in Oregon.

Early in the next session Dr. Linn, true to the pledge he had voluntarily given, not to permit our claims to this country to slumber, brought up his bill again in the Senate, and pressed it with great ardor and perseverance, and on various occasions combated the objections made to it by several senators, and urged with force and eloquence; among these were Mr. Calhoun, Mr. Archer, Mr. McDuffie, Mr. Crittenden, Mr. Conrad, Mr. Choate, and Mr. Berrien; but he was ably supported by his colleagues, Mr. Benton, Mr. Young, Mr. Walker, Mr. Sevier, Mr. Buchanan, and Mr. Phelps.

After much conflict the bill was passed by the Senate, Feb. 6, 1843, by a vote of 24 to 22.

Thus, after laboring incessantly for five years, from the 7th of Feb. 1838, when he first brought in a bill authorizing the occupation of Oregon, he at last had the satisfaction of seeing his bill passed by the Senate, and his persevering efforts crowned at least with partial success. Well might he feel a just pride and a throb of joy, and well might his friends congratulate him upon the passage of that measure he had taken so deep and lively an interest in, and the consummation of which seemed to be the most important object of his public life. Speaking of this measure, Colonel Benton as magnanimously as truthfully said in his speech at St. Louis, at a meeting of the citizens convened to testify their respect for the memory of Dr. Linn, "But how can I omit the last great act as yet unfinished, in which his whole soul was engaged at the time of his death? The bill for the settlement and occupation of Oregon was his, and he carried it through the Senate when his colleague, who now addresses you, could not have done it. This is another historical truth fit to be made known on this occasion, and which is now declared to this large and respectable assembly under all the circumstances which impart solemnity to the declaration. He carried that bill through the Senate, and it was the measure of a statesman. Just to the settler, it was wise to the government. * * * * * * * * Alas, that he should not have been spared to put the finishing hand to a measure which was to reward the emigrant, to protect his country, to curb England, and to connect his own name with the foundation of an empire. But it is done! the unfinished work will go on; it will be completed, and the name of LINN will not be forgotten; that name will live and be connected with Oregon while its banks bear a plant, or its waters roll a wave."

And the work did go on. Dr. Linn had given it such an impetus that it could not stop. He had aroused the public mind to the importance of securing this beautiful and valuable country from the grasp of Great Britain. The people demanded that the government should take possession of and occupy it; that it should be secured to us, and to us exclusively; and that an American government should be established there for the protection of American citizens, which has been done. That country is now our own exclusively; and out of it have been formed two territories, Oregon and Washington, which will ere long come into the great republican family of States, and become the seat of agriculture, manufactures, commerce, learning and wealth.

Well might Col. Benton pronounce the great work undertaken by Dr. Linn, and so long persevered in, "the measure of a statesman." With that measure is his name inseparably connected; and so long as the green hills of Oregon and Washington are covered with flocks and herds, and their fruitful valleys wave with golden harvests, will the name of LINN be held in grateful remembrance by every American who proudly surveys the majestic hills, the rich valleys, the noble streams, the gigantic forests, and the deep and spacious bays of the North-West, and exultingly exclaims,

> "This is my own, my native land."

CHAPTER V.

DUELLING.—THE CILLEY DUEL.

On the 24th day of February, 1838, took place an event in the vicinity of the city of Washington which shocked the public mind over the whole country, and cast a gloom upon every countenance within the limits of the national metropolis. Such was the deep and solemn impression made by the tragical event alluded to, that it still lingers in the memory of those who were then upon the stage of action, and a recurrence to the subject again brings up something of the painful emotions so keenly felt at the time.

The reader will understand that I allude to the death of the Hon. Jonathan Cilley, a member of the House of Representatives from the State of Maine, in a duel with Mr. Graves, a representative in Congress from the State of Kentucky; commonly called "the Cilley duel."

Growing as it did out of the heated political conflicts of the day, and taking place between two gentlemen between whom there existed no enmity whatever, and had been no controversy of any kind,—upon a mere punctilio, resulting in the death of one who bore malice against no human being, least of all against him by whose hand he fell, who was equally free from all unkind feeling towards him, every circumstance attending the tragedy was calculated to produce deep and painful sensations.

The subject was brought before the House, referred to a select committee to investigate and inquire into the facts and report to the House, which was done, and a bill was brought in, passed, and sent to the Senate for the prevention and punishment of duelling in the District of Columbia. This bill having been taken up for consideration in the Senate,

Mr. CLAYTON expressed his objections to duelling in a very pointed manner, and his sincere desire to do all in his power to suppress it. He very much doubted, however, the efficacy of the bill before them. Such was the severity of some of its provisions, that it would be next to impossible to procure conviction under it. One of the provisions sought to make the sending of a challenge felony, which was only a misdemeanor in the eye of the common law. He admitted the practice of duelling to be both illegal and immoral; yet he contended that it was not of that class of crime which should subject the offender to the cell of a penitentiary, and make him the associate of the vilest felons. There was nothing in the offence that was either base, or mean, or sordid; neither were likely to be engaged in it persons whom we would dare to send to a penitentiary to be classed with thieves and vagabonds. The moral sense of the community would be shocked at such a measure, and such a law would be rendered a mere nullity from the interference of the executive prerogative. He deprecated duelling, and would go all reasonable lengths against it, and he thought some legal provision necessary. He would vote for the bill as amended by the judiciary committee, though he believed it would not have the good effect its friends designed.

Mr. LINN said the senator from Delaware (Mr. Clayton) had treated the subject with so much sound practical sense, that little else could be said on the subject. What community (asked Mr. L.) could be found that would pronounce a man either a murderer or a felon, who might have chanced to kill another in fair and equal combat? He was persuaded that no man acting on his responsibility as a juror would render such a verdict. Many of the States had passed severe penal laws in relation to this matter, and yet in what State had they been enforced? Other States had adopted milder remedies, such as disfranchisement of citizenship, rendering the guilty for ever incapable of holding any office of honor, trust or profit; and such laws he maintained had a more wholesome action than those severe and unjust enactments, because the one was generally carried into effect, while the other were but a dead letter upon the statute book. To illustrate the effect of public opinion on this subject, Mr. L. instanced a case that had taken place in his own State, where a small man, for a supposed offence, was cruelly lashed by a large one, the result of which was a challenge and a duel in which the first assailant fell mortally wounded. The survivor was found guilty under the laws of Missouri, when a petition signed by an immense number was presented to the legislature for his pardon, and this was granted almost by acclamation. And such, said Mr. L., would be the result in all cases where the law inflicts penalties against which the public feeling revolts. He was aware that duelling was not defensible upon the principles of Christianity, neither was war, and yet how frequently had war been engaged in by Christian nations. If such a bill could be introduced as would strike at the root of the evil, and one whose penalties would be likely to be enforced, he would cheerfully give it his support.

Mr. SMITH of Conn. having spoken long and vehemently in favor of the bill, and denominated duellists *murderers* and *assassins*,

Mr. LINN replied, repudiating the idea of calling men murderers and felons because they had fought duels; some of the purest and best men on earth, he said, had been engaged in them, and were they to be so stigmatized? The question before them was, how the practice of duelling could be prevented? and to this he would answer, not by cruel and sanguinary laws which would in no instance be carried into effect. He thought there were cases of deadly insult which few men would not be ready to resent at all risks, whatever the penalties aginst duelling might be; and from the warmth the gentleman from Connecticut had exhibited, he was quite sure he would be one of the last men to pass such an insult over unnoticed.

There was subsequently much discussion upon amendments proposed to the bill, in which Mr. Linn took part. It finally passed the Senate without a division; its title being, "a bill to prohibit the giving or accepting, within the District of Columbia, of a challenge to fight a duel, and for the punishment thereof." This became, and is now, a law. Whether this law, or the "Cilley duel" has had the effect to render duelling less frequent in the District of Columbia, there may be differences of opinion; but that no duel has since taken place within the District, is a fact well known. Several challenges have passed, however, between members of Congress, and one duel (between Mr. Clingman and Mr. Yancey) has been fought outside of the District; happily with no injury to either party.

Dr. Linn said in the course of some remarks upon the duelling bill, that if gentlemen were determined to fight a duel, this bill would not prevent them; that they could easily invite each other to take tea at some place outside the District, or to meet them for some other apparently harmless and legitimate purpose, but with an understanding between them that it was for a hostile purpose. And such has been the case in two or three instances. Nevertheless it can hardly be doubted that the obstacles which the law interposes, and the penalties it inflicts have operated, in conjunction with public opinion, since "the Cilley duel," to greatly, if not entirely, check the practice among members of Congress. It is, however, to be observed that the practice of duelling is, and has been for twenty years past, on the decrease in every section of the Union.

It may be the most fitting place here to mention, that about three years after this period, namely, in 1841, Dr. Linn was himself drawn into an affair of this kind as the friend and second of one of the parties. I refer to the well-remembered misunderstanding between Mr. Clay, and Col. King of Alabama. But while he acted as the second of the latter, he was the friend of both, and used his best efforts to bring about an honorable and satisfactory understanding between these distinguished senators. Happily his own, aided by the good offices of Mr. Archer, Mr. Preston, and other friends of Mr. Clay, brought about mutual explanations and a reconciliation, and averted a hostile meeting.

OFFICIAL REPORTERS.

Dr. LINN, during the whole ten years he occupied a seat in the Senate, devoted himself assiduously to the business before the body, and especially to those subjects that more immediately interested his own constituents and the people of the great West. It was exceedingly rare that he was absent from his seat when a vote was taken; and in his constant attendance, fidelity to his duties, and refraining from unnecessarily occupying the time of the Senate in desultory talk or long and elaborate speeches, he set an example which the public have great reason to wish should be closely followed by many who now fill the places of those who have passed away. Dr. Linn was absent on one occasion, when a vote by ayes and noes was taken in the Senate, on a subject on which he was desirous to record his vote. On returning to the Senate Chamber, and finding the vote had been taken in his absence, he rose, and stated he should have been glad to have recorded his vote, and the courtesy of the Senate, might, if appealed to, accord him the privilege of doing so; nevertheless, as he was absent, and as he thought every Senator ought, if he could, to be present whenever a vote was taken, he should not ask the privilege of voting; as a reason for his absence, he said he had had occasion to step to his committee room to get a paper he then needed, not expecting that the vote would be so soon taken; and thus he had deprived himself of the privilege of voting.

Dr. Linn stated truly, and what every Senator would bear cheerful witness to (June 17, 1840), that "It was very seldom he trespassed upon the time or the patience of the Senate, except on business, and then he endeavored to use no more words than were barely sufficient to explain to the Senate the subject he had in hand, or the object he desired."

This casual remark, dropped unpremeditatedly, presents to us the great rule and maxim of his senatorial life; and it furnishes us with the reason why we meet with so few speeches from him in the published debates of the Senate, for the time he was a member of the body. His purpose was, not to enlarge, elaborate and expand the language which clothed his ideas, like the ample folds which cover the diminutive body of some fine lady, but to condense and compress them into the fewest words possible. He indulged in no ambitious desire to produce an effect or impression upon the Senate or the galleries, by any display of rhetoric.

"The applause of listening Senates to command,"

was neither his ambition nor his vocation; though, from the evidences he occasionally gave, no one could doubt that had he been ambitious of acquiring reputation as an orator, he could easily have attained that object, possessing as he did, a large fund of scientific, literary, critical, and historical information, a lively imagination, correct taste, an easy and copious flow of language, a good voice, an impressive presence, and an agreeable manner.

On the occasion of some complaint being made by senators, of the incorrect manner in which their remarks were often reported, Dr. LINN said he did not rise to make any complaint against the reporters on either side of the House, but to say that the discussion going on, proved conclusively to his mind, that the reporters should be sworn officers of the Senate, and compelled to furnish each member with notes of what he said. "Our constituents," said Mr. L., "have a right to know what we say, as well as what we do. The journal showed all their votes, but what was said in support or explanation of them, went to the public in a very imperfect manner. He thought that the body would see the propriety of his suggestion. If this plan were adopted, each member would have notes furnished him, and then the responsibility would no longer rest on the reporters, but where it should, upon those who spoke. Every difficulty would be obviated by the course indicated, and each member held responsible for the sentiments, opinions and facts, stated by him in debate. He said he would be glad if some member would move a resolution to appoint a committee to inquire into the expediency of making reporters sworn officers of the Senate.

In pursuance of this suggestion from the Senator from Missouri, Mr. Walker said, he submitted the following resolution:

Resolved, That a select committee be appointed to inquire into the propriety of selecting an equal number of reporters, of both political parties, who shall be sworn to report correctly, as far as practicable, the proceedings of this body.

Though the Doctor's plan was not then carried into effect, it has since been adopted with modifications, and is now in operation. Every word now uttered in either House of Congress, is taken down with wonderful accuracy and despatch.

PRE-EMPTION TO SETTLERS ON THE PUBLIC LANDS.

In the subject of Pre-emption to settlers on the Public Lands in the new States, Dr. Linn manifested a warm interest, and devoted to it much time. There were few of greater concern to the hardy pioneers who pushed forward beyond the conveniences of roads, bridges, settlements, neighborhoods, schools, churches, and medical aid, subduing the wilderness, marking out the way and preparing it for the great wave of emigration, which advanced with such mighty force and steady onward power in their rear. The subject came frequently before Congress, and was much and ably discussed. On the one side, it was contended, that these pioneers were trespassers upon the public lands, that they went upon them in their own wrong, in defiance of law, and for the purpose of securing for themselves and their families the choicest locations; that, if they suffered hardships and privations, no one, least of all, had the government requested them to expose themselves to these, or to push forward beyond and in advance of the great stream of emigration and settlement, and locate upon the lands before they were surveyed and brought into market. It was also urged against the pre-emption system, that it was giving away our choicest lands to foreigners, to whom it was an invitation to come and take them, almost without money and without price; and thus, in a manner, building up whole States with persons of foreign birth.

Mr. Benton, having introduced "a bill to establish a permanent prospective pre-emption system," sustained it in an able, argumentative speech, in reply to which Mr. Mangum spoke at length.

Mr. Linn then defended the bill and advocated the pre-emption system of disposing of the public lands. He said the country had been settled on the pre-emptive system from the beginning; and he wished to keep the beginning, the middle, and the end together. In allusion to the epithets applied by some gentlemen to the settlers, of "squatters" and "land-stealers," and of the opinions of others in contradiction to his statement, that a small civil force, and an enforcement of the laws, would preserve the public land from encroachment, he said that it was a scriptural injunction to man, to possess the earth and replenish it; but if it were "land stealing," this was a nation of land stealers from the beginning, for they had either stolen it or cheated the Indians out of it; and, therefore, the appellation would apply equally to their forefathers. That the movement of the people would be onward, he again asserted; and he denied that the laws were a sufficient safeguard of the public lands. Jurors could not be found to convict in such cases, which were uniformly decided against the government, at an expense of many thousand dollars. Would they, then, send an army to destroy the "squatters?" If he had an enemy in the world (and he believed he had not many), he would wish him no greater infliction than the scorpion stings of conscience with which the execution of such a commission would be succeeded. It was not unusual by legislation, to heal breaches in the law. Charters were sometimes violated, and legislation was resorted to to heal the breach. Here, then, was a breach of the law by the settlers, and they were asked to pass that bill to heal that breach."

The bill having been ably discussed by Mr. Benton, Mr. Clay of Alabama, Mr. Mangum, Mr. Buchanan, Mr. Clay of Ky., Mr. Wright, and other senators,

Mr. Linn rose to make a few observations, and to notice some of the remarks of the honorable senator from Kentucky (Mr. Clay), which referred to what he, Mr. L., had said on a former day, in regard to the application of force to carry into effect the prohibitory laws against those who settled on, and used the public lands, and for whose benefit pre-emption laws had been passed by Congress from time to time. Mr. L. had then expressed the opinion, that it was physically impossible to remove, by force, those who are usually termed "squatters" upon the public domain. He had often expressed that opinion here and elsewhere; it was the settled conviction of his mind. And he now put the question to the honorable senator from Ky. (Mr. Clay), whether he would, were he in the executive chair of the United States, wield the military power of the government, in an endeavor to dispossess them? "He would like to see the man who would avow such an intention. The orders undoubtedly might be issued; but could the officers of the army execute them, even if they would? He apprehended not. On this subject it might be well to advert to what had been said so well, by his friend from Arkansas (Mr. Sevier), the other day, of this experiment, when tried only in a very small way. Orders were given to the military, and the officers attempted, nay, did remove the settlers from what is called Langley's Purchase, which had been wrenched from the Territory of Arkansas by a treaty with some tribes of Indians within the borders of an old State, and for the benefit and accommodation of that State. The district of country thus severed from the territory was three hundred miles in length and forty miles wide. The officers had no sooner executed their orders, and turned their backs, than the inhabitants returned to the lands which they claimed. Their houses had been burned; they rebuilt them. Their crops had been cut up and destroyed; they replanted them. They were driven off a second time, and a second time they returned. Thus they persevered until the government gave up the contest; and finally granted to each family as an indemnity for their losses, three hundred and twenty acres of land; whilst those who had respected the laws, and quietly quitted their homes, in obedience to the orders of the government, will receive but one hundred and sixty acres, by the bill which passed this House only a few days ago. Now, if the power of the government could not enforce its prohibitions in the single State of Arkansas, at that time a feeble and dependent territory, how was it likely to succeed through the extended line from Lake Superior to the Sabine River? Before such an operation could ever be attempted, you must augment the number of your army, for the whole military force of the country, as it now stands, would be totally inadequate to accomplish such an object. The very idea has in it something ludicrous, if not Quixotic, to those acquainted with the nature of the subject. It would certainly be a most amusing spectacle to behold our gallant and chivalric officers, occupied in driving the helpless women and inoffensive children from their homes and habitations, whilst their husbands and fathers were ready with their rifles to pour upon them certain destruction from the woods and thickets! The very attempt would lead to their extermination, thereby adducing a new proof that there is but one step from the sublime to the ridiculous. The truth is, that the law prohibiting such settlement was *practically* a dead letter, and must remain so.

In our early history, there was no law prohibiting our people from settling where they pleased on the unoccupied public lands. The first law upon that subject was passed in 1807, and seemed to be intended against those who claimed lands under the French and Spanish grants in Louisania, and the object was to prevent those who had only an inchoate title under such grants, from going upon the public domain, and locating and surveying such claims *as had not been surveyed;* and a most iniquitous law it was. He would speak with respect of the legislation of Congress, but such was his opinion of that law, and he conceived it might be easily proved. He now repeated his assertion, that the attempt to pass any law to restrain the American people from settling on the public lands, was worse than useless. Congress might employ itself in passing such edicts as often as it pleased, but it never could have one of them effectually enforced.

As to pre-emption laws, there were now whole districts occupied under them, which would have remained a howling wilderness for years but for the settlers having preceded your surveyors, and it is now an important policy to bring those lands into market. They would yield the treasury millions of dollars for the benefit of the country.

Antecedent to the year 1820, the public lands were sold upon a credit system or a system of part cash—one quarter, and the remainder credit. This was in its operation a pre-emption law, *because* it enabled the poor man to take possession of a choice piece of land on the payment of a few dollars, and allowed him the period of five years to pay up the remainder by instalments, which he could easily accomplish from the produce of his labor. The general principle of pre-emption itself was the principal plan of the old thirteen States of the revolution, which enabled them successfully to battle with the mother country in the revolution.

Virginia had her pre-emption laws which extended to Kentucky at an early period. Much of the lands situated in the Green River country sold for a few cents the acre under the head-right occupancy, which was no more nor less than a pre-emption law. By the old laws of Pennsylvania, and most of the other Atlantic States, a mere nominal payment of "a penny" or "a peppercorn," or the girding a few trees, or the building of a log cabin, was considered an ample equivalent for the land. The public lands were not then expected to produce any amount of money; that was not the object in view, but to get them settled as speedily as possible; nor would they ever have yielded the government a single dollar, but for the enterprising, hardy settlers, who literally buried themselves in the woods and wilds, and who, at the expense of privation, hardship, suffering and hard labor, prepared the wilderness for becoming the abode of such as followed them in the second line of emigration, and who preferred to *purchase* "improvements," rather than go into the wilderness to *make* them.

Regarding this question in an enlarged, national point of view, it appeared to him that every reasonable encouragement should be given to the extension of our settlements to aid in the development of our resources. Under the invitation of the government, already adverted to, the extensive and fertile regions in Upper Illinois, Wisconsin and Iowa, were rapidly peopled. The flourishing and populous towns of Galena, Dubuque, and many others, sprang into existence like magic, and in a few years the wilderness was made to blossom like a garden. Look for one moment at the results. This people dug from the bowels of the earth hidden riches, and from that time have increased the production of lead until it amounts annually to twenty or thirty millions of pounds, being perhaps sufficient to render us independent of foreign nations for this important material necessary to our defence in time of war, and entering largely into consumption in the arts. Massachussetts and other manufacturing States are as much interested as we of the West are, or more even than we are, as they supply us with manufactured articles in return for the raw materials which we send them.

Mr. Linn here referred to Daniel Boon, the hardy pioneer first of Kentucky, and next of Missouri, who, impelled by his love of danger, sought out a lonely spot in the latter State on the extreme border of civilization, "squatted" on the public land, and contributed to its defence. Mr. L. regretted that this hardy and adventurous pioneer had not lived a few years longer to see this broad Union extending itself from one great ocean to the other.

Boon, Mr. L. said, was a living type, an impersonation, as it were, of the spirit which had settled this continent. He rejoiced to see the same spirit in full force and operation to this hour. God forbid he should ever see it stopped; but that could not be done. The whole force of the government could not arrest it. He thought that, as Americans, we ought to feel proud as we witnessed the onward march of the Anglo-American race and its rapid progress for the benefit of the human family. He should rejoice to see it scale the rugged tops of the Rocky Mountains, and pour itself into the fertile valleys of the Oregon country. Let the race of free American pioneers go onward West, carrying their love of liberty and all their free and beneficent institutions with them; and he would encourage their progress by every proper means, to the utmost verge of the continent.

In no one had the hardy pioneer of the West, the inmate of the *log cabin*, a more true, reliable, and devoted friend than in Dr. Linn. For them he seemed to feel more than an ordinary interest, and never did a subject come up which in any way concerned them that he did not watch it with jealous care, and see that their interests were duly provided for. Had they all been his own children he could hardly have manifested greater concern for them, and acted the part of a more watchful guardian. And it was this faithful watchfulness of their interests, and his ever prompt and earnest advocacy of their rights, that won for him the devoted attachment of those stalwart, brave, industrious, unpolished, yet warm-hearted sons of the wilderness and the prairie, who well knew that, though they were far away from the Halls of Congress, and could not make their wants and grievances known, there was one there who would never sit in silence and see them wronged; and hence it was that the people of Iowa and Wisconsin relied on Dr. Linn, and considered him as much *their* senator as if they had elected him, and he was responsible to them. But as he was *not* responsible to them and they could have no voice in re-electing him to the Senate, what could have prompted him thus to take so lively and active an interest in their behalf? It was, first, a warm and generous nature, which was amply repaid for doing good by the consciousness of having done his duty; and secondly, the deep interest which Dr. Linn felt and took in every thing which concerned the great West, with which he was and had been, from birth up, identified. It was his country, and not only his country, but his particular portion of it, his home, and had been the home of his fathers, by whose blood it had been won and possessed. The fathers of many of those who now filled the West, had bravely fought side by side with his ancestors, father and grandfather, had been mutually roused by the terrible midnight war-whoop of the savage, had mutually and desperately defended their wives, children and homes, and had mingled their blood together on many a desperate battle-field, and in many an ambush and hand-to-hand encounter. The strong bonds of attachment which are formed in times of mutual danger, trial and peril, —by mutual suffering, and by that interchange of good offices, kindnesses and sympathies, which, while it does honor to, softens, improves, and ennobles the human heart, are the most enduring of all human ties except those of love and family affection; and such were the bonds that once united the people of the West, as well as those of "the old thirteen States;" and it was the remembrance of the past, and the influence of its history, which so knit Dr. L. to all who were identified with that section of the country; they were to him as brothers, not as strangers; and his solicitude for their welfare, his watchfulness of their interests, his defence of their rights, his indignant repelling of all imputations cast upon them, such as "land stealers," and the like, were amply repaid, first, by the consciousness of having performed his duty, and secondly, by the grateful attachment manifested for him by the warm-hearted, though rough-clad, and rough-mannered people of the West, who still mourn his loss and cherish his memory in affectionate and grateful remembrance; and nowhere more warmly than in that far off land whose shores are washed by the waves, whose hills are fanned, and whose golden fields are gently swayed to and fro in light and shade by the refreshing breezes from the almost boundless Pacific.

The following letter from the Hon. Silas Wright to Mrs. Linn, shows the estimation in which Dr. L. was held by his brother senators, at least by those of his own party.

SENATE CHAMBER, WASHINGTON CITY,
March 10, 1841.

My dear Mrs. Linn,—I have been trying to find time to write you a long letter, from the 1st. of Jan. to this time, and you will say the effort must have been a faint one, or the letter would have reached you before this day; my good Lady, you are to get no letter now; I have so much to say to you that if I should commence a letter many a duty for which my friends here yet hold me to a rigid performance, would be neglected; we are now in the minority here, and I have looked forward to that time as one of leisure to us all, and we have not found that leisure yet. I now write to you from my seat in the Senate, and in the hearing of one of the most exciting debates to which I ever listened; so I must leave you to the Doctor to report all we have done here, but I cannot resist dropping you a few lines to make you a *little proud* about your good husband, whom you know that I love like a brother, and I do assure you that Dr. Linn has done himself great honor in his eloquent and heart-touching debates in the Senate during the short session. I am so happy to find that he has gained confidence in himself, which has made him become one of the most powerful, useful, and truly eloquent debaters in our Body. You know that he has been working like a slave in attending to the private business of Missouri, and has long resisted the entreaties of Mr. Buchanan and myself, with your ardent wishes, to participate more in the debates of the Senate: not in the habit of public-speaking, the Dr. feared that he might not do it well; he must now feel the great injustice that he has done himself, and that long since, had it not been for his *sensitive modesty*, that he would have taken the stand that he now holds in the Senate, as one of the most powerful members of that body, and most certainly possesses more popularity than any other member of Congress. You know, my dear Mrs. Linn, that I never flatter, and was I not fully aware of the truth of all I say about my kind friend the Doctor, I would not write it to you. I have often wished that every Missourian could see how your good husband labors for the prosperity of their noble State; then indeed would they know how to appreciate the wonderful industry of the hardest-working member of Congress.—One more word and, my good lady, I must finish this hasty communication. The President sent us your note to read with the injunction for its preservation, and to be returned to him; so you see how much value he attaches to it, and you must now permit me to say that you have a very happy talent in communicating your friendly feelings, and at the time your note reached him, every evidence of kindly feeling from his friends was most gratefully *felt*. He is now a private citizen, and let me say to you, that I truly think he has sustained his fall from the highest human elevation to that which he now holds, in a manner, and with an equanimity of temper and spirit, which adds more to his valuable reputation than all the acts of his previous life. But my good Mrs. Linn, you know *how much* I am his friend, and if I am now extravagant in his praise, you will make an allowance, and in every event I beg you to believe that

I am equally your friend,

SILAS WRIGHT, JR.

To Mrs. Elizabeth A. R. Linn, St. Genevieve.

BOARD OF COMMISSIONERS ON PRIVATE CLAIMS.

Bills had been introduced during several sessions of Congress to establish a Board of Commissioners to hear and examine claims against the United States, which had in every instance received the support of Dr. Linn, and in some instances he had spoken in favor of their passage. At the last session of the 26th Congress, a bill of this kind having been introduced, and come up for a third reading, it was earnestly opposed by Mr. Calhoun, Mr. Mangum and other senators. Mr. Linn advocated its passage; he said the bill had passed at the last three or four sessions after full discussion, besides being four times reported upon,—twice by the Committee on Claims, and twice by the Judiciary Committee; and he was therefore surprised that the senator (Mr. Calhoun) should again oppose it, as he had done year after year, without offering any measure as a substitute.

Mr. L. contended that great injustice was now done to the private claimant by the present system, than which none could be worse in its operation, and until something better should be proposed as a remedy for the evils now felt, he would support the present bill. He regretted that honorable senators had not seen the distress of the widows and children of land claimants, occasioned by the delay in the disposal of their claims;

for he was sure if they had, they would give to this subject that disposition which would lead to a speedier determination of private claims, while a due regard should be paid both to the rights of the citizen and the government.

He stated that there were 1500 or 2000 private bills of various kinds reported in the House of Representatives at the last session; and he himself reported a bill six years before which had not yet been acted on. He did not impute neglect of duty to any one; but he was satisfied that, in the first place, this body was too large and too transient, and in the second place, too political to despatch business of that kind in the prompt and speedy manner that it ought to be disposed of, and to give to all cases that examination and scrutiny which are necessary to a just understanding of them. The questions involved in private claims were sometimes of an abstruse and intricate character, and time was necessary to acquire such a knowledge of the facts and principles involved, as would enable senators to come to right decisions upon them. Sometimes senators here would acquire that knowledge, but circumstances might operate a postponement of the action of the Senate upon the claim, when the terms of those senators who had made themselves acquainted with the case might expire, or, if they held to the doctrine of instructions, they might be instructed out of their seats, which would then be occupied by new men, who would have to go through anew the same course and labor of investigation that their predecessors had, and so on for years. He thought it due to claimants, and due to good faith, that justice should neither be refused nor unreasonably delayed. It was cruel to keep men attending here year after year and generation after generation, as they attended the Court of Chancery in England, appealing to Congress for the payment of what is justly due, and made sick and disheartened by hope deferred. For his part, he said, his profession, as well as his habits of thought, led him to look at and regard individual suffering; but there were some who appeared to act like the soldier on the field of battle, who treads indiscriminately and without a thought for their suffering, alike on friend and foe, in the pursuit of his object, or in the discharge of his duty.

After further discussion in which Dr. L. earnestly endeavored to secure its passage, the bill was laid on the table, and of course was defeated. But though, as in the case of Oregon, Dr. Linn did not live to witness the success of a measure he so warmly advocated and deemed of so much importance to individuals as well as just to the Government, yet the time came, many years after his voice had been hushed in the grave, when a measure similar to the one he advocated,

—differing only in being called a "Court of Claims" instead of a "Board of Claims," became a law, and is now in full operation. That the final passage of a law establishing the Court of Claims was brought about in some measure by his advocacy and that of others of such a measure years before, no one acquainted with the habits of the Senate and House of Representatives, and the slow progress measures of a general character make in those bodies, can doubt. Time is required for such things to mature; and discussion is as necessary to their success as ploughing, harrowing, &c., is for the production of a crop of wheat.

Swamp, or Drowned Lands.

Among other matters of public importance and interesting to the people of the West, which occupied the attention of Dr. Linn, was that of draining the extensive marshes, lakes, lagoons and swamps, to be found on the Mississippi River and some of its tributaries, caused by an overflow of these streams in the spring and summer annually. They were fruitful sources of those chills and fevers, and sometimes of malignant bilious fevers, with which all in their vicinity and for many miles around were annually visited, and which, some seasons, prove so fatal. As a physician of large experience, Dr. L. knew the importance of removing the cause of these malignant diseases and restoring salubrity to the atmosphere. With that view, and as he well knew the government could not undertake an enterprise of the kind, he turned his attention to the subject and brought in a bill by which to accomplish the purpose he had so much at heart. The following is the bill:

A bill to surrender to the States of Missouri and Arkansas alternate sections of certain public lands, reported as not worth the expense of survey, for the purpose of increasing the value of the public domain.

Be it enacted, &c., That there be, and hereby are, granted to the States of Missouri and Arkansas, respectively, every alternate section of the public land situate within the counties hereafter stated, which have been reported by the deputy-surveyors to the surveyors-general, as not worth the expense of survey, upon the condition that all the moneys arising from the sale of said lands be expended, under the direction of the Legislatures of those States respectively, in the improvement of the water courses running through the said public lands, by the construction of canals and bridges, removal of rafts and other obstructions to their navigation, for the purpose of draining and preventing inundations of the said lands, to wit: to the State of Missouri, each alternate section within the counties of Cape Girardeau, Scott, Wayne, Stoddard, and New Madrid; and to the State of Arkansas, each alternate section within the counties of Mississippi, Crittenden, Saint Francis, Poinsett, Green and Randolph, respectively.

Mr. LINN said that this bill provided for the accomplishment of objects alike beneficial to the giver and the receiver; but the people of the far Western States had on certain occasions, when the subject of the public lands occupied the attention of this body, been stigmatized as "land pirates," "plunderers of the public lands," &c.; so that a member from that section of the country always felt some trepidation in bringing forward any proposition relating to the public domain. He trusted, however, that the beneficent purpose sought to be accomplished by the measure he had proposed, would commend the bill to the favorable consideration of honorable senators representing all sections of the country.

The district of country embraced within the bill was, with few exceptions, a very extensive land tract of alluvion, at times almost entirely overflowed by the waters of the Mississippi River, the main and little St. Francis, and the Castor, (which run through its whole length nearly parallel with the Mississippi,) and also with many smaller streams which fall into it from the neighboring high grounds, all of which find their way to the Father of Waters through lakes, lagoons, and filthy quagmires. It has, doubtless, for ages been subject to inundation; but this has been more particularly the case since the earthquakes of 1811 and 1812, the focus of which seemed to be placed in this basin, and the vibrations of which radiated to the extreme verge of the republic.

The transforming effects of these mighty phenomena were manifested in this district by the upheaving of the bed of the Mississippi, staying the course of its waters for several hours and causing them to overflow its banks; by which broad and deep lakes, sixty miles in length, were made, where stood the day before magnificent forests of cypress and other trees; the bottom of the river St. Francis was thrown up, and its waters scattered over a wide space; and dry ground was formed where swamps and lakes existed before; extensive areas, sunk below the general level, were subsequently filled with water; craters were opened, from which were vomited mud, sand, and coal, and many other effects were produced, to detail which is not now necessary.

The lakes and marshes are all connected with each other and with the St. Francis, by sinuses or bayous, receiving its overflowing waters and those of the Mississippi River, which annually inundate hundreds of thousands of acres, equalling in fertility any soil in the world.

The St. Francis and its tributaries, which course

this tract, are choked up with rafts like those on the Red River, with fallen timber, drift wood, and other obstructions. Such is also the case with the bayous which connect the St. Francis with the marshes and lakes, and the lakes with each other. By removing these rafts in the St. Francis River, and the drift wood and fallen timber in the bayous, and by deepening the connexions between the lakes, which would serve as so many canals—the principal feeder of which would be the St. Francis—much standing water would be liberated, and a continuous stream would then flow on through all these different inosculating branches to the Mississippi and thereby reclaim large portions of this rich territory, in a few years to be covered with a dense population, where *now* there is nothing but a melancholy waste, inhabited by savage beasts and venomous reptiles, and infecting the neighboring counties by its noisome exhalations.

In its present condition your surveyors have turned from portions of it in utter despair, as uninviting, unhealthful, and useless. Although it has been the theatre of the grandest and most destructive operations of nature, and is seamed all over with marks of Divine wrath, it is still blessed with a mild climate and great fertility of soil, and is of easy access to the ocean; and with the transforming effects of man's industry, will, like Holland, become a busy scene of prosperity and happiness, and, perhaps, equally as remarkable for its rivers and canals.

Will Congress have the *enlightened selfishness* to grant the aid necessary to render its *own property* of some value? The whole of this tract, however, is not affected by the periodical inundations. There are ridges of forty or fifty miles in length, above the reach of the water at its greatest height; there are also islands of rock, of various heights and dimensions, rising out of this marsh, like islands in the ocean; but so surrounded by water as to be cut off from all communication with each other and with the Mississippi, except in boats which must be navigated through dense forests and tangled jungles; in consequence of which these bodies of fertile lands are almost tenantless.

The opening of all the different sluices to give vent to the accumulating waters, cutting canals, building bridges, throwing up dykes, draining marshes, &c., would eventually reclaim the whole or nearly the whole, and fit it for the abode of our people whose energies bid defiance to every thing but impossibilities.

The objects contemplated by the bill are of great importance to the citizens of Missouri and Arkansas. The Legislatures of both States have sent memorials here upon the subject; and the question again presents itself: Shall all this work necessary to make the tract useful, be thrown upon the people living in that section, who feel a deep interest in the undertaking? or, will the Government extend its aid by contributing a portion of this (at present) unproductive domain towards this object? It might with much reason be urged that the entire tract had better be granted to the States in which it lies, than that it should remain in its present deplorable condition. But it will be perceived that a grant only of each alternate section is asked for; and should the grant be refused, there is little probability that, for a century to come, the Government will make any effort to reclaim this land. Will it, then, be so ungenerous as to throw upon individuals a labor which it should undertake itself?

This great alluvion stretches from Cape Girardeau in Missouri, to Helena in Arkansas—a distance of three hundred and fifty miles in length, and from thirty to fifty in breadth; and with the exception of a narrow belt lying along the borders of the Mississippi, and certain isolated spots scattered throughout, may be considered as worse than useless—nay, a positive nuisance.

Mr. LINN said, that the inhabitants of Southern Missouri had for years been looking anxiously for the Government to take some steps to clear the St. Francis, Big, Black and Current Rivers, of the obstructions in the way of successful navigation. He had brought the subject repeatedly before Congress, and, in 1836, an appropriation was made for the examination of these streams. An officer, Captain Guion, had made a hasty survey late in the autumn and had made a report, which Mr. L. now caused to be read; and haviug been read, Mr. L. proceeded:

The engineer examined the river St. Francis, and the country through which it passes, at a very unpropitious season, and the report is to be taken with many grains of allowance, especially, when speaking of the impracticability of making certain portions of the St. Francis navigable.

But even admitting that the difficulties in removing obstacles and giving to the St. Francis a permanent channel in certain points were insurmountable, still, much could be done to improve the water communication. Black River is a large and deep tributary of White River, and navigable to the only "raft" in it at all seasons of the year. Remove this one obstacle and boats could ascend it and its principal tributary (the Current) to the copper mines in Missouri, at all seasons with small boats.

But, sir, the beneficial effects of removing the "rafts" in the St. Francis and Big Black Rivers, and the redeeming from periodical inundation such an extensive surface of rich alluvion, do not stop here. By removing the obstructions in the way to the navigation of the St. Francis and Black Rivers, you will be enabled to reach by water, the very centre of the great mineral region of Missouri, which is drained by these rivers and their tributaries, and which is of unparalleled richness in copper, zinc, iron, lead, manganese, and many other mineral substances, and thereby add greatly to the value of the public lands. Will not Congress, then, act the part, in this matter, of a liberal and provident landlord, and embrace this opportunity and the proposed means to improve its own domain?"

Mr. SEVIER expressed his satisfaction that his friend from Missouri had interested himself in this important subject. He could say, from personal knowledge, that the views he had presented were entirely correct; and that the tract of country proposed to be granted, in part, was, in its present condition, wholly unavailable to the Government.

The bill was then referred to the Committee on Public Lands, but no further action appears to have been taken upon it during the session. But a bill was a few years after brought in and passed, by which the United States surrendered all the swamp, or inundated lands, to the States in which they were situated respectively, a measure which has resulted in the reclamation and draining of hundreds of thousands of acres of land which was utterly valueless to the Government, and a positive nuisance to large tracts of country around, on account of the malaria which arose from its putrid marshes and lagoons, and spread itself for miles around, carrying the seeds of disease and death wherever it lighted. The measure was also intended to enable the States bordering on the Mississippi River, to erect dikes along its banks to prevent the annual overflow which inundates so large a tract of country, and sometimes does great damage by forming new channels for the river. Few measures have been productive of more real benefits to those sections of the country immediately interested than this; and had Dr. Linn lived, he would have effected it instead of leaving its accomplishment to others; but having initiated it, and pointed out the way and the great importance of the measure, it may, without injustice to those who followed him, be claimed as his own. True, others might have thought of it and brought it forward; and so might some other person than Professor Morse, have been, in time, the author of the Magnetic Telegraph; but no other did till he led the way; it was then, after his death, easy to follow, and take up what he had left uncompleted.

In common with the party to which he belonged, Dr. Linn was strongly opposed to what was denominated "the Distribution Act," which provided for the distribution of the proceeds of the sales of Public Lands, and which was a *whig* measure. Dr. L. thought that these proceeds, so far as they were not needed to defray the expenses, or to pay the debts of the General Government, should be applied to strengthen the common defence of the country; and he therefore introduced a bill in December, 1841, to repeal the distribution sections of the act mentioned, and pledging those proceeds to purposes of national defence.

Mr. L. expressed his views in regard to the Distribution Act, to which he was opposed: he thought it an indirect mode of assuming the State debts. It was known that this country had an immense extent of sea coast and territorial border, stretching from the Atlantic to the Pacific, to protect, requiring a large expenditure; and it was not to be denied that its foreign relations were in a precarious situation; that at a moment's warning a war might be precipitated upon us; yet they had frittered away the means of national defence, and now hesitated to retrace their steps, when prudence, policy and duty, demanded the retraction. It was said, that when the crisis should come, the States would be ready to supply the General Government with the means of defence; but he thought it was the better policy for the Government to prepare itself for any *crisis* of this kind, so that it need not be dependent upon the States when it came.

Mr. L. had suggested that the bill be referred to the Committee on Military Affairs, as the Committee on Public Lands were opposed to it and already committed against it.

Mr. CALHOUN was in favor of referring it to a special committee.

Mr. PIERCE rose to express his gratification, that thus early in the session something had been proposed in behalf of national defences, a matter so long neglected, while every section of the Union had been agitated and embroiled with contests for party supremacy. The proposition of his friend from Missouri (Mr. LINN) gave earnest of patriotic, and at the same time, of prudent and judicious action upon one of the most important questions that could possibly claim the attention of the republic. Whether the means of defence were to be derived from the public lands or from any other source, it was a clear case that the country could not be left longer in its present condition. It had no adequate preparation from one extremity of the seaboard to the other, to defend itself against aggression. And let it be remembered, that aggression, if resolved upon at this day, with the application of steam to ocean navigation, and the improvements in military science, must, in the nature of things, be sudden and tremendous. * * * * *

No gentleman could doubt that, in our present defenceless state, the only power from which at present we had any thing to apprehend, might and probably would destroy, laying aside all considerations of the loss of life and incalculable amount of human suffering, more property in a single night—in a single city—than would be required to place ourselves in a condition of comparative protection and security. It had been said by gentlemen distinguished in the naval as well as land service, that we were not at this moment *relatively* better prepared for a conflict with Great Britain than we were at the commencement of the late war, thirty years ago. The nation felt this to be a hazardous and shameful condition, in which it ought not to be permitted to remain. The most appropriate disposition of the bill, it struck him, was that indicated by the Senator from South Carolina (Mr. CALHOUN). Let it go to a select committee.

Further debate ensued upon the subject of distribution and the propriety of referring the bill to a select or a standing committee, or to the Committee of the Whole. Upon the vote being taken, the Senate refused to refer the bill, but made it the order of the day for some few days ahead. As it provided for the repeal of the Distribution Act, and a majority of the Senate at that time were in favor of, as they had a few months before passed, that act, it met with decided opposition, and consequently failed. But Dr. L. had, nevertheless, performed what he deemed his duty to his constituents and to the country, and might console himself with the reflection that it was not in the power of mortals always to command success, even when most merited. But public men are often doomed to witness the failure of measures they deem eminently useful and important to the country, sometimes because others do not take the same view of them that they do, and sometimes because proposed by one who belongs to a party in the minority, and the majority are unwilling to allow an opponent the credit of a good measure even though the country may be benefited thereby. Nothing is more common than this, however contrary to the theory of a republican government, which is based upon the supposition that every citizen, whether in a public or private station, will have the true interests of the republic at heart, and honestly advocate and support whatever is calculated to promote the general good and prosperity of the whole nation, no matter by whom suggested or originated. In practice, however, one party advocates, while another opposes measures, simply because they are "party measures;" because the party proposing is to have the credit of whatever good they may be productive of, and may thereby gain strength with the country. I do not intend to affirm that this is always, and with all public men, the rule of action; but I am reluctantly compelled to say, that the prosperity and success of the party to which public men attach themselves, to which they owe their official positions, and look for a continuance of favor, is too often quite as near their hearts and exerts as great an influence upon their actions, as the prosperity and best interests of the country. "The heart is deceitful above all things," and never more so than in the breast of a politician who has long sought to attain, has attained, and is ambitious to retain, a station of honor, profit or trust, which gives him eminence, influence and consideration in the nation or with those among whom he resides. There naturally arises, also, an attachment on the part of the individual to the party to which he belongs, and with which he acts; its prosperity or adversity, success or defeat, weal or woe, are his; he exults when it triumphs, is cast down when it is prostrated, and becomes so identified with it that whatever its fate, that fate is his. No wonder, then, that it should sometimes, and, indeed, not unfrequently, usurp the place of country, and its opponents be looked upon almost in the light of public enemies, and treated as if they were at least domestic foes.

Dr. Linn was a very decided party man; he believed the measures and principles of the party to which he belonged to be such as were calculated to promote the general good, and he therefore advocated them with the zeal and ardency which belonged to a warm heart, honest impulses and strong feelings. He was devotedly attached to General Jackson personally, and supported his measures with an ardor due to the honest convictions of his judgment and the warmth of his personal friendship for the man. But while he did so, such was the kindliness and sincerity of his nature, such the urbanity of his demeanor, such the generosity and nobleness of his disposition, and the ever pleasant expression of his countenance, that though his language in debate sometimes savored of a tartness foreign to his heart, his opponents ever gave him credit for the strictest honor, honesty, sincerity and manliness, and as a man held him in high esteem.

ARMED OCCUPATION OF FLORIDA.

In 1842, the Florida war being considered at an end, and yet the few Indians remaining in that territory continuing to commit depredations and murders upon the inhabitants sparsely settled along the frontiers, who were too few and far between to render each other much protection, if any, indeed, against the sudden incursions of the savages, it was deemed necessary to adopt some measure that would tempt young, hardy, bold and athletic men to take up their abode in the vicinity of the Indians and defend the country against their depredations. The great object was to push forward the white settlements into the unsettled parts of the territory, and thus to gradually crowd out the Indians, while a hardy body of pioneers were located along the line of advancing settlements who could cope with the savages, even in their own peculiar mode of warfare.

With that view, Mr. Benton from the Committee on Military Affairs, introduced a bill giving lands to such as would settle upon them in that section of Florida. Mr. B. said the principle of the bill had several times received the sanction of the Senate; similar bills having been several times passed by that body within the last three years. It was now recommended by the President and Secretary of War; and with the more reason as the number of Indians in the Peninsula of Florida was greatly reduced, and the troops partly withdrawn. There were not Indians enough in the territory to justify military operations. But there were too many to justify settlements by cultivators and others, until inducements were held out to them sufficient to justify people incurring the risks and the privations incident to such settlement. The bill, he said, proposed these inducements; namely, a quarter section of land, subsistence for one year, [this was afterwards stricken out by the House,] and arms and ammunition for such as should need them. Mr. B. said the necessity for the bill was becoming more and more urgent by the massacres that were now taking place in that part of Florida.

The bill having passed the Senate and come back from the House amended, was again opposed in the Senate, and to some of those who spoke against it Mr.

Linn replied. He contended that the Government had acted heretofore upon the principle of making donations of land as an inducement to settlement. It was that policy which had contributed to secure the rapid settlement and sale of the public domain. It was a policy which had caused no actual loss to the Government. Mr. L. said he had incorporated that very principle in his Oregon bill; and he sincerely hoped senators would not oppose it on that ground. He trusted that the past policy of the Government would not be disregarded. After speaking of the effectiveness of the bill as it passed the Senate, and the amendments by the House, he alluded to the policy the Government had pursued, of granting bounty land to the soldiers who defended the country during the last war. This was the same in principle. The settlers would go there under the inducement held out by the bill—a bounty in land—and fight for the soil, and save the blood of regular military forces, which had been withdrawn from the contest at present. Those men would fight for their land, and love it the more because they had to fight for it. After giving a graphic description of the character, energy, and boldness of the men who would be induced to go into Florida under this bill, Mr. L. showed that they would make a most effective force to grapple with the Indian, knife in hand, and drive him from his fastnesses. He argued that the Government would have to do either one thing or the other—to hold out an inducement for necessitous, enterprising, and bold men to go to Florida, and save the defenceless women and children from the cruelties of the savage, or speedily enlist another body of men and give them this very bounty, and pay them from the treasury a heavy sum of money, to fight until the last Indian was driven from the territory. It was folly to suppose that an enemy as scattered as these Indians were, with small parties here and there, and every where, could be operated against by a regular military force. You could never dislodge them until you shall select a body of men that will follow them in their hammocks, seek out and discover their lurking places, beat up their quarters, dog them from one fastness to another, until they found there was to be no peace nor rest for them, and no security for them but in coming in and giving themselves up. Scattered as the Indians now were, it would keep 10,000 regular men operating at all points, to be of any service. Mr. L. dwelt on the mode of Indian warfare, showing that they could keep in active operation a very much larger number of men than they counted themselves, as it was their custom to strike a serious unexpected blow, and then suddenly disappear, striking perhaps another unlooked for blow in a few hours after, at a point quite distant from the first, and then, in the midst of these interminable fastnesses, whose labyrinths none could thread but themselves, elude pursuit, and laugh at their pursuers. But surround them with a cordon of hardy, fearless, advancing settlers, or let the column gradually advance upon them only from one direction, clearing up the country as it rolls onward, and the Indians would soon find they must surrender, or seek other quarters.

Mr. Woodbridge of Michigan, said, so far as the bill contemplated a donation of land as an inducement for the settlement of Florida, it met his hearty concurrence; and it established no new principle in that respect. On a similar principle, 100,000 acres of land were given to secure a settlement at the junction of the Ohio, as early as 1787 or '88—the Government then having to contend with just as savage an enemy as the Indians of Florida.

As Mr. Linn was much interested in the settlement of Florida,—and we have already seen how active he had been to introduce the culture of new plants in that region, and thereby encourage the settlement and increase the productions of the territory,—and as he was also desirous that Congress should approve the principle of encouraging settlements by donations of land to settlers,—a principle embraced in his Oregon bill,—he was much gratified by the Armed Occupation bill becoming a law, having passed the Senate by a vote of 24 to 16.

Although the measure has not been productive of all the beneficial effects anticipated by its friends, it was not without some good results. Even to get the land settled, without deriving any income or remuneration from it, is a much greater benefit to the country than any price in money that could be obtained for the land if sold, had the Government obtained four or ten times its real value; for,

> "What constitutes a State?
> Not high raised battlement or labored mound,
> Thick wall or moated gate:
> Not cities fair, with spires and turrets crown'd:
> No:—men, high-minded men—
> * * * * * * *
> Men who their duties know,
> Knowing too their rights, and, knowing, dare maintain."

Those lands were not such as emigrants would voluntarily settle upon and pay for, or accept as a donation, upon condition of placing their families upon them in their natural, unhealthy condition; they had first to be drained, or the overflowing waters diked out, and when this was done, when, as "in the beginning," the land and the waters were separated, and "the dry land" was made to appear; "and the earth brought forth grass and herb, yielding seed after his kind, and the tree yielding fruit, whose seed was in itself, after his kind," then those drowned lands become valuable, being very rich and productive, and tempting to the husbandman. Many of these swamps, lakes and lagoons, the habitations of alligators, snapping turtles, copper-headed, moccasin, and other poison snakes and reptiles, have been drained and turned into fruitful fields, as Dr. Linn predicted they would, and others will, in time, undergo this desirable metamorphosis.

DESTRUCTION OF STEAMBOATS ON THE MISSISSIPPI AND THE OHIO RIVERS.

While the Ohio and the Mississippi Rivers, and their tributaries, were the great highways upon which the commerce of the immense and fruitful country which they drained, was compelled to travel,—by which alone its exports could reach a market, and its imports be received, as was the case for many years, and until railroads in some measure supplanted these great natural highways,—the immense losses which occurred in consequence of the existence of numerous snags and sawyers in those rivers, and the great delays which took place in the season of low water in consequence of the "sand-bars" which then obstructed the navigation, were felt as a most serious evil by the people of the West, and the attention of Congress was again and again called to the subject, and its aid and the agency of the General Government invoked to render the necessary relief, by clearing out these snags and sawyers, and deepening the channel over, or by some means removing, these "sand-bars." Appropriations were made from time to time by Congress for this purpose; but as there was a class of men, of politicians or statesmen, in Congress, and sometimes occupying the Presidential chair, who denied that Congress had the constitutional power to appropriate the public moneys for purposes of this kind, those appropriations were always strenuously, and sometimes successfully opposed, and the objects intended to be accomplished were never more than half accomplished, and then left in such a manner, that what had been done might as well not have been done; the money expended was but thrown away, and this fact served as an argument subsequently, against making further appropriations for the same or similar purposes.

On the 17th of January, 1843, Mr. Linn rose in the Senate and stated, that he had been requested to present to that body a memorial from the city of St. Louis, signed by nearly fifteen hundred of its most intelligent and useful business men. He knew many of the gentlemen who had put their names to this memorial; and he could assure the Senate, that the utmost confidence was due to any statement they endorsed. The prayer of the memorial is, that Congress may make an appropriation for improving the navigation of the great western rivers. The memorialists state that, especially in the Missouri and Mississippi Rivers, within the last four years, the accumulation of snags has been so great as to render navigation not only dangerous in the extreme to commerce, but hazardous, in consequence of the great number of lives lost among the passengers. They further state, said Mr. L., that, in the year 1839, there were forty steamboats lost; in 1840, there were forty-one; twenty-nine in 1841, and in 1842, twenty-eight. The value of the boats would average $25,000 each, making a total loss of $3,000,000. But this is not all: they further state, that almost every boat engaged in the Missouri trade has been injured, more or less, by snags, the repairs of which cost about $260 each, which makes a total loss of $3,710,000, in the course of four years.

Between the 11th September, and the 13th of October, in the past year, the following boats were lost between the city of St. Louis and the mouth of the Ohio; to wit:

Sept.	11.	Mentor, boat and part of the cargo, loss	$34,000
"	13.	New Orleans, sunk within 100 yards of the Mentor, loss	45,000
"	22.	Pre-emption, near the same place	25,000
"	"	Robert T. Lytle, near the same place	7,000
"	26.	Fort Pitt, within $\frac{1}{4}$ of a mile of the same place	25,000
Oct.	6.	Louisville	8,000
"	7.	Osage Valley,	40,000
"	13.	Eliza—sunk—40 or 50 persons drowned, loss	50,000

These losses, amounting to $234,000, occurred in less than five weeks.

Mr. Linn continued. They further say, that the most formidable obstructions in the Western rivers are at St. Louis, or near that place; but they nevertheless sympathize with their fellow-citizens throughout the great valley of the Mississippi, and feel called on to co-operate with these, in urging this honorable body to do justice to the West, by making ample appropriations for the immediate improvement of our rivers,—the Missouri, the Ohio, and the Upper and Lower Mississippi. They observe that they can safely say that the commerce on those rivers and their tributaries, forming twenty thousand miles of interior navigation, cannot amount to less at the present time, than two hundred millions a year. The removal of snags, the clearing of logs from the banks caved in, and the improvement of the harbor of St. Louis, (all commenced several years ago,) cannot be completed unless by the aid of the Government, and under its authority. They say that the rapids of the Upper Mississppi could be improved by a slack-water navigation, or a canal, which would enhance the value of the public lands.

This subject, Mr. Linn said, was taken up by the population of the whole valley of the Mississippi. Every man, woman and child, in that valley was directly interested in the improvement of the great

Western rivers. This population must and will be heard on this important matter. He could not face his constituents without doing all in his power to obviate the crying and melancholy evils complained of. He could not return home unless he exerted himself with all the ability and energy he possessed, to procure this appropriation.

Nearly four millions of property, Mr. L. said, had been destroyed in less than four years,—a greater loss, he presumed, than has occurred from storm or tempest on our Atlantic coast. This can be obviated by Congress on the Western waters, whilst God alone can command the storms of the great deep. The greatest amount of loss will be found between St. Louis and the mouth of the Ohio,—a distance of two hundred miles. A snag-boat at work at a few points designated emphatically, "steamboat graveyards," would have prevented all the destruction of property and loss of life complained of in this and other petitions. Captain Shreve eradicated one year all the snags that formerly obstructed these points, by which the navigation was rendered comparatively safe. This can be done again. It was vainly hoped that the iron steamboats would have resisted the snags and sawyers, which stand in some places like a forest of enormous trees. This has been tested, and the boats are found incapable of resisting the force of the snag. The Valley Forge iron boat was lost this winter; but had been since raised. Scarcely a Western newspaper can be taken up, in which some account of a fresh wreck cannot be found. Last night he observed in one the loss of the Henry Clay, valued at $40,000, without estimating the cargo. Two hundred millions of dollars are involved in the trade carried on by steamboats on these rivers—thirty millions belonging to St. Louis.

The right of Congress to make appropriations for the purpose of improving rivers and harbors, the great highways of commerce, both external and internal, having been questioned by some of our statesmen, and become, partially, one of the dividing questions between the political parties of the country, it is thought to be not out of place here to give, very briefly, the views of several senators as expressed on this occasion. Since this debate occurred Mr. POLK and Mr. PIERCE, while exercising the duties of Chief Magistrate of the nation, have vetoed bills making such appropriations on the ground of their unconstitutionality.

Mr. SMITH of Indiana, following Mr. Linn, said, he fully and heartily concurred with the memorialists, as well as in the very just remarks of the senator from Missouri. The subject was of great importance to the whole country, but especially so to the Great West. He had long thought that this important matter had been too much neglected by Congress. Such had been the loss of property and sacrifice of human life, in consequence of the neglect of the Government to remove the obstructions from the Western waters, and to provide safe harbors on the Western lakes, that there was and would be, but one voice on the subject, and he trusted that the time had arrived for effective action on the subject. He would not go into an examination of the details of the memorials referred to, but the facts are most startling, and he recommended their careful examination to the committee to whom they were referred.

Mr. HUNTINGTON,—chairman of the Committee on Commerce, said, he could assure the Senate that the subject had not escaped the Committee on Commerce. Several memorials were before the committee, where the most anxious desire to do justice in the matter prevailed.

Mr. ALLEN (of Ohio), expressed his satisfaction at the assurance just given by the chairman of the Committee on Commerce, that the subject would be carefully considered. He would move the printing of the memorial. He hoped the committee would embody all the facts, information and reasoning of the several memorials in one general report, showing the extent, importance, and value of the navigation of the Western waters, and the loss of life and property occasioned by the obstructions, for the removal of which the appropriation is asked.

Mr. Barrow stated, that it was the purpose of the committee to do what the senator had expressed a wish should be done. Every member of the committee, as far as he could observe, was well disposed towards the object in view, and all were aware of the importance of the navigation of these Western waters, and of the necessity of doing something to arrest the losses complained of. The duty of collating the materials and facts, and of making a report, had been assigned to him by the committee, and he was engaged in preparing it.

Mr. Calhoun said, in the absence of a representation of the State of Tennessee in this body, he thought it proper to call the attention of the committee to one of the main branches of the Mississippi River, which had apparently been entirely overlooked; he alluded to the Tennessee River. That river was, he believed, of more importance than any other of the branches of the Mississippi, with the exception of the Ohio. There were no less than six States interested in the navigation of that river. It was a larger stream than the Ohio, and if the same expense were bestowed upon it, as upon the Ohio River, he would not be at all surprised to see, in the course of ten years, the commerce upon that river exceed that of the Ohio. He hoped the committee would establish some principle upon which the navigation of these *real internal seas*—for such to all intents they were—might be improved; and to see how far this great river was entitled to their attention, on the principle thus established.

Mr. Benton called the attention of the committee to the appropriation of $100,000 made at the last session for removing obstructions, and complained that nothing had been done under this appropriation.

Mr. Walker called the attention of the committee to a navigable tributary of the Mississippi, flowing 600 miles through a country that furnished a larger contribution of cotton to the commerce of the South, than either the Tennessee or the Red River, or the Arkansas. He alluded to the Yazoo River. He entered into a variety of details showing the importance and value of the navigation of this river, and those tributary to it.

Mr. W. thought this a question of as great importance as could come before the committee on commerce. The navigation of these great inland channels of communication with the Ocean, furnished more produce for exportation than the Atlantic coast.

Mr. Crittenden hoped that something would be done in relation to the great rivers of the West—the Mississippi and the Ohio, and perhaps some others; but if they were going to include all the inferior streams, it was perfectly evident, as had been well said by the Senator from Alabama (Mr. King), they would not be able to legislate upon the subject at all. These rivers are our great inland ocean, and they had as much right to claim the assistance of the government as those living on the Atlantic coast had. He hoped the committee which had charge of the subject would confine themselves to the great object of the improvement of these large rivers.

Each of the senators who spoke on this occasion, not only recognized the right but the duty of Congress to make appropriations to improve the navigation of these Western rivers. Mr. Calhoun, it will be noted, denominated the rivers of the West "GREAT INTERNAL SEAS," and as such he admitted the duty of the government to make appropriations for the improvement of their navigation and the security of life and property upon them.

But the necessity for these appropriations is not now perhaps so important; not that the obstructions to the navigation upon the waters of the West do not now exist to the same extent as formerly, but from the fact that the construction of railroads connecting the great commercial cities of the West with the great cities on the Atlantic, and thereby enabling the people of the West to send forward their produce and receive goods in return at all seasons of the year, and in much less time than formerly, is shifting the commerce from the rivers to the railroads, and bids fair to render the former highways of trade and commerce wholly useless except for those residing immediately on the banks of these streams, and for cities which have no other channel of communication; as, for instance, between St. Louis and New Orleans, Natchez, Memphis, Little Rock, &c., and between St. Louis and St. Paul. But how long it may be ere St. Louis shall be connected with each and all of these cities by railroads, remains to be seen; probably not many years, however; and then we shall seldom hear of the destruction of steamboats by snags and sawyers upon the Mississippi River, and the loss of a great number of lives with the total loss of boat and cargo. The time is not distant, when, instead of ten or twenty steamboats arriving at the wharves of that city per day from New Orleans, Pittsburg, Cincinnati, Louisville, Memphis, Natchez, Galena, Burlington, Davenport, Dubuque, St. Paul, and from the Rocky Mountains, fifty or sixty, perhaps a hundred, trains of rail cars will daily come rushing into that city from almost every part of the compass, and from every part of our great Republic, even from San Francisco, the mouth of the Columbia River, Puget's Sound, Salt Lake, &c., &c. And who will now undertake to say that the city of Mexico itself, will not be the terminus of one of these numerous routes of rapid intercommunication?

CHAPTER VI.

GENERAL JACKSON'S FINE.

It is a matter of history, that in 1815, soon after the battle of New Orleans, and while General Jackson was still in that city, he deemed it his duty to adopt and pursue such a course of measures as brought him in conflict with the civil authorities, and that a fine of one thousand dollars was imposed upon him by Judge Hall, U. S. District Judge, for an alleged contempt of the judicial authority. Parties and party feeling ran excessively high there at the time. On the one hand, it was alleged that the General acted in the most arbitrary and tyrannical manner towards some of the citizens of Louisiana, and especially in proclaiming martial law and imprisoning a member of the Legislature; on the other hand, it was asserted in justification of his proceedings, that there were treasonable designs afoot, and that the measures taken by General Jackson were necessary to the security of the city. Judge Hall having been applied to for a writ of *habeas corpus* in behalf of Louis Louallier, who, as was alleged, was held in illegal imprisonment, granted the same, and was therefor arrested and confined by order of General Jackson, and after six days confinement in the guard-house, was conducted by a file of soldiers out of the city, and beyond the lines of the camp. It was for this act, this alleged interference with the judicial authority, that the general was afterwards cited before, and fined one thousand dollars by the judge. All the circumstances attending these transactions, the eminent stations of the two prominent men concerned, the General and the Judge, the conflict that it involved between the military and the civil power, all were calculated to excite an unusual degree of feeling and asperity between those who enlisted on the one side or on the other. Accordingly, when the fine was imposed and paid, the sum was almost instantly raised by the friends of General Jackson, and handed to him; but instead of putting the money in his own pocket, he ordered it to be applied to charitable purposes.

His friends throughout the Union had insisted upon the injustice of this fine, but it was not till after he had retired from public life that the refunding of this fine by the United States was proposed and warmly advocated in various State legislatures and public meetings. No subject lay nearer the heart of Dr. Linn than the refunding of this fine to General Jackson, and he consequently took an active part in procuring the passage of the bill for that purpose. In his inmost heart, aye, in his heart of hearts, he believed the fine wrongfully imposed; that the general was at the time and in doing that for which he was fined, acting the part of a true, bold and determined patriot, bent upon saving New Orleans from the enemy at any hazard to himself personally, and feeling thus, it was natural that one possessing his ardent temperament, and entertaining the warmest feeling of personal attachment to the ex-President, should at least show no lukewarmness in a matter which so deeply concerned the latter.

On the other hand, those who opposed the refunding of this fine, were equally honest and sincere in their conviction that it had been rightfully imposed; that General Jackson had most unwarrantably attempted to place the military above the civil and judicial power of the country, and in imprisoning a U. S. judge in his camp for granting a writ of right, committed a most flagrant breach of the laws and a most unjustifiable act of arbitrary power.

The friends of the measure did not place it upon the ground that General Jackson had a constitutional right to do what he did: Dr. L. in the course of the debate said "that the friends of this measure had not argued it on the ground of the act for which the fine was incurred being constitutional. He apprehended not one of his friends had taken that position, and that therefore the senator from Delaware (Mr. Bayard) was in error in supposing it so advocated. What he and his friends did say was, that General Jackson, under the circumstances in which he was placed, acted nobly, and merited the approval and gratitude of the whole country, so fully, unequivocally, and repeatedly awarded to him then, and ever since the transaction. He was not the man voluntarily to abandon his duty to his country in such a crisis, and take refuge behind the letter of the constitution for his excuse after both country and constitution were destroyed by an invading enemy." And Mr. Buchanan said, "It had never been contended on this floor that a military commander possessed the power, under the constitution of the United States, to declare martial law. No such principle had ever been asserted on this (the Democratic) side of the Senate. * * * We do not contend, strictly speaking, that General Jackson had any constitutional right to declare martial law at New Orleans; but that, as this exercise of power was the only means of saving the city from capture by the enemy, he stood amply justified before the country for the act. We place the argument not upon the ground of strict constitutional right, but of such an overruling necessity as left General

Jackson no alternative but the establishment of martial law, or the sacrifice of New Orleans to the rapine and lust of the British soldiery."

This subject was, on several occasions, brought before Congress by Dr. Linn, whose remarks upon it, delivered in the Senate on the 14th of May, 1842, are here inserted.

Remarks of Mr. Linn, of Missouri, on the bill to indemnify General Jackson for the fine imposed on him at New Orleans in 1815, *delivered in the United States Senate, May* 14, 1842.

The following bill being under consideration, viz:

A BILL to indemnify Major General Andrew Jackson for damage sustained in the discharge of his official duty.

Be it enacted by the Senate and House of Representatives of the United States of America in Congress assembled, That the proper accounting officers of the Treasury Department be, and they are hereby, directed to ascertain the amount of the penalty or damages awarded by the district judge of the United States, at New Orleans, in the year eighteen hundred and fifteen, against Major General Andrew Jackson, then commander-in-chief of that district, for official acts in that capacity, and paid by him at that time; and that the sum so paid, with interest at six per cent. per annum, be paid to Major General Andrew Jackson, out of any moneys in the treasury not otherwise appropriated.

Mr. LINN said he desired to occupy the attention

of the Senate a short time by a few observations, in reply to the Senator from Louisiana (Mr. Conrad.)

If this were the first case of the kind (said Mr. L.) which had occurred in the history of the country, I might, perhaps, be induced to pause while in the act of extending sheer justice to an injured citizen. But, sir, our statute-books abound in precedents—cases in which military and naval officers, as well as other agents in almost *every* department of the Government, having, in the discharge of their duty, incurred the penalty of the law, and been obliged to pay fines, have called upon us for relief, and have seldom, or never, called in vain.

In the case now presented to the Senate, what are we required to do? Nothing, sir—nothing but a simple, naked, and unencumbered act of *justice* to a citizen who has been fined by a court for an act done while in the performance of his duty, and while rendering most valuable and important services to his country. This is the only true and proper light in which the subject can be viewed; and it can serve no good object to intermix extraneous matters, as proposed in the amendments, with the plain question. It is not necessary to make any allusion to the judge by whom the fine was imposed; and the bill is, therefore, silent as to Judge Hall. It neither condemns his motives nor his acts. It is possible, as I remarked the other day, that the Judge and the General, in the discharge of their peculiar duties, may have both been right. *We all know that the General was right.* In regard to the former, we are not called upon, and it is worse than useless now to express an opinion directly or indirectly; and as to the latter, should we now refuse to extend to him the simple act of justice which the bill provides, or clog it with derogatory amendments, we would trample upon every generous emotion which moved the bosoms of the fair daughters of New Orleans when they gathered their jewels to ward off the blow aimed at their gallant preserver by an indignant judiciary—every noble and generous impulse which has moved a free people to elevate him, by their suffrages, above the sentence of the court.

I repeat, an investigation into the motives or the acts of Judge Hall is uncalled for; and I will not contribute to such an investigation. The question has but *one* bearing or point to which we must look. It is confined to this inquiry: Was the declaration of martial law *necessary* to the safety of New Orleans? It would be a waste of time to seek, here or elsewhere, for a man who will give a negative answer to this question; for all, I believe—even the Senator (Mr. Conrad) himself—will admit that General Jackson had good and sufficient ground for believing that martial law was necessary; that his imperative duty was, to *save the city*—and, as a means, that duty required him to establish martial law. But, if, at this day, it should be contended that the grounds of the General's belief were insufficient, to what source, I would ask, must the error be traced? There was no error in the case; many good reasons existed, and they were communicated to General Jackson by the *highest civil authorities of the State*—Governor Claiborne among the number; and were by those authorities deemed to be of such a nature as to render the establishment of martial law indispensably necessary to its safety.

Of this indispensable necessity, the most incredulous will be convinced by reading the letters of Governor Claiborne to General Jackson. In that of the 8th of August, 1814, he says:

"On a late occasion I had the mortification to acknowlege my inability to meet a requisition from General Flournoy; the corps of this city having, for the most part, *resisted* my orders; being encouraged in their disobedience by the Legislature of the State, then in session; one branch of which, the Senate, having declared the *requisition* illegal and oppressive, and the House of Representatives having rejected a proposition to approve the measure. How far I shall be supported in my late orders, remains yet to be proved. I have reason to calculate upon the patriotism of the interior and western counties. I know, also, that there are many faithful citizens in New Orleans; but there are others, in whose attachment to the United States *I ought not to confide.* Upon the whole, sir, I cannot disguise the fact, that if Louisiana should be attacked, we must principally depend for security upon the prompt movements of the regular force under your command,

and the militia of the Western States and Territories. At this moment, we are in a very unprepared and defenceless condition; several important points of defence remain unoccupied, and, in case of a sudden attack, this capital would, I fear, fall an easy sacrifice."

On the 12th of the same month the General was told—

"On the native Americans and a *vast majority* of the Creoles of the country, I place much confidence; nor do I doubt the fidelity of many Europeans who have long resided in the country; but there are others, much devoted to the interest of Spain, and whose partiality to the English is not less observable than their dislike to the American Government."

In a letter of the 24th, the same ideas are repeated—

"Be assured, sir, that no exertions shall be wanting on my part; but I cannot disguise from you that I have a very difficult people to manage; to this moment, no opposition to the requisition has manifested itself, but I am not seconded with that *ardent zeal* which, in my opinion, the crisis demands. We look with great anxiety to your movements, and place our greatest reliance for safety on the energy and patriotism of the Western States. In Louisiana there are many faithful citizens: these last persuade themselves that Spain will soon repossess herself of Louisiana, and they seem to believe that a combined Spanish and English force will soon appear on our coast. If Louisiana is invaded, I shall put myself at the head of such of my militia as will follow me to the field, and, *on receiving, shall obey your orders.* I need not assure you of my entire confidence in you as a commander, and of the pleasure I shall experience in supporting all your measures for the common defence. But, sir, a cause of indescribable chagrin to me is, that I am not at the head of a willing and united people: native Americans, native Louisianians, Frenchmen and Spaniards, with some Englishmen, compose the mass of the population—among them there exists much jealousy, and as great differences in political sentiments, as in their language and habits. But nevertheless, sir, if we are supported by a respectable body of regular troops, or of Western militia, I trust I shall be able to bring to your aid a valiant and faithful corps of Louisiana militia; but if we are left to rely *principally on our own resources*, I fear *existing jealousies* will lead to distrust so general, that we shall be able to make but a feeble resistance."

If there be any upon whose minds there lingers a doubt upon this question, let him look at the picture which New Orleans presented at that day. A quarter of a century ago, the organization of the society of that city was peculiar; in its composition there was much that was foreign to our institutions, in act and in feeling; for in it was infused a mixture from the continent of Europe, of men not native to our soil—from France, Spain, Portugal, Britain, and Germany—many of whom felt a deep gratitude to England for the overthrow of Bonaparte. Indeed, when we reflect upon the situation of New Orleans as it then was, in regard to this portion of its population *alone*, we might well be justified in lauding the declaration of martial law by General Jackson, even aside from the fact that he was urged to do so by the civil authorities of the State, and by others of its most gallant and patriotic sons.

If, sir, my memory serves me, something fell from

the gentleman from Louisiana, which indicated a desire, on his part, that the friends of Gen. Jackson should *establish* the fact that he was justified, on legal constitutional grounds, for adopting the course which he pursued at New Orleans. He would require us to point out the law under which the General acted. I trust the Senator will be satisfied with the fact, that many emergencies arise in war—and, indeed, some in peace—in which the high civil and military servants of the people are, from *necessity*, compelled to "take the responsibility" of doing some act for the safety of the country, which is beyond the pale of their ordinary duties, and, if the Senator pleases, beyond the law. Again: I could refer the Senator to the cases in which Generals Wilkinson, Brown, and other officers on the frontiers of the State of New York, have been amerced for arresting and imprisoning persons on *suspicion* of being spies or traitors.

There are precedents innumerable where officers have been found guilty of breaches of law in the discharge of their duty, and, therefore, calling for the interference of a just Government. Of these, it is only necessary to introduce a few, where the Government did interpose and give relief to the injured officer. These cases commenced as early as August, 1790, and have continued down to the present time. Thus, in April, 1818, Major General Jacob Brown was indemnified for damages sustained under sentence of civil law, for having confined an individual found near his camp, suspected of traitorous designs.

At the same session, Captain Austin and Lieutenant Wells were indemnified against nine judgments, amounting to upwards of $6,000, for having confined nine individuals suspected of treachery to the country. In this case it was justly remarked by the then Secretary of War, (John C. Calhoun,) that "if it should be determined that no law authorized" the act, "yet I would respectfully suggest that there may be cases, in the exigencies of war, in which, if the commander should transcend his legal power, Congress ought to protect him, and those who act under him, from consequential damages;" in which the committee of the House of Representatives, as stated by their chairman, the lately deceased member from North Carolina (Mr. Williams) concurred.

In the case of General Robert Swartwout, in 1818, the committee by whom it was reported stated that "it is considered one of those extreme cases of necessity in which an overstepping of the established legal rules of society stands fully justified."

In May, 1820, General James Wilkinson was indemnified for damages recovered against him by General Adair, on account of false imprisonment.

In March, 1823, Colonel Robert Purdy was indemnified for damages, for having arrested and imprisoned an individual found near his garrison, whose acts had done injury to the subordination of that post, and were calculated to violate law. In this case it was remarked that, "admitting the court to be correct, both as to jurisdiction and the definition" of the character, &c., yet the committee are of opinion the petitioner is entitled to relief, because they are satisfied he acted with the sole view of promoting the public interest confided to his command.

In March, 1823, Lieutenant Robert F. Stockton, of the navy, was indemnified for damages sustained on account of the capture and detention of a vessel and crew. The committee, in this case, remarked, that, "having maturely considered the case," they "are of opinion that in the capture," &c., "he was actuated by an honest determination to discharge, in a proper manner, the trust reposed in him by the Government."

Cases in point might be further multiplied, were it deemed necessary, to show the entire willingness of the Government, at all times, to protect its faithful officers and agents in the discharge of their official duties.

Sir, in all these examples, the Congress of the United States have paid or remitted their fines, by the usual preliminary course of investigation and report by a committee. The same principles governed, and the same proceedings occurred, in all the cases. The public good was *presumed* to be the governing motive of the officer, and the grounds of the act complained of. And in all these instances, in which provision was made to refund the fines, no difference in *principle* can be found from that involved in the case now presented. And in respect to this fine, which was exacted from General Jackson, I would ask, *are Senators prepared to make his case an exception?*

I would have avoided, if possible, saying any thing in reference to the deeds of General Jackson; neither do I wish to point the Senate to the halo with which those deeds have surrounded his venerable head and illumined his country. My voice will not be heard in utterance of his praise, to induce Senators to support the bill which they are now considering. Nor is it necessary; for even those who have opposed obstacles to its passage—obstacles which have surprised me, and which I doubt not will be viewed with astonishment by a vast majority of the people of this republic—have admitted his just claim to honor and fame, and the gratitude of his countrymen. His actions proclaim for themselves their enduring fame; gratitude has stamped them upon our memories; and the true and steady hand of History will grave them deeply upon her imperishable tablets. His good name cannot *now* be sullied; it is placed in the scroll which contains the list of those whom freemen and patriots delight to honor.

His reputation, like a star, far above the clouds of detraction which float around our censorious world, will shine with a brighter radiance as the flight of time shall hallow his memory.

I have given a few out of many precedents; though I am free to confess that, when this bill was submitted to the consideration of the Senate, I did not anticipate that gentlemen would take a course which would render them necessary. I have one now before me; and, as it is of peculiar applicability, and supported by an opinion from a source to which Senators will attach a sincere veneration, I will ask their particular attention to it. The case arose from the arrest of certain individuals suspected of treason by General Wilkinson; and, in defence of the course pursued by the General, President Jefferson expressed his opinion in the letter which I will read with the permission of the Senate.

Extract of a letter from Mr. Jefferson to John B. Colvin, Esq.

"To proceed to the conspiracy of Burr, and particularly to General Wilkinson's situation in New Orleans. In judging this case we are bound to consider the state of the information, correct and incorrect, which he then possessed. He expected Burr and his band from above, a British fleet from below; and he knew there was a formidable conspiracy within the city. Under these circumstances, was he justifiable, 1st. In seizing notorious conspirators? On this there can be but two opinions—one, of the guilty and their accomplices; the other, that of all honest men. 2d. Sending them to the seat of Government, when the written law gave them a right to trial in the Territory? The danger of their rescue; of continuing the machinations; the tardiness and weakness of the law; apathy of the judges; active patronage of the whole tribe of lawyers; unknown dispositions of the juries; an hourly expectation of the enemy; salvation of the city, and of the Union itself, which would have been convulsed to its centre, had that conspiracy succeeded—all these constituted *a law of necessity* and self-preservation; and rendered the *salus populi* supreme over the written law. The officer who is called to act on this superior ground does, indeed, risk himself on the *justice of the controlling powers of the Constitution;* and his station makes it his duty to incur that risk. But those controlling powers, and his fellow-citizens generally, are bound to judge according to the circumstances under which he acted. They are not to transfer the information of this place or moment to the time and place of this action; but to *put themselves into his situation.* We know here that there never was danger of a British fleet from below; and that Burr's band was crushed before it reached the Mississippi. But General Wilkinson's information was very different; and he could act on no other.

"From these examples and principles, you may see what I think on the question proposed. They do not go to the case of persons charged with petty duties, where consequences are trifling, and time allowed for a legal course; nor to authorize them to take such cases out of the written law. In these, the example of overleaping the law is of greater evil than a strict adherence to its imperfect provisions. *It is incumbent on those only who accept of great charges, to risk themselves on great occasions, when the safety of the nation, or some of its very high interests, are at stake.* An officer is bound to obey orders; yet he would be a bad one who should do it in cases for which they were not intended, and which involved the most important consequences.

The line of discrimination between cases may be difficult. *But the good officer is bound to draw it at his own peril*, and throws himself on the JUSTICE of his country, and the *rectitude* of his motives."

Now, sir, viewing ingenuously the whole course of General Jackson at New Orleans, and contrasting the principles involved in his case with Judge Hall, with those expressed in the letter of President Jefferson, could any man doubt that the General rested upon the rectitude of his intentions and the justice of his country? None, sir—none can doubt it. The almost entire population of Louisiana rose to sustain and honor him; his countrymen, by conferring upon him the highest mark of their confidence, have approved his every act at New Orleans; and we are now called on to render to him an act of justice—an act which that venerated statesman and patriot warrior of the Republic believes necessary to remove from the page of his life a passage which the decision of a court may have blurred, and which may, by *possibility*, create an injurious doubt as to the rectitude of his intentions, in the minds of some when he shall rest in his grave. The country has manifested its confidence in his uprightness, by bestowing upon him the highest office in the gift of the people—and that confidence they have never had cause to repent. His history should become familiar to the youth of our land; it furnishes one of the best examples by which to shape their course as citizens of the Republic; and presents, in the most prominent manner, that great reward which is extended to honesty of purpose, disinterested love of country, and persevering efforts to promote its welfare—a reward greater than that which has ever been given by any other country, to any man, for like virtues. Though left an orphan at an early age, these virtues, and these efforts alone, unaided by wealth or by connexions, (for not a drop of his blood flows in the veins of any living creature,) have placed him at the head of our most distinguished citizens, and made him one of the ornaments of our young Republic. Oh, sir, he is a noble production of our glorious political institutions.

In reverting to the question before the Senate, I would remark, that the declaration of martial law, by General Jackson, involved *all* the consequences to which the Senator from Louisiana has thought proper to allude.

And here I may be permitted to introduce additional facts, to demonstrate the necessity of the measure. They are taken from the answer of General Jackson to the rule of the court, and have never been questioned:

"If examples can justify, or the practice of others serve as a proof of necessity, the respondent has ample materials for his defence; not from analogous construction, but from the conduct of all the different departments of the State Government, in the very case now under discussion.

" The Legislature of the State, having no constitutional power to regulate or restrain commerce, on the — day of December last, passed an act laying an embargo; the Executive sanctioned it; and, from a conviction of its necessity, it was acquiesced in. The same Legislature shut up the courts of justice for four months to all civil suitors; the same Executive sanctioned that law; and the judiciary not only acquiesced, but solemnly approved it.

" The Governor, as appears by one of the letters quoted, undertook to inflict the punishment of exile upon an inhabitant without any form of law, merely because he thought that an individual's presence might be dangerous to the public safety.

" The judge of *this very court*, duly impressed with the emergency of the moment, and the necessity of employing every means of defence, consented to the discharge of men committed and indicted for *capital crimes*, without bail, and without recognizance; and probably under an impression that the exercise of his functions would be useless, *absented* himself from the place where his court was to be holden, and postponed its session during a regular term.

" Thus the conduct of the legislative, executive and judiciary branches of the Government of this State have borne the fullest testimony of the existence of the necessity on which the respondent relies.

" The unqualified approbation of the Legislature of the United States, and such of the individual States as were in session, ought also to be admitted as no slight means of defence, inasmuch as all these respectable bodies were fully apprised of his proclamation of martial law, and some of them seemed to refer to it, by thanking him for the energy of his measures."

What an extraordinary picture does this state of facts present! Here is a Governor who exiles an individual on suspicion of his entertaining dangerous designs—a Legislature laying an embargo upon the commerce of the country, and shutting up the courts of justice—and a judiciary voluntarily laying aside the ermine, and absenting themselves, to avoid the performance of a solemn duty; and this directly in violation of the law and the Constitution—and all these events passed, as they should—without condemnation from any quarter; because, where virtuous intentions were, these acts were most virtuous; whilst the *General* who had the courage to take the high responsibility of saving his country, has a mark of disapprobation set upon him by a member of this very *judicial tribunal* which had evaded the performance of the duties imposed upon it by the laws and the Constitution; and you—you, sir—hesitate to efface it, or, departing from all precedent, propose to attach conditions which neither he nor his friends can accept.

The gentleman from Louisiana [Mr. Conrad], in his allusions, would seem to desire to have it appear that General Jackson continued the operation of the law longer than was absolutely necessary. There was a rumor of peace; the enemy had been driven from before the town; and the gentleman thinks, or would have us infer, that the rigor of the martial law should have been somewhat relaxed. For what? That individuals might be permitted to promote a *little* disaffection—to raise a small speck of hostility against the watchful and brave veteran—to give a slight degree of encouragement to the poor defeated enemy—and to be permitted to do this by publications in newspapers, by handbills stuck upon the walls of the town, or in any other *peaceable* way which their ingenuity might suggest? I repeat, the declaration of martial law involved the consequences which followed; and, in regard to the proceedings of Judge Hall, we need not waste our time in fine-spun disquisitions about his writs, his arrest, or his *banishment* from the camp, and *imprisonment* or *confinement* to the remaining portion of the United States and its territories. The Judge, as well as every other person within the precincts of the camp, were, *for the time*, subject to the operation of the law. When he issued his process, in order to take from the military an individual who had been arrested and secured for the purpose of preventing him from giving aid to the enemy, or *endangering the safety of the country*, the time had not arrived for the Judge to assume his functions. From the moment of its adoption to that in whch it ceased, the martial law was paramount; and there could, under such circumstances, be no contempt of court. If there was any contempt, it was a contempt committed by the Judge against the necessarily paramount authority which existed within the precincts of the camp—an authority created by the necessities and dangers of that portion of the country. And, sir, in regard to the intimation that General Jackson should have acted upon the rumor of peace, and immediately relieved his camp from the operation of martial law, I have to say, that the fact that the rumor was suffered to pass unheeded, is a strong and convincing evidence not only of his capacity to command, but of his unslumbering vigilance, and his entire devotedness to the *safety of the country* and the glory of its arms. And if I were to select any portion of his eventful history for an evidence of his great qualities as a commander, it would be that which represents him as casting to the winds rumors which lulled into security those about him, while a powerful and mortified enemy, smarting under the infliction of a chastisement which had torn from their brows the blushing honors which they had so bravely gathered upon the fields of Europe, were crouching within a single bound of the plain from which they had been driven, and, with hot blood and braced sinews, were eager to spring upon and tear those who had so recently humbled them. No, sir; none of the attributes which mark the character of General Jackson could subject him to the machinations of the enemy, however subtle. His vigilance was as untiring as his honesty was incorruptible. And appreciating, as he should, the *vast responsibility* which rested upon him, he was not to be diverted from his duty by a rumor,—nothing but *certainty* should, or did satisfy him. It has been correctly said by a late distinguished member of the Senate, that the post held by General Jackson—the outlet of the Mississippi—was more important than any other in our vast country; and so long as that noble river continued to bear its vast tribute to the ocean, so long would the defence of New Orleans remain one of the brightest pages of our country's history.

I would here call the attention of the Senate to another portion of the answer of General Jackson, touching his conduct and his views of duty after the rumor of peace had reached New Orleans.

"He thought peace a probable, but by no means a certain event. If it had really taken place, a few days must bring the official advice of it; and he believed it better to submit, during those few days, to the salutary restraints imposed, than to put every thing dear to ourselves and country at risk upon an uncertain contingency. Admit the chances to have been a hundred or a thousand to one in favor of the ratification, and against any renewed attempts of the enemy; what should we say or think of the prudence of the man who would stake his life, his fortune, his country, and his honor, even with such odds in his favor, against a few days' anticipated enjoyment of the blessings of peace? The respondent could not bring himself to play so deep a hazard; uninfluenced by the clamors of the ignorant and the designing, he continued the exercise of that law which necessity had compelled him to proclaim; and he still thinks himself justified, by the situation of affairs, for the course which he adopted and pursued. Has he exercised this power wantonly or improperly? If so he is liable—not, as he believes, to this honorable court for contempt, but to his Government for an abuse of power, and to those individuals whom he has injured, in damages proportioned to that injury.

"About the period last described, the consul of France, who appears by Governor Claiborne's letter, to have embarrassed the first drafts, by his claims in favor of pretended subjects of his king, renewed his interference; his certificates were given to men in the ranks of the army—to some who had never applied, and to others who wished to use them as the means of obtaining an inglorious exemption from danger and fatigue. The immunity derived from these certificates not only thinned the ranks, by the withdrawal of those to whom they were given, but produced the desertion of others, who thought themselves equally entitled to the privilege; and to this cause must be traced the abandonment of the important post of Chef Menteur, and the temporary refusal of a relief ordered to occupy it.

"Under these circumstances, to remove the force of an example which had already occasioned such dangerous consequences, and to punish those who were so unwilling to defend what they were so ready to enjoy, the respondent issued a general order, directing those French subjects who had availed themselves of the consul's certificates to remove out of the lines of defence, and far enough to avoid any temptation of intercourse with our enemy, whom they were so scrupulous of opposing. This measure was resorted to, as the mildest mode of proceeding against a dangerous and increasing evil; and the respondent had the less scruple of his power, in this instance, as it was not quite so strong as that which Governor Claiborne had exercised, before the invasion, by the advice of his attorney general, in the case of Colonel Coliel.

"It created, however, some sensation; discontents were again fomented, from the source that had first produced them. *Aliens and strangers became the most violent advocates of constitutional rights; and native Americans were taught the value of their privileges, by those who formally disavowed any title to their enjoyment.* The order was particularly opposed—in an anonymous publication. In this, the author deliberately and wickedly misrepresented the order, as subjecting to removal all Frenchmen whatever, even those who had gloriously fought in defence of the country; and, after many dangerous and unwarrantable declarations, he closes, by calling upon all Frenchmen to flock to the standard of their consul—thus advising and producing an act of mutiny and insubordination, and publishing the evidence of our weakness and discord to the enemy, who were still in our vicinity, anxious, no doubt, before the cessation of hostilities, to wipe away the late stain upon their arms. To have silently looked on such an offence, without making any attempt to punish it, would have been a formal surrender of all discipline, all order, all personal dignity and public safety. This could not be done; and the respondent immediately ordered the arrest of the defender. A writ of *habeas corpus* was directed to issue for his enlargement. The very case which had been foreseen—the very contingency on which martial law was intended to operate—had now occurred. The civil magistrate seemed to think it his duty to enforce the enjoyment of civil rights, although the consequences which have been described would probably have resulted. An unbending sense of what he seemed to think his station required, induced him to order the liberation of the prisoner. This, under the respondent's sense of duty, produced a conflict which it was his wish to avoid.

"No other course remained than to enforce the principles which he had laid down as his guide, and to suspend the exercise of this judicial power, wherever it interfered with the necessary means of defence. The only way effectually to do this, was to place the Judge in a situation in which his interference could not counteract the measures of defence, or give countenance to the mutinous disposition that had shown itself in so alarming a degree. Merely to have disregarded the writ, would have but increased the evil; and to have obeyed it, was wholly repugnant to the respondent's ideas of the public safety, and to his own sense of duty. The Judge was, therefore, confined, and removed beyond the lines of defence."

While, on the one hand, no one can doubt that, in establishing martial law at New Orleans, General Jackson was actuated by motives of duty and patriotism, and while it cannot and will not be denied that, in all cases in which our military officers have been amerced, in consequence of performing a duty deemed necessary and proper, we have extended relief to them in the manner now proposed,—we are not, on the other hand, required, by any consistent view of the facts, either to censure, to exonerate, or to applaud Judge Hall, and whatever may be my views of his course, I feel that there would be an inconsistency in departing from all precedent in this simple act of justice to the venerable patriot now standing upon the verge of his grave; and, therefore, I repeat, I do not desire to call in question, on this occasion, the conduct of the Judge. I sincerely hope that he, too, was guided by a desire to discharge the duties of his station; for, in view of the circumstances, under which this collision of adverse authorities occurred, there is an attractive moral grandeur presented in the idea of its harmonious adjustment.

In time of war, how numerous are the instances where our commanding officers are obliged, by the *force of circumstances,* to assume a high, and, unless guided by an enlightened discretion, a dangerous responsibility! And in all cases, where they have kept within the limits which that discretion prescribes, the legislative authority has interposed its arm, and saved them from harm. Indeed, I cannot recall to my mind a single instance where compensation has been withheld. But it is urged that the General was much too fond of assuming responsibilities. Yes: his whole life was one continued scene of acts performed for the benefit of his country—of responsibilities voluntarily assumed for its glory and honor. When or where was it unwisely or wickedly assumed? I challenge an answer. And I may here be permitted to name an instance in which General Jackson *assumed the responsibility*, which, I doubt not, contributed in a great measure to the glorious result at New Orleans, though the incident occurred some time previous to that event.

In the autumn of 1812, a portion of the Tennessee volunteers, under General Jackson, were dismissed at Natchez, to which place they had been ordered for the protection of the lower country. They were far from their homes and connections, and disbanded, by the order of the Government, without arms, or rations, or assistance of any kind, and left to make their way back through a wilderness country—liable to sickness by the way, and attacks from hostile Indians. Under these circumstances it was that the General *assumed the responsibility*, at the imminent risk of his private fortune and public character, of supplying them with arms, ammunition, food, and as many horses and wagons as sufficed for their transportation. Can it be doubted that this provident and generous act of the General endeared him to the brave Tennesseans, and, in 1814, made them prompt to respond to his call for volunteers for the defence of New Orleans? Had the dismissed troops at Natchez, in 1812, been forsaken by him in their distress, as they had been by the Government, and left penniless, and without food, far from their friends and homes, can any one suppose that they would have again placed themselves under a commander who had thus neglected them? No, sir; they would have turned in disgust from a service where devotion to country and innumerable hardships were repaid only with neglect and ingratitude by their General and their country.

I would also call attention to another incident in

the history of this great man—an incident which shows that he possessed, in a most remarkable degree, a trait of character which so peculiarly distinguishes a great warrior. I allude to the incident which occurred during the Creek war, when his troops, harassed by fatiguing marches, and irritated by scanty food and the machinations of uneasy spirits, were about to revolt and leave his standard. In the moment of suffering and anger, and overlooking their duty to their country, they openly refused to be longer detained in its service; at the moment they were about to abandon him, he seized a musket, and, placing himself before the revolted brigade, one thousand five hundred strong, told them what they owed to their country; and declared that he would slay the first who attempted to abandon his duty; they might fly from that duty, but they should only do so by passing over his dead body. The troops, convinced by his stern reasoning, mortified at the humbling contrast which their conduct presented to his, and admiring the devotion and firmness of their commander, returned to their duty.

Such is the man to whom we are called on now to extend justice—a man who never shrank from a duty when his country's good demanded its performance—though that duty involved a *responsibility* however fearful—though it may have required him to lay down his life. For his devotion to his country, that country has honored him—he has received the highest honors in its gift; and he requires no painting, as suggested by the Senator from Louisiana, to commemorate his public services, or to perpetuate in the bosom of his countrymen the gratitude which true patriotism feels towards the true patriot—a gratitude which will extend through all generations, as long as a love of country shall exist, and his deeds, delineated by the pencil of *Truth*, shall remain recorded upon the page of history.

If, indeed, historical paintings are to be made, in order to illustrate the character of General Jackson, I would suggest that the incident to which I have just alluded furnish the subject for one. Let him be shown standing, unaided, with a musket in his hands, sternly opposing fifteen hundred angry, half-famished men, and, at the hazard of his life, checking their revolt, and bringing them back to reason and duty. This would tend to exhibit his undaunted courage, his firmness, and his unyielding determination in the discharge of a high trust.

I would also point to another trait of his character —his patient hardihood while in the service of his country—proved by another incident in the Creek war, which could be made the subject of an interesting painting, and would represent him destitute of food, fatigued by marches and by watchings, and supplying the pressing calls of hunger by the acorns which he gathered as he passed under the forest trees, rather than abandon an exposed frontier to the tomahawk and scalping-knife of a savage and remorseless enemy. If you would represent him as the friend of order and the protector of the law, and at the same time exhibit his magnanimity of soul, place upon canvas that bright moment of his history, when, at New Orleans, he bowed to the sentence of the judge, and, while with one hand he yielded an unjust penalty to the demands of the law, with the other he staid the angry waves of popular commotion, advancing to overwhelm the tribunal by whom the penalty was exacted. Would you commemorate his humanity? Then represent him in his tent, after one of the bloody battles with the Creeks, taking charge of an infant Indian boy, found upon its dead mother's breast, and which its own relations advised should be knocked on the head. That same boy who, nourished on the food of the camp by him and his officers, and watched with care and tenderness, survived the dangers of a campaign—by him was fostered and educated—and, at seventeen years of. age, died in the bosom of his preserver's family, beloved and lamented. Can the whole range of history furnish a picture surpassing this in moral beauty?

It was not, sir, my intention to say aught that would tend to arouse the political antipathies of any one, or open the fountains of bitterness, now nearly dried up.

I trust I have not. I have considered the question before the Senate, from the very beginning, as one which, of all others, should be discussed without a reference to political misunderstandings; and for the reason, that the character of our country is involved in the manner of its discussion, as well as in the result. For it does not follow that those who were opposed to General Jackson during his political or civil life, are called on to throw obstacles in the way of this bill. May they not with candor and justice, yield their support to it? To me it seems that the whole case lies in a very narrow compass:—a case which, guided alone by common sense and justice, was decided upon *instantly* and *correctly* by the whole population of New Orleans, before whose eyes all the circumstances transpired. This decision has been confirmed by the entire country; and it remains only for us, by the cold act of justice which we are now called upon to perform, to confirm this universal verdict, and to deprive all time to come of a vestige of the wrong which has been done him. Aside from the imperative duty which devolves upon us, I would ask Senators if there is one here who would hesitate in giving his vote for this bill, were it *but* to cheer the heart of the venerable patriot, and render more calm his last moments, by the reflection that the evidence of his country's confidence and justice is now entire? Exalted old man! Though we may never again look into those eyes which never winked at danger, nor behold again that venerable and dignified form, now bending with the load of years over the verge of eternity, the recollection of you, or your glorious deeds, can never be effaced from our memories!

How many precedents we have to direct us in our duty!—how great the debt which would urge us to adopt them! A little while since we voted twenty-five thousand dollars to the family of General Harrison, as a *mere* donation. Yet a little while more, and the greatest light of the land will be set in the gloom of the grave. At such a time, and under such circumstances, ought the money taken from General Jackson, without trial, by the decision of an incensed judge, to be withheld? Not that he has asked us for it, or wants it as a pecuniary aid; but because it will tend to smooth his way to the grave, by showing that the Senate of the United States looked upon his conduct at New Orleans as justifiable—his motives as pure—and as an example to future generals to do likewise under similar circumstances. Let gentlemen refuse this, and were I disposed to make that refusal a political question, I would take in one hand this bill, and in the other the act giving to the heirs of General Harrison twenty-five thousand dollars; and, going before a grateful people with them, could any one doubt what would be the result? No, sir, no. General Jackson is above the charity of the Senate, as he is beyond its praise or blame ; neither he nor his friends desire any thing more than justice at your hands. They consider your treasury as disgraced while it retains the money wrung from him in the performance of a noble duty nobly performed. Then let it be returned, and in no ungracious or ambiguous spirit ; return it in the same manner as you have to all others under similar circumstances—even to your humblest custom-house officers. By so doing, you will avoid the imputation that, had he been less—much less—in the eyes of the world than he is, your justice would have been more freely dispensed."

The efforts made by Dr. Linn to procure the passage of the bill to remit General Jackson's fine, were labors of love. His whole heart and soul were in it. Viewing the subject in the light that he did, he considered the fine as a great piece of injustice inflicted upon him, and that this injustice had been suffered to go unremoved and unrebuked for a long period of time. General Jackson was now standing on the verge of the grave, and if the removal of what he considered "the only obloquy that rested on his name "was to be effected before his death, so as to afford him any satisfaction, it must be done with the least possible delay. Such were the motives that prompted the action and the zeal of Dr. Linn. They were honorable, manly, just and humane.

To do *justice* was his great object; and it would probably have been one of the happiest moments of his life had he lived a few months longer, when the bill to remit the fine became a law, and he could have informed his friend, the General, that the fine was at last remitted, and the obloquy resting upon his name had been wiped out by his country's own hand and act. But though the bill passed the Senate it did not pass the House, at that time, nor become a law until February, 1844, about four months after the Doctor had been called hence. He had, however, given it such an impetus by advocating it with so much zeal and earnestness, that its final passage was undoubtedly due to his efforts in endeavoring to effect the consummation of the measure.

What General Jackson's feelings were towards him on account of the part he had taken, will be seen in the following letter addressed by him to Mrs. Linn very soon after the bill had passed the Senate, every sentence of which glows with warm and grateful regard.

Letter from Gen. Andrew Jackson to Mrs. Linn.

HERMITAGE, June 14, 1842.

MY DEAR FRIEND,—Although very feeble in health, I cannot refrain from dropping you a few lines to express my pleasure and gratitude for the greatest act of friendship that I ever received, which has been bestowed on me by your dear, patriotic husband, and my faithful and kind friend, Dr Linn, in the late bill which he brought through the U. S. Senate, indemnifying me in discharging my official duty in establishing martial law in the City of New Orleans, when called there to defend it, during our late war with England. The Doctor's speech in my behalf to the Senate on this occasion has made my heart overflow with gratitude and love to him, and as long as I live I will cherish and revere him as my best friend. I have often told you and the Doctor that although the Eternal One had blessed me with so many good friends and dear objects to love, that I sometimes felt very desolate when I reflected that not a drop of my blood flowed in the veins of one of the human family; and all that I had to leave my country was a good name. And how can I express all the gratitude I feel to the benefactor who has wiped off the only obloquy that I thought might rest on my name? You, my dear Mrs. Linn, who know me so well, can judge of my deep and grateful feelings towards your husband for this noble act of kindness to me. How often have I said to you that from the first moment I beheld Dr. Linn I felt my heart drawn most warmly to him. I have written to him, expressing my great desire that he would come to see me, and to be sure to bring you and your children with him. I hope that your little daughter looks like her lovely departed sister Jane, who was as dear to me as if she had been my own child. My daughter unites with me in much love to you and yours, and sincerely hopes that you and the Doctor will come to see us very soon. God bless you all.

Your affectionate friend,

ANDREW JACKSON.

To Mrs. E. A. R. Linn.

But Dr. Linn's labors did not cease with the failure of the bill at the time the foregoing speech was delivered. It was brought forward again by him at the next session—1842–'3, when, after debate in the Senate in which he bore a conspicuous part, it again passed that body, February 28, 1843, 28 to 20, but failed in the House. His effort on this occasion, just at the close of the last session of the 27th Congress, and the last of his senatorial career, was the closing act of his public life. Little as he could foresee that when the bill passed the Senate his pubic labors were virtually finished, it can scarcely be doubted that, could the fact have been known to him, he would not have desired that any other act of his in the discharge of his duty as a senator, should have been his *opus coronus*. Upon the passage of the bill, had the future been revealed to him, he would have said to senators with whom he had been so long and so agreeably associated, "My labors are now closed. I have conscientiously endeavored to perform my duty as became an American senator: my only guide has been the public good: I have endeavored to be just, and have not feared to be so: all the ends I have aimed at have been my country's, my God's, and truth's. The destinies of our beloved country are in your hands:—obey the Constitution; preserve the Union; may it be perpetual: may it grow in greatness; abound in wise, patriotic, able statesmen, and set a noble example to all others of JUSTICE, MODERATION, WISDOM, INTELLIGENCE, and VIRTUE."

APPENDIX.

PROCEEDINGS OF CONGRESS, OF THE CITY OF ST. LOUIS, OF THE ST. LOUIS MEDICAL SOCIETY, OF THE LEGISLATURES OF WISCONSIN AND IOWA, AND OTHER CORPORATE BODIES,

ON THE OCCASION OF

THE DEATH OF DR. LINN;

ALSO,

LETTERS OF CONDOLENCE ADDRESSED TO MRS. LINN, FROM DISTINGUISHED MEN, ON THAT OCCASION.

APPENDIX.

TRIBUTES OF RESPECT

TO THE

MEMORY OF DR. L. F. LINN.

U. S. SENATE.—December 12, 1843.

THE journal having been read Mr. BENTON rose and said:

Mr. President, I rise to make the Senate a formal communication of an event which has occurred during the recess, and has been heard by all with deep regret. My colleague and friend, the late Senator LINN, departed this life on Tuesday, the 3d day of October last, at the early age of forty-eight years, and without the warnings or the sufferings which usually precede our departure from this world. He laid him down to sleep and awoke no more. It was to him the sleep of death! and the only drop of consolation in this sudden and calamitous visitation was, that it took place in his own house, and that his unconscious remains were immediately surrounded by his family and friends, and received all the care and aid which love and skill could give.

I discharge a mournful duty, Mr. President, in bringing

his deplorable event to the formal notice of the Senate; in offering the public tribute of my applause to the many virtues of my deceased colleague, and in asking for his memory the last honors which respect and affection of the Senate bestow upon the name of a deceased brother.

LEWIS FIELD LINN, the subject of this annunciation, was born in the State of Kentucky, in the year 1795, in the immediate vicinity of Louisville. His grandfather was Colonel William Linn, one of the favorite officers of General George Rogers Clarke, and well known for his courage and enterprise in the early settlement of the great West. At the age of eleven, he had fought in the ranks of men in the defence of a station in Western Pennsylvania, and was seen to deliver a deliberate and effective fire. He was one of the first to navigate the Ohio and Mississippi from Pittsburg to New Orleans, and back again—a daring achievement, which himself and some others accomplished for the public service, and amidst every species of danger, in the year 1776. He was killed by the Indians at an early period; leaving a family of young children, of whom the worthy Colonel William Pope (father of Gov. Pope, and head of the numerous and respectable family of that name in the West) became the guardian. The father of Senator Linn was among these children; and, at an early age, skaiting upon the ice near Louisville, with three other boys, he was taken prisoner by the Shawanee Indians, carried off and detained captive for three years, when all four made their escape and returned home by killing their guard, traversing some hundred miles of wilderness, and swimming the Ohio River. The mother of Senator Linn was a Pennsylvanian by birth; her maiden name Hunter; born at Carlisle; and also had heroic blood in her veins. Tradition, if not history, preserves the recollection of her courage and conduct at Fort Jefferson, at the Iron Banks in 1781, where the Indians attacked and were repulsed from that post. Women and boys were men in those days.

The father of Senator Linn died young, leaving this son but eleven years of age. The cares of an elder brother supplied (as far as such a loss could be supplied) the loss of a father ; and under his auspices the education of the orphan was conducted. He was intended for the medical profession, and received his education, scholastic and professional, in the State of his nativity. At an early age he was qualified for the practice of medicine, and commenced it in the then Territory now State of Missouri ; and was immediately amongst the foremost of his profession. Intuitive sagacity supplied in him the place of long experience ; and boundless benevolence conciliated universal esteem. To all his patients he was the same ; flying with alacrity to every call, attending upon the poor and humble as zealously as on the rich and powerful, on the stranger as readily as on the neighbor, discharging to all the duties of nurse and friend as well as physician, and wholly regardless of his own interest or even his own health, in his zeal to serve and to save others.

The highest professional honors and rewards were before him. Though commencing on a provincial theatre, there was not a capital in Europe or America in which he would not have obtained the first rank in physic or surgery. But his fellow-citizens perceived in his varied abilities capacity and aptitude for service in a different walk. He was called into the political field by an election to the Senate of his adopted State. Thence he was called to the performance of judicial duties by a federal appointment to investigate land titles. Thence he was called to the high station of Senator in the Congress of the United States—first by an executive appointment, then by three successive almost unanimous elections. The last of those elections he received but one year ago, and had not commenced his duties under it—had not sworn in under the certificate which attested it—when a sudden and premature death put an end to his earthly career. He entered this body in the year 1833, death dissolved his connection with it in 1843. For ten years he was a beloved and distinguished member of this body, and surely a nobler or a finer character never adorned the chamber of the American Senate.

He was my friend, but I speak not the language of friendship when I speak his praise. A debt of justice is all that I can attempt to discharge: an imperfect copy of the *true man* is all that I can attempt to paint.

A sagacious head and a feeling heart were the great characteristics of Dr. Linn. He had a judgment which penetrated both men and things and gave him near and clear views of far distant events. He saw at once the bearing—the remote bearing of great measures, either for good or for evil, and brought instantly to their support or opposition the logic of a prompt and natural eloquence more beautiful in its delivery and more effective in its application than any that art can bestow. He had great fertility of mind, and was himself the author and mover of many great measures—some for the benefit of the whole Union—some for the benefit of the great West—some for the benefit of his own State—many for the benefit of individuals. The pages of our legislative history will bear the evidences of these meritorious labors to a remote and grateful posterity.

Brilliant as were the qualities of his head, the qualities of his heart still eclipse them. It is to the heart we look for the character of the man; and what a heart had LEWIS LINN! The kindest, the gentlest, the most feeling, and the most generous that ever beat in the bosom of a bearded man! And yet, when the occasion required it, the bravest and the most daring also. He never beheld a case of human wo without melting before it, he never encountered an apparition of earthly danger without giving it defiance. Where is the friend, or even the stranger, in danger or distress to whose succor he did not fly, and whose sorrowful or perilous case he did not make his own? When—where—was he ever called upon for a service or a sacrifice and rendered not, upon the instant, the one or the other as the occasion required?

The senatorial service of this rare man fell upon trying times—high party times—when the collisions of party too often embittered the ardent feelings of generous natures; but who ever knew bitterness or party animosities in him? He was, indeed, a party-man—as true to his party as to his friends and his country; but beyond the line of duty and of principle—beyond the debate and the vote—he knew no party and saw no opponent. Who among us all, even after the fiercest debate, ever met him without meeting the benignant smile and the kind salutation? Who of us all ever needed a friend without finding one in him? Who of us all was ever stretched upon the bed of sickness without finding him at its side? Who of us all ever knew a personal difficulty of which he was not, as far as possible, the kind composer?

Such was Senator Linn in high party times among us. And what he was here among us he was every where and with every body. At home among his friends and neighbors; on the high road among casual acquaintances; in foreign lands among strangers; in all and in every of these situations he was the same thing. He had kindness and sympathy for every human being; and the whole voyage of his life was one continued and benign circumnavigation of all the virtues which adorn and exalt the character of man ; piety, charity, benevolence, generosity, courage, patriotism, fidelity, all shone conspicuously in him, and might extort from the beholder the impressive interrogatory, *For what place was this man made ?* Was it for the Senate or the camp ? For public or for private life ? For the bar or the bench ? For the art which heals the diseases of the body, or that which cures the infirmities of the State ? For which of all these was he born ? And the answer is, For all. He was born to fill the largest and most varied circle of human excellence ; and to crown all these advantages, nature had given him what the great Lord Bacon calls a perpetual letter of recommendation—a countenance not only good, but sweet and winning—radiant with the virtues of his soul—captivating universal confidence ; and such as no stranger could behold—no traveller, even in the desert, could meet, without stopping to reverence, and saying : Here is a man in whose hands I could deposit my life, liberty, fortune, honor. Alas ! that so much excellence should have perished so soon ! that such a man should have been snatched away at the early age of forty-eight, and while his faculties were still ripening and developing !

In the life and character of such a man, so exuberant in all that is grand and beautiful in human nature, it is difficult to particularize excellencies or to pick out any one quality or circumstance which could claim pre-eminence over all others. If I should attempt it, I should point, among his measures for the benefit of the whole Union, to the Oregon bill ; among his measures for the benefit of his own State, to the acquisition of the Platte country ; among his private virtues to the love and affection which he bore to that half-brother—the half-brother only—who, only thirteen years older than himself, had been to him the tenderest of fathers. For twenty-nine years I had known the depth of that affection, and never saw it burn more brightly than in our last interview, only three weeks before his death. He had just travelled a thousand miles out of his way to see that brother; and his name was still the dearest theme of his conversation—a conversation, strange to tell! which turned, not upon the empty and fleeting subjects of the day, but upon things solid and eternal—upon friendship and upon death, and upon the duties of the living and the dead. He spoke of two friends whom it was natural to believe that he should survive, and to whose memories he intended to pay the debt of friendship. Vain calculation! Vain impulsion of generosity and friendship! One of these two friends now discharges that mournful debt to him; the other [General Jackson] has written me a letter, expressing his "*deep sorrow for the untimely death of our friend*, Dr. LINN."

Mr. BENTON then moved the usual resolutions of respect.

Mr. CRITTENDEN then rose and said: I rise, Mr. President, to second the motion of the Hon. Senator from Missouri, and to express my cordial concurrence in the resolutions he has offered.

The highest tribute of our respect is justly due to the honored name and memory of Senator LINN; and there is not a heart here that does not pay it freely and plenteously. These resolutions are but responsive to the general feeling that prevails throughout the land, and will afford to his widow and his orphans the consolatory evidence that their *country* shares their grief, and mourns for their bereavement.

I am very sensible, Mr. President, that the very appropriate, interesting, and eloquent remarks of the Senator from Missouri (Mr. BENTON) have made it difficult to add any thing that will not impair the effect of what he has said; but I must beg the indulgence of the Senate for a few moments. Senator LINN was by birth a Kentuckian, and my countryman. I do not dispute the claims of Missouri, his adopted State; but I wish it to be remembered, that I claim for Kentucky the honor of his nativity; and by the great law that regulates such precious inheritances, a portion, at least, of his fame must descend to his native land. It is the just ambition and right of Kentucky to gather together the bright names of her children, no matter in what lands their bodies may be buried, and to preserve them as her jewels and her crown. The name of LINN is one of her jewels; and its pure and unsullied lustre shall long remain as one of her richest ornaments.

The death of such a man is a national calamity. Long a distinguished member of this body, he was continually rewarded with the increasing confidence of the great State he so honorably represented; and his reputation and usefulness increased at every step of his progress.

In the Senate his death is most sensibly felt. We have lost a colleague and friend, whose noble and amiable qualities bound us to him as with "hooks of steel." Who of us that knew him can forget his open, frank, and manly bearing—that smile, that seemed to be the pure, warm sunshine of the heart, and the thousand courtesies and kindnesses that gave a "daily beauty to his life?"

He possessed a high order of intellect; was resolute, courageous, and ardent in all his pursuits. A decided party man, he participated largely and conspicuously in the business of the Senate and the conflicts of its debates; but there was a kindliness and benignity about him, that, like polished armor, turned aside all feelings of ill-will or animosity. He had political opponents in the Senate, but not one enemy.

The good and generous qualities of our nature were blended in his character ;

> "———and the elements
> So mixed in him, that Nature might stand up
> And say to all the world—*This was a man.*"

HOUSE OF REPRESENTATIVES.

A message from the Senate, announcing the death of Dr. LINN, having been received,

Mr. BOWLIN, of Missouri, rose and addressed the House as follows :

I rise with no ordinary emotions—occasioned, partially by the novelty of my own position ; but more, much more, by the recollection of the painful and melancholy event which now demands the tribute of our grief. It is, indeed, a painful, a most painful event to me ; and one calculated, from its associations, to spread the gloom of melancholy over the councils now assembled. We have convened here for the discharge of our public duties, and we look around us in vain for all those companions in our labors whom we were wont to have met. The hand of Death, inexorable Death, has been amongst us.—In the other end of the Capitol, a seat is vacated ; ah ! vacated, and that for ever. The heart of its occupant, which in life ever beat responsive to the calls of charity and humanity, now beats no more ; and the tongue, whose patriotic eloquence has charmed the Senate, is now stilled by the dull, cold hand of Death.

The Hon. LEWIS F. LINN, late Senator from Missouri, as announced by the resolutions on your table, is no more. He died suddenly at his residence in St. Genevieve, on the 3d day of October last, just as he was preparing to leave for this, the field of his distinguished labors. The manner of his death was peculiarly afflicting to his friends. It was as sudden as it was unexpected. In the midst of life and usual health—with no note of warning to his friends—without the usual premonitory symptoms—without, perhaps, an admonition to himself—in the midst of his family and friends, and in the mid career of his usefulness and honor, he is suddenly summoned from us to that land of spirits where "the weary are at rest."

Having spent a restless and sleepless night, he had the curtains of the bed drawn to secure to him a morning's repose. He fell into a sleep, a profound sleep, from which he never awoke. And though his couch was watched with the sleepless eye of affectionate devotion, separated only by a curtain, yet his spirit passed away so calm, so tranquil, that it was difficult to tell the precise moment of its flight. But though he died with no eye upon him, save that of his God, yet the mildness and serenity of his countenance proclaimed the consolation to his friends, trumpet-tongued, that he departed in peace, and with scarce a struggle.

Of his life: It was one continued scene of uniformity and beauty. But I will not trespass upon the province of his biographer, further than to touch some of its prominent points. He was born in the State of Kentucky in the year 1795, and inherited from that chivalrous and gallant people many of the noble qualities that adorned him in after life. In the year 1809—a mere boy—he emigrated to Missouri, and cast his fortune among a people eager to discern, and proud to reward merit. In 1814, at the age of seventeen years, he entered the tented field, and, side by side with a near and esteemed relative, now an honorable member of this House, (Gov. Dodge,) was engaged gallantly fighting the battles of his country; and though a youth, too young to have his deeds chronicled in history, yet the memory of them is cherished in the hearts of the people of his adopted State.

After the war he applied himself to the acquisition of his profession; and by the force and energy of his mind and his well-regulated habits of industry, soon placed himself in the front ranks of that learned and honorable profession. As a physician he was prompt and determined, yet mild, courteous, and cheerful; by the versatility of his genius throwing around the couch of sickness and death every thing to inspire hope and dispel gloom. No man was ever more highly esteemed or more dearly loved within the circle of his practice. Long, long, will the memory of his virtues be engraven on the hearts of those people who knew him longest, and knew him best.

He was next called, by the people of his county, to the Legislature of his adopted State, where, in a short session, he gave early promise of that character as a legislator, which has since so brilliantly shone in the councils of the nation. His career there was marked by an enlightened policy, a lofty patriotism, and a firm and unswerving devotion to those fundamental principles upon which he believed was based the liberty of his country. The generous confidence of his constituents was only equalled by the disinterested fidelity of the representative, in executing the trusts committed to his charge.

In 1832, he was appointed one of the board of commissioners to adjust the private land claims of the ancient inhabitants of Upper Louisiana, (now Missouri.) To the discharge of the complicated duties of this office he brought a mind well stored with information upon the subject, and an energy that never flagged. In this place he accomplished much, in settling the vexed questions of titles to our lands, and by the suavity of his manners, and the uniform urbanity of his demeanor, won from all the homage of an exalted respect. Indeed, it would be difficult to portray the veneration in which his memory is held by those early first pioneers of the country who laid in the wilderness the foundation of a great republic.

If it were allowable, upon an occasion of this kind, to speak of one's self, I might be permitted to say that it was at this period of his life, I had the good fortune to make his acquaintance, and establish a mutual friendship which existed through life. A stranger in a strange land, he extended to me the hand of fellowship and welcome, and encouraged me by his counsels, and animated me by the buoyancy of his own generous heart. A few weeks changed our then relative positions—he to the Senate, I to the editor's chair ; and it is due to his memory to say, that change of position worked no change of relations ; and I can as proudly bear testimony that, whilst acting as a sentinel upon the acts of public men, I found in his career every thing to applaud, nothing to condemn.

Doctor LINN was appointed to the Senate in November, 1833, and continued in that station until the period of his death—an uninterrupted period of nearly ten years ; during which time he passed through three elections before the Legislature of Missouri, each time increasing in strength, as he increased in the confidence of the people. He entered that body, of which he was destined to become so distinguished a member, laboring under many disadvantages, arising alike from education and from habits. The angry ocean of party politics he found lashed into a commotion the most furious ; the Senate filled with men of gigantic minds, cultivated intellects, and a long experience in legislation ; and, to crown all, so much possessed of feelings which political animosities had engendered as to render personal and social intercourse difficult and constrained. Yet, by his evenness of temper and firmness of purpose, combined with his social disposition and urbanity of manners, he soon acquired a most enviable respect from those with whom he had to act.

Of his general labors in the Senate, and the enlightened patriotism that directed them, the archives of the country bear abundant testimony. On all local subjects he labored faithfully and efficiently for his immediate constituents. His unabated efforts in obtaining post roads, forts, and military roads upon the frontier ; the acquisition of the Platte country ; the improvement of our rivers and harbors ; the adjustment of the land claims of the ancient inhabitants of Upper Louisiana, bear witness to the people of Missouri of the zeal and fidelity of him whose loss they so sadly deplore.

But the great question which called forth all the energies of his mind was the occupation of the Oregon Territory. Looking at the subject with a prophetic spirit, and the eye of a statesman, he saw, in the distance, the time when that beautiful land of hill and dale, of mountain breeze and crystal stream, should bloom and blossom as the rose, beneath the cheerful hand of industry ; and he struggled hard to plant alike on the beautiful plains the American citizen and the American flag. This was the great work to which he had for years devoted all the energies of his soul ; and, without repining at the awards of Providence, we all must regret, seriously regret, that he was not spared to witness its accomplishment. But he has left it for others to perform, with his own great efforts as beacon lights to guide them on their way, and associated with the cause of Oregon the glory of a name.

"A light, a land-mark, on the cliffs of fame."

But he is gone; and while we deplore his loss, let us not be unmindful of those who are left to mourn—ah! deeply mourn, a husband's and a father's death. Who can assuage their grief? Who pluck the rooted sorrow from their hearts? He alone who "tempers the winds to the shorn lamb." To His mercy and Divine protection we most humbly commend them.

Resolved unanimously, That, as a testimony of respect for the memory of the Hon. L. F. LINN, deceased, the members of this House will wear the usual badge of mourning for thirty days; and that the House do now adjourn.

So the resolution was agreed to.

And the House adjourned.

LEGISLATURE OF IOWA.

Mr. Foley, the attentive and worthy member of the House of Representatives from Jackson County, presented the following resolutions, which passed the House unanimously on the 19th instant, and were concurred in by the Council on the 20th.

Resolved, by the Council and House of Representatives of the Territory of Iowa, That each member of the respective Houses be requested to wear crape on the left arm for the space of 30 days, as a testimony of respect to the memory of the Hon. Lewis F. Linn, late a Senator of the United States from the State of Missouri.

Resolved, That we respectfully tender the bereaved and afflicted family of the distinguished statesman, the assurances of our sympathy and condolence, and that a copy of these Resolutions be forwarded to the widow of the deceased by the Speaker of the House of Representatives and the President of the Council.

During the pendency before the House of the foregoing resolutions, Mr. Rogers from Dubuque arose and made the following brief and appropriate remarks :

Mr. Speaker :—I hope the Resolution of my friend from Jackson, will pass without a dissenting vote. They are an appropriate tribute of respect to the memory of a much lamented and distinguished public man.

Dr. Linn was the warm and devoted friend of this Territory. His zeal, on all occasions, in our behalf, won for him the name of the "Iowa Senator," and our citizens will not soon forget the services which rendered the appellation deserved. His loss is nearly as severely felt by us, as by his own State. Cut down in the vigor of life—in the midst of his usefulness—with great and glorious projects upon his hands unfinished ; dropping from the theatre of his brilliant and patriotic labors, and from companions that loved and admired him, like an orb suddenly shaken from the heavens. He has gone to the grave followed by the universal regrets and sorrows of the whole people of the Great West.

Death should terminate all animosities. I hope, on this occasion, we will sink the partisan into the patriot, and remember that we are Americans, having a deep and abiding interest in the character of our public men—their fame is our moral inheritance—let us cherish it with patriotic pride.

Mr. Speaker, I had but a word to say. I believe that the adoption of these resolutions will have a good effect upon the living—encouraging them in the faithful discharge of their duties, and at the same time evince a deserved respect for departed worth.

House of Representatives,
Iowa City, Jan. 4th, 1844.

To Mrs. Lewis F. Linn.

Madam,—In pursuance to the order of the Legislature of this Territory, we herewith inclose you a copy of a Joint Resolution passed by the same, in testimony of respect to your departed husband.

In connection therewith, we trust it will not be improper for us to say, that though dead, he will long live in the memory of the Citizens of this Territory. Time cannot efface the remembrance of services like his—and in their love his memory will find "a monument more lasting than brass."

Allow us furthermore, to assure you, Madam, that you mourn not alone, over the loss of one, so gifted, and whose promise of extended usefulness, was so fair. Though he fell in the midst of his unfinished plans, the whole West, whose champion he was, feels that it has lost its ablest defender and its most zealous and untiring advocate.

That he died universally regretted, and after a well-spent life, are not, however, we feel assured, the only sources of consolation to you. Religion presents her soothing and consoling influence. She points to a higher and nobler sphere of enjoyment, and she tells of a holier union, hereafter, of the loved ones that have separated upon earth. May you in eternity enjoy that union, with the husband who has been thus suddenly and unexpectedly called away.

With sentiments of respect and esteem we remain your obedient servants,

JAMES P. CARLETON,
Speaker of House of Representatives.
FRANCIS SPRINGER,
President of the Council.

LEGISLATURE OF WISCONSIN.

The proceedings of the Legislature relative to the death of Dr. Linn, were due to the memory of the deceased, for the solicitude which he ever manifested for the welfare of this Territory, as well as for the benefits which it has derived from his labors.

The remarks of Mr. Strong of Wisconsin, as well as the sentiments embodied in his resolutions, will be responded to by every citizen who has noted the official course of the truly upright and generous Statesman to whose memory they are offered.

Mr. Strong of Wisconsin rose, to offer certain resolutions, and prefaced their introduction with the following remarks.

Mr. President—I rise for the purpose of asking leave of the Council to offer certain joint resolutions, expressing the great regret which the Legislative Assembly feels for the death of that great and good man, Lewis F. Linn, late a Senator in Congress from the State of Missouri, and to present some slight tribute of respect for his memory; and I feel sure, that all who know his character, and especially all who have had the pleasure, as I have, of forming his personal acquaintance, will readily unite with me in performing this melancholy duty.

He was emphatically the friend of Wisconsin, as he was of the whole West; the active part he has always taken on the floor of the United States Senate, in support of every measure which had for its object the advancement of our interests, cannot but have endeared him to every citizen of the Territory, and have satisfied all that in him we have lost a friend whose place we can scarcely hope to see filled. Dr. Linn, wherever he moved, whether in political or private circles, was the beloved of all, and it can be said of him with as much truth probably as of any man that ever lived, that he was without an enemy. But an overruling Providence has removed him from earth; and as we can do no more, I hope we shall do no less, than offer to his memory the humble tribute of respect contained in the resolutions I hold in my hand.

Mr. Strong then submitted the following, which were adopted:

Resolved, By the Council (if the House of Representatives concur), That the Legislative Assembly of the Territory of Wisconsin have learned, with feelings of the greatest regret, the death of the Hon. Lewis F. Linn, late a Senator in Congress from the State of Missouri; that by his death his family have been deprived of a most affectionate and amiable head; Congress of a true Patriot and able Statesman; his own State of a most faithful and efficient Representative; the whole West of a firm and ever ready advocate of its best interests, and the Territory of Wisconsin in particular of one who has been on all occasions its resolute and devoted friend; and to whom it is deeply indebted for his zealous activity in her behalf, in the body of which he was a member.

Resolved, That as a testimony of the respect which the Legislative Assembly of the Territory entertain for the memory of the Hon. Lewis F. Linn, both Houses will immediately adjourn, after resolving that each member, shall wear crape on his left arm in respect to his memory, for thirty days. The Council thereupon adjourned.

TRIBUTES OF RESPECT TO LEWIS F. LINN.

The citizens of St. Louis, without distinction of party, are requested to meet at the Court House on Wednesday evening, the 11th instant, at 7½ o'clock, to express their regret at the sudden death of the Hon. Lewis F. Linn, U. S. Senator from Missouri.

St. Louis.

How many of those immortal minds, whose genius has illustrated the history of our race, have lived and died with no other consolation than that of seeing their opinions making way and giving freedom and happiness to men! How few indeed have lived long enough to see this! but rarer yet has it happened that the author of a great truth has survived to witness its general acceptation, or reap the reward which a distant posterity alone bestows in its homage and veneration of his name.

The foregoing sentiments of an able contemporary, are particularly applicable to the recent and sudden death of the Hon. Lewis F. Linn. His favorite measure was the immediate occupation and settlement of the Oregon Territory by American citizens. His enlightened mind led him to perceive the importance of maintaining our title to that region by encouraging its early settlement, and extending to those who might check our progress westward, before we had reached the Pacific Ocean. The correctness of his "Oregon Bill," has already been fully proved by the impetus given to emigration thither, even by the probability of its adoption by the Federal Government; but he was not spared to witness its enactment— to behold the triumph of those views which he had so long urged with determined zeal and far-reaching patriotism. We trust, however, that the action of the next Congress will award to his memory the highest praise which it can bestow—the approval of his views on the Oregon question; that it will not be left to "a distant posterity" to pay that tribute to his name which is so eminently due.

We know that the annals of the world show melancholy proofs of the fact, that great men are not always appreciated by the age in which they live; but there are many instances on record, and the history of our Republic furnishes not a few, that those who devote their lives to the service of their fellowmen and of their country, are not always neglected by their contemporaries.

Although Dr. Linn had not the gratification of witnessing before his death, the triumph of that policy which he has the honor of having first suggested, and to the advocacy of which he long devoted the energies of his whole mind, yet his constituents, regardless of party associations cheerfully award to him the meed of their heartfelt and cordial approbation. He possessed, to an extraordinary degree, those attractive qualities which endeared him to all who knew him, and which won the confidence and regard even of those who cherished different opinions, and who consequently were often found arrayed in opposition to his views. Although he never deserted the party to which he was sincerely attached, yet his opponents respected his gentlemanly bearing, his chivalric character and his true greatness, which would not suffer him to stoop to mean and paltry devices for success, or indulge in coarse and bitter invective to wound the feelings of those who could not view all public questions in the same light with himself. His mind was too enlarged, his soul too pure, and his aspirations too noble, to permit him to descend to the humiliating acts which have often degraded the Statesmen of our own and other lands. All gave him credit for sincerity and patriotism, and Missouri, which twice honored him with a seat in the U. S. Senate, will not cease to cherish his memory as one of her brightest ornaments. He was a Statesman without reproach, a patriot without ignoble ambition, and in a word, one of "the noblest works of God—an honest man." Long may he be remembered as "the model Senator" of Missouri.

A WHIG.

[*From the Missouri Reporter, St. Louis.*]

Yesterday the mournful intelligence reached this city, that the Hon. Lewis F. Linn, United States Senator from Missouri, died at his residence, in St. Genevieve, on the 3d instant. We learn that after dinner, on the day of his death, he retired to his room, and was shortly afterwards discovered to have passed without a groan to a purer and better world.

Dr. Linn suffered severely last spring from an attack of chronic rheumatism, and on his recovery made a visit to Philadelphia, New York and other eastern cities. On his return home, about a fortnight ago, he appeared to be entirely restored to health, and his family and friends had just begun to congratulate themrselves on his renewed strength and activity, and the public on the bright career which still awaited him, when the sad truth broke upon them, that he whom they so fondly admired, had closed his pilgrimage on earth.

It was the good fortune of Dr. Linn to enjoy the confidence and esteem of all parties, notwithstanding he was a member of the United States Senate during the most exciting sessions ever known in our political history. With attainments of a high order and intellect, gifted by nature with unusual endowments, and a heart pure and unsullied, he won the affection of all associated with him, and became an especial favorite of the people of this State, to whose interests he had devoted himself with untiring industry. His unremitting exertions to advance the interests of the Great West, long ago caused the citizens of this State to regard him as their especial champion in the Halls of Congress, and to speak of him with feelings of the highest regard and enthusiasm. Twice had he been elected to the U. S. Senate with little or no opposition; both his political friends and opponents recording their votes in his favor with the greatest cheerfulness. No man in Missouri ever commanded more general and sincere respect, and none ever possessed a more wide-spread or deserved popularity. The planters and the merchants, the frontier settlers and the emigrants to Oregon, found in him one who labored for their prosperity with an ambition unalloyed by selfishness—with no ulterior or sinister objects to gratify, and with no other desire than to perform his duty to his constituents faithfully, honestly and unostentatiously. His efforts in behalf of Oregon will for ever identify his name with our Pacific Territory. His was the labor of first urging on the National Government the importance of the occupation and settlement of that lovely region, and to him belongs the honor of arousing the attention of the whole country to that great question. It is to be deeply regretted that he was not spared to witness, the triumph of that great measure, which he originated, advocated, and urged forward with zeal, till the indifferent became interested, the doubtful convinced, and the hostile prepared to abandon all opposition to it. But nothing can rob him of the honor which is so eminently his due—nothing can separate his name from the future glory of our Pacific Territory. The first city whose foundations shall be laid west of the Rocky Mountains by American citizens, will bear his name, and those emigrants to Oregon, now on their march across the Western prairies, will form the nucleus around which will soon be gathered a happy and thriving population, to attest hereafter the sagacity, forecast, and patriotism of the lamented Linn.

To the citizens of Missouri and the whole nation, the death of Dr. Linn is a heavy calamity. No one in Missouri can fill the void thus created. His public life affords a model worthy of imitation; his conduct as Senator an example to be followed by all who may succeed him. He was courteous, chivalric, brilliant and profound; an uncompromising but conciliatory advocate of his political principles; a debater of great power, but unostentatious in his manner; a Statesman without vanity, a politician without bitterness, a man, like the Chevalier Bayard, "*sans peur, sans reproche.*"

The sadness visible on every countenance yesterday, when his death was announced in our city, and the low and mournful tones in which all spoke of the public loss sustained by his sudden decease, proved the sincerity and depth of the affection universally felt for one so worthy and so pure. Most sincerely do we sympathize with her who has lost an idolized husband, and with those who have been deprived by this afflictive dispensation of Providence, of an affectionate and honored parent. If it can afford any consolation to the bereaved family to know that others mourn with them in the hour of their grief, they have the best assurance which can be given, that every Missourian feels the deepest sorrow at the loss of one so distinguished and so loved.

St. Louis, *October* 16*th*, 1843.

To Mrs. L. F. Linn.

Respected Madam,—The people of St. Louis at the Court House of the County in public meeting assembled, made it my duty to forward to you a copy of its proceedings had expressive of their love and respect for the memory of the Honorable Lewis F. Linn, their Senator, and your illustrious and excellent husband, and to signify to you, Madam, how deeply and how sincerely they sympathize with you in this your and their great bereavement.

In attempting to execute the solemn duty I am so oppressed with a sense of my inability to do justice to the feelings of deep sorrow felt by the citizens of a city and a county whom he has served so long, so faithfully and so well, that I fear to increase that grief, so natural for you to feel, and which we so much respect, rather than to afford consolation to the wounded spirit of one whose deep sorrow and affliction has rendered her still more dear to the hearts of a susceptible and stricken people.

Giving utterance to my profound veneration for the memory of the dead, and praying that Almighty God may graciously afford Divine Consolation to the living, I dare intrude no further upon the sanctity of your grief.

Be pleased to accept herewith a copy of the proceedings of the people of the city and county of St. Louis, and be assured of the deep sympathies of each one of the citizens composing that vast assemblage, and their profound respect for your sorrow.

I have the honor to be your obedient and humble servant.

JNO. M. WIMER.

At an unusually numerous meeting of citizens of St. Louis, convened at the court house on Wednesday evening the 11th inst., for the purpose of testifying their respect for the memory of Hon. Lewis F. Linn, late one of the senators in the Congress of the United States from Missouri, and whose death took place on the 3d inst., on motion of Judge James B. Bowlin, Hon. John M. Wimer, mayor of the city, was called to the chair; and N. Paschall was appointed secretary.

The chairman then addressed the meeting to the following effect:

"We are convened here, fellow citizens, in consequence of the receipt of the mournful intelligence that the warm, the devoted and active friend of St. Louis, the Hon. Lewis F. Linn, one of our Senators, has been taken away by the hand of death. It is the greatest loss and the severest chastisement ever inflicted upon St. Louis. The blow was sudden and desolating—the more so, when we consider that our friend, virtue's ornament, was removed by Providence in the midst of life and in the full career of usefulness and honor. It becomes us as a people to meekly bow to the awful and inscrutable dispensation and humbly invoke Divine assistance to aid and suitably to demean ourselves in this our great affliction.

"The pomp of obsequies are of no advantage to the

dead, but they often afford consolation to the living. What tokens of respect for the deceased will be suitable for the occasion, and expressive of the deep emotions of regret felt by the citizens of St. Louis, it is the business of this meeting to consider."

Lewis V. Bogy, Esq., then offered the following resolution, which was unanimously adopted :

"*Resolved*, That a committee of nine persons be appointed by the chair for the purpose of preparing and reporting a preamble, and resolutions appropriate to the occasion."

Thereupon the chair appointed Messrs Bogy, Blair, Drake, Bowlin, Milburn, Geyer, Ayres, Dobyns and Ranney, said committee : The committee having retired Mr. Benton was called upon from all parts of the room, and in obedience to the call addressed the meeting :

He said, that great as the grief of all present was, he had more to lament than any one. As a citizen of the State he felt in common with all other citizens the sorrow which oppressed their bosoms ; as a senator still having some time to serve, he felt the loss of a colleague from whom he always received the kindest, the most cordial, the most efficient aid ; as a friend he had to lament the loss of one of his earliest friends. He (Mr. B.) had arrived in Missouri above a quarter of a century ago, while the lamented deceased was still a youth at school ; and from the first moment of his arrival had found in him, and in all his connections, the most generous friendship, never interrupted for an instant, and which never glowed with more warmth than in the last interview, a few weeks before, when they spent the day together. The loss of such a colleague and of such a friend was to him the addition of a private to a public loss, and doubled the weight of the grief which he felt.

The worthy mayor, said Mr. B., who presides on this melancholy occasion has opened the subject with just and appropriate remarks. The respectable committee which has been appointed, will report resolutions which will cover the merits of the deceased and attest our feeling ; and some one of the committee will doubtless be designated to illustrate with his observations the resolutions which shall be submitted. He would not trench upon his province ; but would confine himself to points, in the public life and character of his deceased friend and colleague, less generally known, but equally honorable to the *man* and the *senator*. He would speak of his generous kindness and amenity, which conciliated good will from all parties—which softened the acerbities of party—which composed many differences—and which flew to the sick bed of every member without regard to party, and joined the assiduities of nurse and friend to the profound skill of the accomplished physician. He would speak of his punctual attendance in his place, and his faithful discharge of every public duty. He would speak of his instant and ready attention to every call from his constituents, whether opponents (for he had no foes) or supporters. He would speak of his success in carrying great measures, which would not have been carried by any one save himself. There was a charm in the goodness of his heart, the gentleness of his manner and the amiability of his temper, which gave power to talents and enabled him to do for his State, what none but himself could have done.

He (Mr. B.) was not using the language of eulogy but speaking the words of truth, and saying that which should pass into history. Perhaps the most important measure ever carried in Congress for the benefit of Missouri was the acquisition of that superb territory known as the Platte country ; the lamented Linn was the author of that measure!—True, he was supported by his colleagues, but they could not have carried it. His colleague in the Senate older than himself, and who addresses you, could not have carried it. It required not only sagacity, and tact, and discretion to carry that great and delicate measure, but it required also the sweetness of temper, which wins hearts, and which our deceased friend so eminently possessed. As an historical truth which should be known now and for ever to every Missourian, this statement is now made on this solemn occasion, to this large and respectable assembly, that the knowledge of it may be spread as wide, and last as long as the acquisition of the Platte has been auspicious and glorious for the State. (Great applause followed the delivery of this statement.)

The old inhabitants of this country—those who viewed all the new emigrants with such kindness on the change of government, and whose grants of land from Spain and France had in so many instances suffered from want of confirmation,—those old inhabitants, and all claiming under them, owe a debt of gratitude to the illustrious deceased, for to him is owing the passage of the last act of Congress, which has done so much towards the final and equitable acknowledgment of these long delayed grants.

This is not the time, said Mr. B., to enumerate the services of the deceased; another occasion will present itself for that act of justice. To mourn the loss of a statesman, a patriot, a friend, a good man—to weep for him, rather than to speak of his public acts—is now the feelings of every one. But how can we omit the last great act, as yet unfinished, in which his whole soul was engaged at the time of his death?—The Bill for the settlement and occupation of Oregon, was his, and he carried it through the Senate, when his colleague, who now addresses you, could not have done it. This is another historical truth, fit to be made known, on this occasion, and which is now declared to this large and respectable assemblage, under all circumstances which impart solemnity to the declaration. (Great applause). He carried that bill through the Senate, and it was the measure of a statesman. Just to the settler, it was wise to the government. The settler has a right to have a home in the new country, which he reclaims from the wilderness and the savage ; the government of the United States can only save its domain on the Oregon by planting its citizens there. Land is the inducement and the reward to emigration, and that land was granted by the bill—liberally granted to the wife, and the children, to the young man and the widow, as well as the husband and the father. That bill is the vindication and the assertion of the American title against the daring designs of England, and it was the only way to save the country. It was carried through the Senate at the last session, and its author was preparing to carry it again. Called this summer to the Atlantic States on private business he availed himself of all opportunities to collect fresh materials for the support of his darling measure. The last day that he spent in this town, only three weeks ago, on his return from the East, he spoke of these materials—of the daring pretensions of England, and of his determination to push the measure which was to save his country's rights with renewed vigor at the ensuing session. Alas that he should not have been spared to put the finishing hand to a measure which was to reward the emigrant, to protect his country, to curb England, and to connect his own name with the foundation of an empire. But it is done ! the unfinished work will go on ! it will be completed and the name of Linn will not be forgotten ; that name will live and be connected with Oregon, while its banks bear a plant or its waters roll a wave.

A great man of the early days of the French Revolution died while he had a great measure depending: it was Mirabeau, who was surprised by death while his bill for the division of estates was still depending before the Legislative Assembly. The terrors of death could not stifle his regard for his bill. He made a bequest of it to a friend. He willed the unfinished work to the celebrated Talleyrand; and this Deputy read to the assembly the speech prepared for the occasion by the great orator, and carried the measure. If inexorable fate had allowed a few minutes to our departed friend, he would doubtless have done the same. Death had no terrors for him, and a moment would have snatched from the agonizing cares of friends and family to have commended and committed the crowning measure of his life to the faithful hands of a successor. He had not that time—not a moment to think, nor to speak!—And now the whole representation from Missouri—the whole delegation from the Great West—must constitute themselves his political legatees—take his great measure to themselves and carry it through.

Mr. B. would still confine himself to points, not so generally known, and among these was the great developement of mind which their lamented friend was undergoing at the time of his death. Of the nine years he had served in the Senate, the last two or three were fullest of improvement to himself and benefit to his country. His faculties were maturing every day, and his delivery becoming truly beautiful. Bred to a profession which did not admit of public displays he required practice to perfect and develop his powers; and practice was doing its part in perfecting genius. A natural gift for speaking was improved into eloquence ; a mind originally good was enriched with the acquisitions of study and observation. Thus improved, he spoke without effort, and seemingly without a consciousness of the power and beauty of his own discourse. The Senate listened to him with astonishment and admiration, and some have been heard to exclaim, *the man is inspired.* A few years more would have doubled his powers. That such a man should have perished in the meridian of his days, and so suddenly and unexpectedly, is for ever to be deplored. He laid down to sleep a few moments, and awoke no more. It was the sleep of death—sleep converted into death—eternal sleep.

On an other occasion Mr. B. said it would be his privilege to speak more deliberately of the merits of the deceased, at present he only followed the impulsions of the heart in giving vent to feelings of sorrow and affection, which found a response in all bosoms, and which so many had met this night to manifest.

Mr. Bogy, from the committee for that purpose, reported the following preamble and resolutions for the action of the meeting.

Whereas, the safety and prosperity of our country mainly depend on the virtue and ability of the statesmen and representatives to whom the duties of government, and the making of laws, are delegated by the people ; and whereas, when Providence has removed from amongst us, to another and a better world, a representative of eminent merit, it becomes our duty to declare in a public and solemn manner, our respect for his memory, and our sense, with all submission to the Divine Will, of the loss sustained ; and whereas an occasion has presented itself of so testifying our sentiments on the sudden death of the Hon. Lewis F. Linn. It is therefore,

Resolved, That we have received the sad tidings of

the recent sudden decease of the Hon. Lewis F. Linn, one of the Senators from this State in the Congress of the United States, with feelings of profound regret, and deplore the event, as a public misfortune.

Resolved, That the conduct and deportment of Lewis F. Linn during his too brief existence, was distinguished in private and professional life, as in high public station, by a rare combination of qualities, commanding our respect, while they won our affections, and that our lamented Senator has given to those who shall succeed him in the councils of the nation, a salutary and bright example.

Resolved, That in his senatorial action, on the relations and interests of these United States and Territories—in their whole vast expanse, from the Lake of the Woods to Cape Sable, and from the shores of the Pacific Ocean to the boundary line of Maine and New Brunswick,—we acknowledge and appreciate the wisdom, energy, and high sense of national right and honor, exibited by Lewis F. Linn.

Resolved, That the efforts of Lewis F. Linn to obtain justice for that portion of our population, whose rights of property were especially guaranteed to them by the treaty of cession of the 30th April, 1803, alone entitle his memory to the respect of every American citizen who can appreciate the value to the individual, or to the mass of national good faith and honor.

Resolved, That we respectfully tender to the bereaved and afflicted family of our deceased Senator the assurance of our sympathies ; and that a copy of the proceedings of this meeting be forwarded to his widow by the chairman with an appropriate letter.

The report having been adopted by the meeting, Gen. Ranney offered a resolution which was afterwards modified to read as follows :

Resolved, That a committee of three persons be appointed by the chairman, whose duty it shall be to select some person to deliver an appropriate address on the occasion of the death of Senator Linn, and to appoint a time and place for its delivery.

The Chair appointed Messrs. Ranney, Hudson and Blannerhasset, to act as this committee.

Judge Lawless, Lewis V. Bogy, Esq. and T. H. Holt Esq., then in succession addressed the meeting in eloquent and happily conceived speeches.

On motion of Dr. Hardage Lane, it was,

Resolved, That the several papers in this city and State be requested to publish the proceedings of this meeting.

The meeting then adjourned.

JOHN M. WIMER, *Chairman.*

N. PASCHALL, *Secretary.*

ST. LOUIS, *October*, *7th*, 1843.

At a meeting of the Medical Society of Missouri held last evening, the death of the Honorable Lewis F. Linn having been announced, the following preamble and resolutions were unanimously adopted.

Whereas, it has pleased an all wise Providence to remove from this life of usefulness by a sudden, and unlooked for death, one of the most estimable of our professional brethren, we the officers and members of the Medical Society of Missouri, deploring in common with the entire community the loss sustained, take this method of expressing our unfeigned sorrow for the event.

Therefore, *Resolved*, That in the death of Dr. Lewis F. Linn, a distinguished member of our body, we are called upon to mourn the loss of one, who for the many ennobling qualities of his heart and understanding, for his high intellectual endowments, and distinguished professional attainments, for his learning, his genius, and his eloquence, must ever be remembered by all who reverence the lofty attainments displayed in the stations he adorned.

Resolved, That this Society sincerely deplore this melancholy dispensation which has deprived our profession of one of its ornaments, and truly sympathize with his distressed family in the loss they have sustained.

Resolved, That as a mark of respect to the deceased the members of this Society wear the usual badge of mourning, for thirty days.

Resolved, That a copy of these resolutions be signed by the officers of this Society, and transmitted to the family of the deceased, and published in the newspapers of the city.

HARDAGE LANE, *President.*
WM. M. MCPHEETERS, Rec. *Secretary.*

MEETING AT ST. GENEVIEVE.

At a large and respectable meeting of the citizens of the town and county of Saint Genevieve in the State of Missouri, held pursuant to notice, at the Court House in the town of Saint Genevieve, on Wednesday, the 4th day of October, A. D. 1843, for the purpose of paying a suitable tribute of respect to the memory of the late Honorable Lewis F. Linn, deceased:

On motion Ferdinand Rozier, Esq., and the Hon. Clement Detchemendy, were called to the chair, and John N. Littlejohn was chosen Secretary, and on a further motion, the Chair appointed the following gentlemen a committee to draft and present to the meeting a preamble and resolutions, expressive of the sense of the meeting, and appropriate to the occasion, to wit, Messrs. Augte. St. Gemme, Esq., Doctor J. Sargeant, Doctor B. Shaw, General J. D. Grafton, William Adams, Esq., Felix Valle, Esq., and Adolph Razier, Esq., who, after having retired for a short time, reported the following preamble and resolutions by their Chairman, to wit:

Whereas it has pleased Almighty God, in the ways of His inscrutable Providence, to remove from us in a sudden manner, by the hand of death, our distinguished and respected townsman and fellow citizen, the HONORABLE LEWIS F. LINN, a member of the Senate of the United States, and whereas, we deem it not only our duty, but our melancholy privilege to be among the first to express, in a public manner, our sense of the loss which is thus sustained, by ourselves, our State and our common country, therefore:

1. *Resolved*, That in the sudden demise of the HONORABLE LEWIS F. LINN, we feel the event as a great affliction, not only to his family, but extending to us his neighbors and personal friends, to the State of Missouri, and to the elevated body of which he was a member in the Counsels of the General Government.

2. *Resolved*, That while as neighbors and citizens we thus deplore the event we have met to reflect and act upon, our sympathy is in a most peculiar manner directed to the bereaved family of our deceased friend, to whom the loss they have sustained, in the husband and the father, is irreparable.

3. *Resolved*, That a copy of these proceedings be signed by the Chairman and Secretary, and forwarded to some one of the editors of newspapers in the city of St.

Louis for publication, with a request that the same may be also inserted in all the newspapers in this State.

4. *Resolved*, That a copy of these proceedings be furnished to the widow and family of the deceased.

All of which was unanimously adopted,—and on motion the meeting adjourned.

FERDINAND ROZIER,
CLEMENT DETCHEMENDY,
Chairman.

JOHN N. LITTLEJOHN, *Secretary.*

At a meeting of the Citizens of Potosi and its vicinity, convened at the Presbyterian Church on Saturday the 14th instant, for the purpose of testifying their respect for the memory of the Hon. Lewis F. Linn, whose death took place on the 3d instant: On motion of W. C. Read, Esq., General Augustus Jones was called to the Chair, and Dr. James H. McGready appointed Secretary. The Chairman then explained the object of the meeting in quite an appropriate manner. Mr. W. C. Read, being called on, addressed the meeting, and in conclusion moved that a committee of seven be appointed by the Chair for the purpose of drafting a preamble and resolutions expressive of the sense of the meeting, whereupon the following gentlemen were appointed, W C. Read, Rev. Mr. Thomas, Rev. Mr. Cowan, John Scott, Col. P. P. Brickey, John Brickey, Esq., and Valentine Haifner, who after a short deliberation made the following report.

Whereas the melancholy intelligence of the death of our Senator, the Hon. Lewis F. Linn, having reached us, and whereas although we should freely and willingly submit to the dispensations of Providence which are always conceived in wisdom and goodness, yet when we see death with all its terrors and fearful forebodings laying waste and cutting down in his prime and usefulness, a public servant, who on all occasions served his fellow-citizens faithfully, and in whom the pride of the community seemed to be concentrated, thereby producing a public calamity which seemed universally to be felt throughout the land, it is but human nature, it is a principle implanted in the human breast to feel a disposition to assemble in congregated masses in peace and friendship, for the purpose of mingling in sentiments of respect for him, and to express a regret for the lamentable occurrence, when he has in obedience to the call of his Maker bid a final adieu to things on earth and left his friends to lament his departure. Therefore be it

Resolved, That in the death of our Senator, the Hon. Lewis F. Linn, Missouri has lost one of her brightest sons, one of her most faithful representatives, and one of her best citizens.

Resolved, That in Dr. Linn we find combined the able and skilful physician, together with a kindness of heart which always manifested the keenest pain at the distress and suffering of his fellow-citizens in their hour of illness.

Resolved, That in the death of our friend we have been deprived of one of the rarest specimens of virtue, charity, and goodness of heart, which adorns the human character.

Resolved, That in his constitution we find the patriot, the philanthropist, and the accomplished and sagacious Statesman.

Resolved, That while he was firm and unswerving in his principles, yet he was kind and courteous to his opponents.

Resolved, That at the next session of Congress, while

there will be a dark gloom cast over the Senate Chamber at the announcement of his death, there will be a vacuum produced which will be hard to fill.

Resolved, That we deeply sympathize with his bereaved family, in the irreparable loss which they have sustained in a kind and affectionate husband and father.

Resolved, That the Secretary of the meeting be directed to transmit a copy of the proceedings of this meeting to the widow of our deceased friend.

Resolved, That the Secretary also be requested to send a copy to his brother, Gov. Dodge, of Wisconsin Territory.

Resolved, That the President and Secretary sign the proceedings of this meeting.

Resolved, That the St. Louis papers be requested to publish the proceedings of the meeting.

The Rev. Mr. Cowan then addressed the meeting in a brief manner. On motion the meeting adjourned.

A. JONES, *President*.

J. H. MCGREADY, *Secretary*.

At a large and respectable meeting of the citizens of Madison County, held at the Court House in Fredericktown, Mo., on the 20th of Oct., 1843, for the purpose of showing the respect due to the memory of our beloved friend and U. S. Senator, Dr. Lewis F. Linn, S. A. Guignon, Esq., was called to the chair and S. D. Caruthers was appointed Secretary. The object of the meeting being made known, by a few appropriate remarks, on motion of Robt. H. Lane, Esq., a committee of ten was appointed to draft a preamble and resolutions, expressive of the regard which we entertain for the memory of the late Hon. Lewis F. Linn: whereupon, the chair appointed the following gentlemen to compose said committee: Messrs. R. H. Lane, T. F. Tong, J. D. Villars, E. F. Pratte, Caleb Cox, D. L. Caruthers, J. P. Davis, Chas. Gregoire, Paul Deguire, and Jas. McFadden. During the absence of the committee, the Hon. John D. Cook was called upon to address the meeting, which he did, in a clear and able manner, making it appear obvious, to every one present, that in the death of Dr. Linn, Missouri, and particularly Southern Missouri, has sustained an irreparable loss. The committee returned, after a few minutes' absence, and through the chairman, R. H. Lane, Esq., reported the following preamble and resolutions:

Whereas the soaring mind of Addison compares the life and exit of a great and good man to the sun, which, on its first appearance gives light and animation to the earth; and, when it makes its final exit, leaves the contemplative powers of man to meditate upon its departed glory, we deem it no misconstruction of the simile in applying this comparison to the Hon. Lewis F. Linn, late U. S. Senator, whose memory, we are, at this time, called upon to lament. His pathway through life was illuminated by the light of genius; and the pure fire of patriotism that glowed in his heart, gave heat and animation to all of his acts for the amelioration of his country: therefore, be it

Resolved, 1. That we deem the death of the Hon. Lewis F. Linn, Senator from Missouri in the Congress of the United States, as a public calamity.

2. That in his brilliant career we behold the enlightened statesman, the pure patriot, and the virtuous citizen.

3. That in his oft-repeated call for the occupation of the Oregon Territory, we recognize the presentation of means for the accomplishment of a glorious end.

4. That on this occasion we tender our condolence to

his bereaved family; and that we submissively bow to the afflicting dispensation of Providence, that bereft us of him.

5. That a transcript of the proceedings of this meeting, signed by the chairman and secretary, be presented to his family.

6. That a copy of these proceedings be sent to Gen. Henry Dodge, half-brother of our deceased friend.

7. That the proceedings of this meeting be signed by the chairman and secretary, and published in the Southern Advocate, and all other papers in this State friendly to Dr. Linn.

The foregoing preamble and resolutions were read, and unanimously adopted. After which, a call was made upon Gen. Augustus Jones to deliver an address: to which he responded in the most feeling and pathetic manner. During his remarks, he reverted back to the scenes of their boyhood:—reminding the enraptured audience of many incidents that occurred during the infantile days of Dr. Linn, which proved beyond a doubt, that he possessed a truly magnanimous soul. He traced him through his long and illustrious career, and told of many of his benevolent acts towards the sick, the wounded, the poor and needy, that would have confirmed in the minds of the most incredulous, that Dr. Linn was well entitled to the appellation of GREAT.

S. C. Guignon, *Chairman.*

S. D. Caruthers, *Secretary.*

Fredericktown, 23*d* *October*, 1840.

Madam,—In accordance with the wish of the meeting held on the 20th inst. at this place, in honor and respect to the memory of your departed husband and our friend, one and all: I herewith enclose you a copy of the proceedings of the meeting; please, madam, accept it in the spirit in which it is tendered, for really it is of friends met to mourn and to deplore the loss of a friend. We are perfectly aware that no one can replace him with you, and are also satisfied that no one will or can replace him in the affection of the people of this State, nor can they have a more faithful friend in the U. S. Senate.

I individually join in the public feeling expressed towards your dear husband, and am sorry that we have been called to meet on so solemn an occasion; but, madam, I trust he has gone to receive the reward due his virtues, and to a world where there is no mourning. Please accept my sincere feeling of sorrow on this occasion, and believe me your friend,

S. C. Guignon.

At a promiscuous meeting of the citizens of Boonville, Cooper County, Missouri, convened at the Court House, on Wednesday evening the 18th of October, 1843, upon the reception of authenticated intelligence of the death of the Hon. Lewis F. Linn, late Senator of Missouri, in the Congress of the United States. Gen. Wm. Shields was called to the chair, and Col. James Quarles appointed secretary. The object of the meeting having been briefly and appropriately stated by the chairman,

On motion of H. W. Crowther, Esq., a committee of twelve were appointed by the chair, to draft a preamble and resolutions expressive of the sentiments and feelings of this community. To wit, H. W. Crowther, Thos. J. Boggs, D. Spahr, B. Tompkins, J. D. Blair, B. G. Wilson, B. W. Sharp, Chas. Cope, B. Emmons Ferry, R. P Bowman, C. H. Smith, and John Andrews.

The committee retired, and after a short interval returned, and reported by Gen. B. Emmons Ferry, the following preamble and resolutions, which were unanimously adopted. To wit:

It having pleased Divine Providence to remove from the scene of his labors and usefulness, the Hon. Lewis F. Linn, one of the Senators of the United States, from the State of Missouri; the citizens of Boonville and vicinity, entertaining a just regard for his private virtues, and distinguished public services, and penetrated with a profound sense of the loss which our country has sustained in the death of one her most able and patriotic men, unite cordially with their fellow-citizens throughout the State, in paying a well-earned tribute to his memory.

Therefore, be it Resolved by the meeting, That, in the death of Dr. Linn, the medical profession, which he adorned by singular and unsurpassed benevolence, has been deprived of one of its most accomplished members, and society has to deplore the loss of one whose manly character, relieved by the most winning gentleness and courtesy, commanded its highest respect, and made him the grace and charm of the social circle.

Resolved, That in his political conduct, Dr. Linn was manly, consistent and sincere, qualities, which, while they entitle him to the confidence and gratitude of his party, win also for him the respect and esteem of his opponents.

Resolved, That the able, persevering, and successful exertions of Dr. Linn upon the Oregon question, have obtained for him a distinguished rank among American statesmen, while from the magnitude and wide-reaching influences of the interests involved in the question, they give him a just claim to the grateful remembrance of the nation, and entitle him to the lasting gratitude of the people of the future Republic of the Far West.

Resolved, That, as citizens of Missouri, we are under a lasting debt of gratitude for the able and efficient services of Dr. Linn in the national councils, by which mainly the cession of the Platte country to the State was achieved.

Resolved, That to the family and relatives of the lamented Linn, we offer our most unfeigned condolence for this sad and sudden bereavement of their household.

Resolved, That these proceedings be signed by the chairman and secretary of the meeting, and that a copy of the same be transmitted to the family of our late distinguished Senator, and also that the secretary be directed to furnish a copy to the editors of the Missouri Register and Boonsville Observer, for publication, and that the other papers in the State be requested to publish the same.

On motion the meeting adjourned.

WM. SHIELDS, *Chairman.*

JAMES QUARLES, *Secretary.*

LETTERS OF CONDOLENCE.

FROM GENERAL JACKSON.

HERMITAGE, *October 16th*, 1843.

MY DEAR FRIEND,—I have just received the Missouri Reporter, which contains the mournful details of your dear husband's, and my revered and very dear friend's death. With a heart filled with the deepest sorrow, I affectionately tender you my condolence on this great bereavement. His loss to you and your dear children is irreparable, and to his country, is so great, in the council of our nation and society, that it cannot be filled. But, my dear friend, we are charged by our blessed Saviour, to mourn, not for the dead, but for the living ; "the Lord giveth and the Lord taketh away, and blessed be the name of the Lord :" he doeth all things well, although we, poor frail mortals, cannot refrain from grief on such afflicting occasions. He was my dearest and most disinterested friend, and as long as I live I will lament his untimely death, with a heart full of gratitude and love for his sincere and warm friendship for me ; and I pray to the Lord to give you and your children strength to bear this awful affliction. But peace be to his name. He cannot return to us, my dear friend, but let us prepare to meet him in a happy immortality, where the wicked cease to trouble and the weary are at rest. My afflictions and debility admonish me that I shall follow my dear friend very soon, and in the Lord's good time, I hope, my poor sorrowing friend, that you and yours may join us in a better world.

My dear daughter sends you her sympathizing love ; she desires me to tell you that she would write to you, but she is in great affliction herself, having just buried a dear interesting babe. All my household unite with me in sincere and tender condolence to you, on this greatest bereavement that you could receive. Do write soon, for you know that, as long as I live, I will feel the deepest interest for you and your children, and when your mind becomes composed from the awful shock of your great affliction, I would be very happy if you would come and see us, and bring your children with you. The Lord bless you and them.

Your affectionate friend,

ANDREW JACKSON.

To Elizabeth A. R. Linn, St. Genevieve.

FROM MR. BUCHANAN.

LANCASTER, *October 14th*, 1843.

MY DEAR FRIEND,—Last evening's mail brought me the Missouri Reporter, containing the mournful intelligence of your dear husband's death. I can scarcely yet recover from the dreadful shock ; so suddenly, so unexpectedly have I been deprived of a very dear friend, who held as high a place in my warmest affections as any other living man, that I can yet scarcely realize the awful truth. He was indeed every thing which constitutes a man, mild and amiable, with great benevolence of heart ; he was the very soul of chivalry and honor, possessing uncommon talents, and extensive information ; he was one of the ablest and most useful members of the Senate, and yet he was so unconscious of his own great power, his loss to his personal and political friends in that body is irreparable. No man in our country can supply his place. He was the rock against whose firmness the storms might beat and beat in vain, and he was ever as prompt and as decided in sustaining his friends in the hour of need, as in defending himself; and yet in him the elements were so combined, that his political opponents were his warm personal friends, and far beyond all question, he was the most popular man amongst his fellow members in the Senate of the United States. But why need I enlarge upon his merits and his great virtues with melancholy pleasure to the partner of his bosom, who enjoyed his most devoted affection, and who was worthy of it all. It is to express my deep, my heartfelt sympathy for her irreparable loss. I know from her great strength of character and Christian principles, that she will not suffer her mourning for the dead to interfere with her duty to the living, neither will she mourn as one without hope. I know that *he* possessed true religious feelings, and we can cherish the belief that he is now with his Redeemer, which, after all the toil and strife of this troublesome world, is at last the one thing needful. She will live for the instruction and benefit of the pledges of their mutual affection, and if Providence should ever place it in my power to extend a helping hand to her or them, I shall esteem it a heartfelt pleasure, as well as a sacred duty to embrace the opportunity.

I hope to hear from you very soon, and if it is not too great a tax on your feelings, write me something about my dear friend's last days on earth.

With sentiments of the purest respect and highest esteem, I remain your most sincere and sympathizing friend,

JAMES BUCHANAN.

To Mrs. Elizabeth A. R. Linn, St. Genevieve.

FROM THE HON. SILAS WRIGHT.

WASHINGTON CITY, SENATE CHAMBER, *June 7th*, 1843.

MY DEAR MRS. LINN,—My good wife unites with me in offering you our heartfelt thanks for your kindness in complying with our request, to give us some account of the last days that your sainted husband passed on earth; you do not know, my good lady, how much of life and feeling that you throw in your composition, and on such an occasion as that we have called from you the *whole picture* of affectionate domestic life, of sensible, refined feeling, tender honor, and pure integrity, and how suddenly and awfully was the whole enveloped in the sable mantle of death and overwhelming grief. We think that we see and feel it all, and cannot speak of it or write about it without bringing on ourselves the overpowering affliction, which belongs to *his last day on earth*, and I feel incapable of writing to you on the subject as I should do. On our assembling here this session of Congress, Mr. Buchanan and myself found the name of a stranger upon Dr. Linn's seat ; we both felt alike, that we could not have that seat so occupied, and I went to the Senator, Mr. Miller of New Jersey, and he cheerfully exchanged with me, (you remember, the Doctor's seat was between Mr. Buchanan's and mine ?) taking my seat and giving me the Doctor's, which I have occupied this session ; and never do I sit down in the chair or open the draw of the desk, that the memory of my friend is not fresh in my mind, and his image before me as I write every line ; it appears to me that I certainly can see him by raising my eyes from the paper, and so far from feeling any of that awe which such impressions have usually made when strongly pressed upon me, my imagination paints nothing but the intense desire to see that winning smile, meet those soft black eyes, and hear that sweet voice, which for ten years met me in this chamber, and contributed so much to my happiness. This has been a most disastrous session of Congress to me, and I cannot express to you how much I have missed my friend ; yet you can and will understand better than any other person, how much I *feel* his loss, because you know how much our tastes, habits of thought, and manner of business were alike. We both had dear and valued friends in the Senate, but not such friends as possessed the intimacy and warmth of feeling which existed between the Doctor and myself. Many would consider the affection that bound us so strongly together as childish, but we knew that it constituted the richest source of happiness, for the heartiness of it extended above and far beyond politics or party feeling, and cemented our friendship with the most profound feelings in human nature. To be deprived of my friend at such a time, when I was heavily taxing all my humble ability to sustain, with other friends, Mr. Van Buren, was a fearful blow to me ; you, who know my sincere attachment to Mr. B., can well imagine my great disappointment at his not being sustained by the Baltimore Convention. I have watched, with great pleasure, the course taken by your admirable brother, Dr. Relfe, and the two Gen. Dodges, in the midst of dark intrigue, fraud and corruption ; the noble relations of my friend and yourself, stood firm in their principles, fearless of all consequences to themselves, and maintained with unwearied efforts, their noble zeal in the cause of Democracy. How often, in reflecting on their admirable course of conduct, I have felt how proud my friend would have been to behold it. And will not you, my poor afflicted friend, take pleasure in hearing of the noble patriotic conduct of relations that are so dear to you? and I know that you will take a mournful satisfaction, on learning how fully his country appreciated the true greatness of your husband's character. When the Democratic Convention discovered that it was not possible to nominate Mr. Van Buren for the Presidency, there was a unanimous expression throughout that body, that, were the lamented Linn now alive, they would not hesitate to nominate him for the Presidency ; for, without the least doubt, he was the most popular man in the Democratic party. His fine talents, the noble and energetic course that he had taken on the Oregon question, with the devoted friendship of Gen. Jackson, would surely carry him in triumph into the Presidential Chair.—But an all-wise Providence has removed him to a better world, and although we must ever mourn his loss, we should struggle not to murmur at the will of God. Mrs. Wright's health is better than usual, she sends you and your children many affectionate regards. When I reach my quiet home, I will write to you one of my long old-fashioned letters.

Your sincerely sympathizing friend,

SILAS WRIGHT.

To Mrs. E. A. R. Linn, St. Genevieve.

FROM THE HON. RICHARD M. JOHNSON.

WHITE SULPHUR, SCOTT COUNTY, KY.
December 25th, 1843.

MRS. LINN.

My dear friend,—Having just returned home in good health, after an absence of ninety-one days, I cannot omit even now, the attempt of expressing the overwhelming sorrow which I feel on the sudden death of my friend and your loved companion, Dr. Lewis F. Linn. If such a loss can be so deeply felt and acknowledged by his country and those who enjoyed his friendship, how much more afflicting must be the sorrow of one who knew him as her bosom friend. Words are not here necessary to convince you how sincerely I regret your great bereavement, and most truly do I condole with you in your sorrow. I shall ever remember with a grateful heart, his friendship blended with yours, to me, and hold myself ever ready when in my power to serve you. Except yourself and family, no one has met with a greater loss than myself, as I felt for him the affection of a brother. I should do injustice to the subject and my own feelings, to say less.

Wishing you every blessing that life can bestow, I am most respectfully your friend,

RICHARD M. JOHNSON.

FROM MR. CLAY.

ST. LOUIS, *April 17th*, 1846.

MY DEAR MADAM,—In the expectation of leaving this

city in a few hours for Kentucky, I called to see you this morning to bid you farewell, and was very much disappointed in not finding you at home, as I desired to again express to you my high satisfaction in meeting you here, and renewing the agreeable intercourse which I enjoyed in your society in Washington city, and I also wished once more, to assure you of my deep sympathy and condolence on account of your great bereavement. I am thankful that Providence tempers your heavy affliction with circumstances of consolation in your promising children. From what I have heard of your son, I hope that he will maintain and add to the reputation of his father, who was a bright ornament to the highest council in our country, while his exalted benevolence made him a benefactor to the afflicted, and his warm social qualities imparted a charm to society, which was more deeply felt than could be expressed.

Wishing you health, happiness, and lengthened days, I am, dear madam, your sincere friend,

H. Clay.

FROM MARTIN VAN BUREN, EX-PRESIDENT U. S.

Lindenwald, *Nov.* 14*th*, 1843.

Many and sincere thanks to you, my dear afflicted friend, for your kind message and the accompanying paper, containing a brief sketch of the last moments of our departed and much valued friend. Be assured, that the whole country sympathizes with you *deeply* and sincerely, in the great loss which both have sustained. The fame which your lamented husband had already acquired, was sufficient to satisfy the wishes of his friends, and did honor to his State and country ; but it still fell far short of that to which he would have risen, could his valuable life have been spared a few years to you. There is not in my judgment, a public man in the country, whose improvement was more rapid, or whose future prospects were brighter. But Providence has decided otherwise, and it is our duty to submit to His decrees without murmuring. That this, difficult as it is, will by you be performed to the uttermost of human power, no one as conversant with the strength of your mind, and the elevation of your principles as I am, will for a moment doubt.

I shall ever remember with melancholy satisfaction, the short visit it was my good fortune to receive from him, last summer, and which he promised soon to repeat.

Remember me most affectionately to your bereaved children, and be assured, that you and they, will always find a sincere friend, in your obedient servant and friend,

M. VAN BUREN.

To Mrs. E. A. R. Linn.

FROM HON. C. G. ATHERTON.

NASHUA, N. H., *October 18th*, 1843.

MY DEAR MRS. LINN,—Mrs. Atherton and myself have been inexpressibly shocked at seeing in a Boston paper of to-day, intelligence of the death of Dr. Linn. From the effect this event has produced on us, who had the pleasure of counting ourselves among the number of his friends, we can appreciate in a remote degree, the terrible severity with which it must have fallen on the wife of his bosom, and on the children of his love. We will not attempt to suggest those topics of consolation which would bid you strive to overcome such an affliction; but trust, that, with the assistance of that fortitude of character, and reliance on Divine Providence, so eminently yours, Time, the comforter, will soften the sharp and now almost insupportable pang of your sorrow, into a melancholy but pleasing recollection of the noble and amiable qualities of your deceased husband. That manly form,—that countenance radiant with genius, those eyes, beaming with intelligence and spirit, and at the same time with kindness and benevolence—they are all present to our minds. His varied and delightful conversation,—his exquisite taste,—his graceful manners, his love of truth, and scorn of all dissimulation and hypocrisy, his heart, that never seemed to know any other than the noblest impulses—these are with us still. They can never be taken away from the recollections of any that once knew him.

Mrs. Atherton would write to you herself, but has been for several weeks quite ill, from the effects of a severe cough. She sends her warmest love and sympathy.

I cannot conclude without expressing my sense of the loss which the public have sustained. The loss of such a man at any time, would be greatly regretted on public considerations; but it is particularly to be lamented in times like the present, when men of his firmness and integrity, and weight of character, are so important in their influence for good on our country.

It was one of the most gratifying anticipations connected with the senatorial term for which I am elected, that I should have the pleasure of listening to Dr. Linn in public, and enjoying his companionship in private. And in feeling how much I have lost myself, let me again assure you of my condolence in your heavy bereavement.

Remember me affectionately to Augustus, and believe me, my dear madam, your friend and obedient servant,

C. G. Atherton.

To Mrs. E. A. R. Linn.

FROM HON. JOHN HENDERSON.

Pass Christian, Harrison Co., Mississippi,
Nov. 5th, 1843.

Dear Madam,—It has been with unaffected sorrow that I. have heard of your sudden bereavement, in the loss of your honored and worthy husband. Regardless of political differences, there was scarcely another member of the U. S. Senate, for whom I entertained a more cordial attachment. And perhaps there is no other one remaining who had won for himself, of those politically opposed to him, so much of personal regard. And this was the more honorable, as all know who knew him, that he gained nothing of private favor, by any concession or compromise of his principles.

Were it here appropriate to speak of his public worth,—my private opinion, thus privately expressed, however complimentary, would be but cold and heartless sympathy in the deep affliction with which your heart must be penetrated. Testimonials of public esteem you will doubtless see recorded to his memory,—but naught but time can heal the secret grief from such affliction. While yet depressed by *all* the gloomy concomitants of your recent calamity—while pangs of sorrow, seemingly inconsolable, are yet brooding in fresh anguish upon your spirits,—I know, my dear madam, of how little avail are words of condolence. But that little is to soothe and mitigate in some degree, the severest of earthly sufferings. And to this end, the profoundest sympathies of Mrs. Henderson and myself, are tendered you in all sincerity.

With considerations of esteem, I am yours, &c.

John Henderson.

To Mrs. E. A. R. Linn.

FROM HON. W. S. ARCHER.

WASHINGTON, *Feb.* 3*d*, 1844.

MY DEAR MADAM,—A painful and most protracted disease has prevented the execution of my purpose, before getting your enclosure, some weeks ago, even at the hazard of an undue obtrusion on your distress, of conveying to you the sincere expression of my condolence on your *great* and irreparable, and my severe bereavement, recently sustained.

I offer no exhortation on the duty of resignation to decrees, which it is not allotted to our province to scan (still less to question), nor any hope of speedy consolation, I know too well the magnitude of your loss and your appreciation of that loss, to indulge the hope that such topics would be of avail. Resignation comes from time, consolation from the hand which can alone effectively raise up the trodden down by calamity, and pour the healing balm into the wounds of the deeply afflicted.

This resignation and this consolation, I do not permit myself to doubt, are destined to be your portion. They will be sent to you through the reward of those affections, to carry to which I know you are going to devote your time and faculties, to impress on your children both *reverence* and *resemblance* of their father. I could invoke for them no more favorable destiny than the last of these results, and sincere is the satisfaction which it would bring to me to learn of the realization. It can be no ill wish even for my little favorite Mary, that she may resemble a character in which the lion lay down with the lamb spirit was embodied and kept controlled by divine grace.

I cannot forbear to add, that the usage of the Senate not permitting more than two persons to be heard on the occasion of obituary notices, and the second to Col. Benton having been selected with propriety from his native State, I was deprived of the satisfaction I should have found in giving expression to my own feelings, separately from the expression which was given by the Body generally. It only remains for me, dear lady, to express the good wishes for your continued health and restoration to happiness—with which I am most sincerely your friend,

WM. S. ARCHER.

Mrs. E. A. R. Linn.

FROM GEN. E. P. GAINES.

FRANKLIN, TENNESSEE, *October* 31*st*, 1843.

MY DEAR MADAM,—My wife and myself have learned, with deep affliction, the sad bereavement you have sustained in the sudden, the premature death of your excellent and beloved husband. If the heartfelt homage of admiration of his countrymen could soothe the sufferings of those most dear to him in his own Missouri, their afflictions should be light, as their sources of mournful consolation are abundant. It has fallen to the lot of few men in America, and certainly no one west of the mountains, to depart this life more admired or more lamented by the people of the United States, than Doctor L. F. Linn. The name of the village at which I write reminds me of an impression which our journey to Washington some years past, affording me an opportunity of the first intimate personal acquaintance with our deceased friend and yourself, that there was a striking similarity in the minds and moral sentiments of Doctors Linn and Franklin. They were indeed alike in many respects. They were both nature's noblemen. If the people of America, as I am sure the people of the WEST and SOUTH, will long mourn the loss of their talented friend and patriotic Senator, how much more deeply must his bereaved family and neighbors, and his immediate constituents, partake of the heart-rending affliction.

My wife and myself desire to unite in offering to you and your family the slender but sincere tribute of that condolence which springs from the heart of friendship. Our experience, however, assures us that the condolence of friends in such cases is unavailing. *Time* alone, added to the consolations which the Christian religion holds forth to the virtuous and the wise, can heal the wounds inflicted on an affectionate heart by the sudden loss of such a friend.

Time has effected for me what I trust it will ere long accomplish for you and your amiable Mary and your noble-hearted Augustus, and every other member of your family. I have reasoned thus:—If we were truly loved by those we have lost—and that we were so loved, ten thousand proofs rise up in the reminiscences of a single day or an hour, that pure love ever watching over and sustaining us as a guardian angel, could not but embrace and sanction whatever moral or religious remedy is essential or proper to the restoration of our health and happiness here and hereafter.

In conclusion, permit me to assure you, my amiable friend, for myself and my wife, that it will be to us a source of much satisfaction to be always recognized by you and your family as your firm and unwavering friends; and when, as we hope soon to have a house and a permanent residence in St. Louis, we shall take constant pleasure in affording you better proofs than we can in this way impart, of our desire and talent for restoring you to that social mood which has so often contributed to the happiness of all who had the pleasure of your daily attention in the same *drawing-room* and at the same *mess-table* for a winter in Washington : a winter replete with festive and social enjoyments, for a large share of which Mrs. Gaines and myself were indebted to you and your lamented husband. We are, dear madam,

With affectionate respect, your friends,

EDMUND PENDLETON GAINES.

A FUNERAL DISCOURSE

ON THE LIFE AND CHARACTER OF THE HON. LEWIS FIELD LINN, DELIVERED BEFORE THE CITIZENS OF ST. LOUIS, AT THEIR REQUEST, ON SUNDAY, THE 19TH DAY OF NOVEMBER, 1843, BY REV. JOHN H. LINN.

WITH the nation at large we are called upon to lament a very afflictive public bereavement, in the death of a great and good man, Dr. LEWIS FIELD LINN, endeared to us by the important public services that crowned his life, and by the many virtues that so eminently adorned his private character.

But we mourn his departure from among us the more, because the inscrutable event has overtaken us at a time when we looked not for it,—when from the past we were looking with eager anticipation to still more important services ; when it seemed certain to all that much benefit to our common country, and to the interests of our wide-spreading Valley especially, was about to ensue from his personal exertions ; when all eyes and all hearts were turned to him, with a quickened impulse and enlarged desires.

In these circumstances—how suddenly ! in a moment ! have all these hopes been blasted by the melancholy, withering intelligence—not that Dr. Linn was sick, dying —but dead, buried.

It is not for weak, erring mortals, like us, to murmur at a dispensation so dark and mysterious as the abrupt extinction of this steadily burning light in the moral and in the political world. But, while this event has come down upon us, at noonday, like the drapery of midnight, we see upon its ample folds the sublime truth written with the finger of Heaven—"It is of the Lord."

The loss we have sustained is as unspeakable as it is unexpected. It has created a void in our community and a chasm in our affections and attachments, which we can never hope to have supplied. He was not one of those ordinary men, who may disappear from the stage of life, without being missed or regretted, beyond the circle of their private acquaintance, and whose place can be easily supplied from the circle they have left behind. Nor is it scarce enough to say, that he belonged to that more limited class, whose abilities, education, and influence have given them a position in the world that few can hope to attain; but in the combination of intellectual and moral worth, he stood among contemporaries, like Saul among the hosts of Israel. He occupied a place which nothing but intellectual strength and moral greatness could have enabled him to secure, and maintain to the day of his death; and we may affirm that among those who can discern the things that differ, who know how to appreciate intellectual vigor, moral worth, honest independence, practical usefulness, real learning, disinterested generosity, and inflexible integrity, no man was more highly or more justly esteemed while he lived, or more deeply regretted when he died.

To give any suitable delineation of him, is a task to which I confess my inadequacy. I was not privileged with his friendship, and with his acquaintance only partially. If I had known him, I could not speak of him as he ought to be spoken of. I could not speak of him as you would justly expect. I could not speak as my own heart would ardently wish; I could not speak as others, who—I will not say have loved him more, for thousands who have not known him personally, have not loved him the less, but who possess more competency—could and would have spoken of him. This inability I regret the less, because his character, in all its aspects, was familiar to your minds. You knew him well; you loved him dearly; you venerated him highly. Many of you recognized in him the warm, devoted, unchanging personal friend. Many of your fathers and mothers he has visited in the hour of sickness and attended their dying beds; and when skill and attention were unable to save, the sympathies of his generous nature proved unfailing.

I hardly need tell you his character. It had a length and breadth about it, which made it obvious to all. Nothing hidden or equivocal—all wide-open, candid, majestic. There was a magnanimity, a strength, a fulness, a freshness, an originality about his modes of thinking and acting, which were as eminent to the eye of observation as the lineaments of his broad and benevolent face. We employ, too, because of its appropriateness, the language of a writer, whose success in describing character has been unparalleled in the world of letters:

> "This was the noblest Roman of them all:
> His life was gentle, and the elements
> So mixed in him, that nature might stand up
> And say to all the world—*this was a man.*"

As you are informed through the public papers, Dr. Linn was a native of Kentucky. He was born in the year

1795, about four miles from the City of Louisville. The enterprising spirit of his grand-parents had carried them in advance of civilization. In the defence of the frontier settlements from Indian aggression, and in the organization of civil and social society, they were required to act a conspicuous part. His mother was born in the town of Carlisle, in the State of Pennsylvania, and emigrating to Kentucky at an early period, was married to Israel Dodge. She was subsequently married to Ashael Linn, and Lewis was the second of three children by that marriage. Though but a boy at the decease of his father, in the household he had been carefully taught the pioneer virtues of industry, frankness, honesty and firmness, and there mind and body were attaining their wonted vigor together.

Such a period in society might be. thought by some unfavorable to the improvement or development of intellect, but in this commnnity it will not be regarded as without its advantages. If to such a place you transport the little community of an educated domestic circle, and supply it with the inventions, discoveries and histories of man, it is doubtful whether the wisdom of the head as well as the heart would not more expand than in the associations of dense society. In a school where the hardier graces of a man were taught at a period eminently favorable to the production of a simple, resolute and elevated character, Senator Linn had his birth and education.

At that time Kentucky was a border country. The emigrant's axe was just claiming its first trophies. The yell of the savage had not yet died away upon the distant forest. A way had not been opened to refinement. The soil had not yet been taxed to supply the imaginary wants of human society, for such demands are few and simple, and always readily and abundantly supplied. The riotings and excesses of luxury were not known, and no contributions for its insatiate appetite had, as yet, been levied. The high claims of honor, held sacred and inviolate, and not the mere restrictions of law, regulated the intercourse of man with his fellow. The monuments of nature stood undefaced by the aggressions of society, the mis-styled triumphs of man.

There, breathing an atmosphere uncontaminated by the baleful presence of oppression and deceitfulness, of fraud and force, his manly and chivalric spirit flourished on the food afforded, and assimilated more and more to the objects of its contemplation. Inclined to study and reflection, his walk, if not with God, was among the sublime and ennobling forms of his greatness. Upon the vast prairie he stood, and along the banks of the beautiful Ohio he wandered, feeling not only the existence, but the presence of his and their Creator. Thus attended, thus surrounded, he advanced towards the era of majority. We claim for him no academic or collegiate honors; for Academies and Colleges were then scarce thought of in the country west of the Alleghanies; but even at that period his intellect may be thought worthy a comparison with those who may be regarded as favored with more imposing facilities. Superior in strength and singleness of purpose, and in the dignity of his whole moral character, it only remained to be tried whether his mind had capacity to take high intellectual rank.

At the requisite age, he began the study of medicine under the instruction of Dr. Galt, of Louisville, Ky.; and it was there that he made more extensively those acquisitions, not only in science, but in the habits of study, which often lie at the foundation of character as subsequently developed, but which so eminently qualified him for future usefulness. At the request of his half brother,

Henry Dodge, the present Delegate from the Territory of Wisconsin, he visited the then Territory of Missouri, as early as 1812. He returned, however, to Kentucky to resume the study of his profession, and when prepared to practise, revisited and settled in St. Genevieve about the year 1815. From that time to the period when he was appointed one of the Commissioners under the Act of Congress, of 9th of July, 1832, to investigate and report on the French and Spanish claims, he devoted himself with great assiduity to the study and practice of his profession.

Warm and generous in his friendships, none could surpass him in sympathy for the afflicted and suffering, and thus controlled, his attentions were unremitting. To skill that was seldom baffled, there was added this essential qualification of a successful physician—a benevolent heart ; a heart that feels his patient's pain as if it were his own ; that looks on the woe-stricken countenance of a wife, and resolves that, if possible, she shall be saved from the desolateness of widowhood ; that looks on weeping children and resolves that no energy shall be spared in saving them from the orphan's destitution ; that looks at a father's and mother's anguish, and resolves that, God assisting, he will save their child.

It was the enthusiasm of this benevolence that diffused over the whole character of Dr. Linn a sacred splendor—adorned and imbued his whole behavior. Never did the love of ease, or study, or friends, present a single temptation to confine him to his books, or detain him with the society of his companions, or at the convivial feast, when he should be watching by the couch of sickness. His manners, always natural and easy, rendered him not only accessible to all, but so prepossessing and delightful that it was absolutely impossible for any, however circumstanced in life, to feel uneasy or restless in his company. Hence the most unreserved confidence always subsisted between him and his patients; and the memorials of his tenderness and skill are to be found in the grateful recollections of all classes of society, in the entire southern portion of our State. For, however much dissimilar views upon religion and politics may affect the state of society generally, it never lost Dr. Linn one friend, or made him less studious or anxious about their wants.

His reputation as a physician had become so extensive, and the demands upon him so frequent—and he was one of those to whom an appeal was never made in vain—that apprehensions in relation to his health, from fatigues and exposures, induced him to accept the appointment of Commissioner, under the Act of July, 1832. To discharge the duties of his office, he removed to this city, in June, 1833, and though the practice of his profession was not entirely abandoned at this, or any subsequent period, we find him entering a theatre upon which he not only sustained himself creditably, but secured an enviable distinction.

It was said by a celebrated Athenian commander, that it was a reproach to a General to have it to say of any event—"I had not expected it." Such censure could seldom attach to Senator Linn. The success of all that he undertook, evinced the versatility of his mind and the energy of his whole character; and if in the political world he had left no other monument of his wisdom and prudence, than recommending the policy to be pursued by the Government of the United States, in confirming grants to the French and Spanish claimants, he would have been entitled to a high place among sound and practical financiers. But having thus been thrown within the confines of political life, without design on his part, unimpelled by ambition, and uncontrolled by selfishness, a wider sphere of usefulness was opening before him.

It is said that the history of our free institutions is contained in the biography of the great men who conduct State affairs, and as examples of integrity and intellect are frequent or rare in living patriots, so will be the duration or decay of Republics. National character depends upon individual exemplifications. Polished Greece and Imperial Rome owe their distinction to the sovereignty of Genius ; and to their poets, philosophers, legislators, historians and heroes, they have chained their immortality. The glory or shame of nations, then, is established by individuals, not by masses that pass in solemn review before posterity. "Nothing," says the same writer, "tends more to the preservation of a nation's untarnished honor in every trial, perhaps nothing so effectually nerves him for the greatest human exertion for his country, more than that he will, after all is over in the tomb, receive not only the justice, but the chaplet of that tribunal. With this bright vision of the future before him, he will pass in safety through temptation, and present an undaunted front to the perils as well as labors of life."

It is with reference to such results, that you have asked for a delineation of the moral and intellectual features of one who has been pronounced a "model statesman," and whom we pronounce, in all the relations of life, a model *man*. But when the eulogy of your speaker shall have gone down with him in forgetfulness to the grave, the youth of America will find in the archives of their country, in unfading and faithful colors, that likeness, not only as a memorial of one loved and lost, but as an example and model for their study and imitation. Always a child of Providence, he was not required to pass the subordinate drudgery of a politician's life ; having served one session in the Senate of Missouri, he was elevated by the suffrage of Heaven to a place in the highest deliberative assembly in the first Government in the world.

LEWIS FIELD LINN was a statesman of Heaven's own selection. In October, 1833, he was appointed by Gov. Dunklin to supply the vacancy in the Senate of the United States, occasioned by the death of the Hon. Alexander Buckner, and took his seat in that body at the Session of 1833 and '4. It is said that Dr. Linn was unaccustomed to the duties of a Legislator, for he had never made politics his study; but all admit that he showed himself equal to the responsibilities of his unsought and unexpected station. His was not the dreary gradation of a novitiate. Comprehending at once, and as if by instinct, the duties of his new position, he soon acquired an honorable stand among the great men who then sat in that body. The impression that he made in our National Councils was felt at home, and the Legislature of Missouri, at its ensuing session, with scarcely a dissenting voice, expressed its confidence in him as a public servant. He was re-elected by a large majority in 1836 and '7, and again, with the approbation of all parties, in 1842 and '3.

Every distinct period in the history of our country has demanded a peculiar order of statesmen, and required some peculiar endowments in those who hold the helm of State. A bold and fearless spirit was needed to ring the knell of despotism in the ear of iron-handed tyranny; and the thundering voice of an eloquent Henry, breaking upon our Legislative halls, woke into life the previously dormant energies of the American people. A spirit of noble enterprise and bold daring was demanded to be ready to stand on trial before kings, and to meet death in any form, and there was hung before the wondering, anxious gaze of patriotism, like the visioned sheet before the entranced Apostle, a bill of rights to be vindicated, and a bill of wrongs to be redressed, signed by a host of worthies, in flaming capitals, flashing terror into the hearts of the enemies of our country. Subsequently, the times demanded men of steady firmness, of unwavering integrity, of unflinching courage, in whose breast the fire of patriotism was an inextinguishable flame, and the great and good Washington was furnished. The days of the Revolution demanded a peculiar order of men. All the other qualifications of every other age seemed to be required in combination. These men were doubtless made, in part, by the times in which they lived, but they would have been adapted to any age, and would have left the impress of their great minds upon it.

It would be pleasant, but might prove a dangerous task, to mark the distinctive periods of our country's history, and delineate the master-spirits that have troubled or quelled this great political ocean But I may, without fear, proceed to inquire what are the qualifications most needed by a statesman in the times in which we live.

The founders of our Government were distinguished for what is sensible and solid, rather than for what is brilliant ; for the useful rather than the visionary ; for what Mr. Locke calls large, sound, round-about sense, and having fought hard for peace and suffered much, they knew how to enjoy it. But for the last few years, there has been an increasing fondness for political combat and partisan gladiatorship. Now, whatever may have been the causes, and whoever may have been to blame, it is apparent that this spirit of contention and strife has been indulged to a melancholy extent, and that the weapons of war are still kept furbished and ready for use. Having tried these weapons long enough to ascertain that they are used with only the advantage that accrues to an army in a dark night, when the life of friend and foe is indiscriminately endangered, the times demand men of peace—statesmen, distinguished for their frankness, candor, honesty, and forbearance. It is said of Dr. Linn, that "firm, yet conciliating, candid, yet courteous, he sat in the councils of our nation at a time when party spirit ran higher than at any other period in the history of our government, and without compromising one jot or tittle of the principles upon which he had been elected to that high office, he maintained terms of friendship and respect with every member of the Senate, with one exception."

Then Lewis Field Linn was such a statesman as the times required. His kind and generous heart felt that this din of political strife had been heard long enough; that enough of that glory had been achieved which can be secured only by arraying brother against brother, altar against altar, and forum against forum; or by skill in noisy polemics and in harsh denunciation, by rending society asunder, and by triumph when victory is always equal to defeat. It was not the Shibboleth of party that he defended, but the great principles of constitutional liberty as he understood and construed them, for which he was the unflinching and unwavering advocate.

An interesting and characteristic incident is related of him, illustrative of the influence he exerted upon his own and the then dominant party in Congress. A number of bills had been put into his hands by a political friend, affecting important personal and local interests, which he felt, to offer himself, would be to jeopard at least. He took them, and in his usual happy and conciliatory manner, began unfolding the package and addressing himself to their merits, when Mr. Buchanan arose and remarked pleasantly—"Doctor, we'll save you the trouble, if you recommend them, we'll pass the whole bundle." This suggestion was in the same spirit seconded by Mr. Clay. And though all this was done playfully, it shows the estimation in which he was held by personal friends and political opponents.

In debate Dr. Linn seemed unconscious of his own strength, for if in this respect he was not distinguished he possessed some advantages. While he did not obtrude himself into every discussion, as if no question, however trivial, could be settled, until his opinion was given, yet neither did any array of opposition, nor any fear of responsibility, nor any apprehension for his popularity, deter him from taking such part in the most important debates as commended itself to his judgment and conscience. He was an unpretending man and therefore diffident. He seldom ventured to speak, and never until he had possessed himself of the facts, and then he never failed to sustain himself creditably, and his arguments were always heard with great deference. He sought his country's good, not his own promotion. He was scarcely ever provoked to personal invective, but when such circumstances did occur, his sarcasm was bold and withering. It was evident to all that he sought, not to defeat and confound his opponents, much less to degrade them in their own estimation or in the opinion of others, but with a look, manner and language which bespoke his own candor and sincerity, to lead them to his conclusions—and his competency was only paralleled by his faithfulness and untiring industry. Says Mr. Buchanan, the distinguished Senator from Pennsylvania, in a letter of condolence to his family : " He was indeed every thing which constitutes a man ; mild, amiable, and benevolent of heart, he was yet the very soul of chivalry and honor. Possessing uncommon talents and extensive information, he was one of the ablest and most useful members of the Senate, and yet he ever seemed unconscious of his own great powers. His loss to his personal and political friends in that body is irreparable. No man in the country can supply his place. He was the rock against whose firmness the storm might beat, but beat in vain ; and he was ever as prompt and decided in sustaining his friends, in their hour of need, as in defending himself. And yet in him the elements were so combined, that his political opponents were all his friends." He adds—and it is a noble tribute—"Beyond all question, he was the most popular man among his fellow members in the Senate of the United States."

The basis of his well-formed public character was his private virtues. The impression left upon the mind of every one who had intercourse with him for a single hour, was, that he possessed honesty which could not be corrupted—integrity which could not be moved by prosperity, nor shaken by adversity.

His stern and inflexible moral principles were written upon every lineament of his strongly marked countenance—upon every word that fell from his lips, and upon every action of his life, whether as a citizen or public servant.

As the result of this last trait, he was possessed of decision of character. He knew—he felt he was right, and then he was never moved from his course by trifles. When any thing was to be done, he was unwearied until its completion ; and this was the case whether one object, or a multiplicity of cares, pressed upon him. But he was never obstinate ; for his decision, energy and unyielding perseverance, were controlled by the native, unaffected benevolence of his heart. And to the presence of these benevolent affections he was largely indebted for that graceful and easy politeness, that unassuming suavity of temper, which were so conspicuous in his intercourse with society, and which so justly and eminently entitled him to the uniformly and universally recognized appellation—"the peace-loving Senator."

The acquisition of the Platte country, and the bill for the occupation and settlement of Oregon, were the prominent measures introduced, and successfully recommended by him, during his short but useful Congressional career. And his colleague, with becoming magnanimity, has testified that these bills were carried through the Senate at a time, and under circumstances, when the gentleness and firmness, the suavity and energy of Senator Linn, made him alone competent for this splendid achievement. In reference to the character, designs and provisions of the Oregon bill, we give you the language of his colleague: "It was the measure of a statesman. Just to the settler, it was wise to the Government. The settler has a right to have a home in the new country which he reclaims from the wilderness and the savage. The Government of the United States can only save its domain on the Oregon by planting its colonies there. Land is the inducement and the reward to emigration—and that land was granted by the bill—liberally granted to the wife and to the children—to the young man and the widow, as well as to the husband and the father." "That bill," he adds, "is the vindication and assertion of the American title against the daring designs of England, and the only way to save the country. And in the conception and recommendation of this bill, he showed himself alike solicitous to secure personal interests and national honor." Well has it been said that the name of Linn will be identified with the rising, spreading glory of that immense territory.

We have followed Senator Linn through his comparatively brief, but distinguished career; in boyhood, acquiring those habits of mind and body that indicated the promise of his usefulness to the world ; in his profession, with a mind richly stored with general as well as professional information, with a heart alive to all the tender and generous sensibilities of our nature, throwing the drapery of kindness over the chamber of affliction, lighting up a milder sun in the sky overcast with the clouds of misfortune, and searching out the causes of distress that he knew not. Like Job, he was eyes to the blind, and feet to the lame, a father to the orphan, and the widow's friend.

Says my correspondent, " Could the world have seen Dr. Linn's house when his death was made known at St. Genevieve, then indeed would his worth have been appreciated. The rich and poor filled his house and yard, from the town and country, to learn if the melancholy news was true—that their friend, their kind physician for so many years, who never charged the widow or the poor man for his individual services—their benevolent fellow-citizen, who had so often put in jeopardy all he had on earth to save their property, was indeed gone from them for ever. Even the poor Africans, whose sick beds Dr. Linn had watched over many a long and weary night, were seen kneeling around the heart-broken widow and orphan children, begging to know if they could serve them in any way." " Surely," adds my correspondent, " such heartfelt affection for any man, such profound sympathy for his family, could not be manifested more strongly for any person, than was evinced by those who followed him to his last home."

At the call of his country he promptly relinquished his profession and entered upon the duties of a public servant ; as a Commissioner, satisfactorily adjusting antagonist claims, involving important private and public interests ; as a Senator, standing forth on this great theatre, acknowledged by all a great and good man, lending the energies of his mighty mind to defend the institutions of his country from all assaults, both from within and without. Devoted to the interests of his constituents, he showed himself a faithful and industrious Representative.

But while the memorials of his tenderness shall thus be gathered up by his friends, in private life ; while love and affection mourn him, yet not as those who mourn without hope ; while the memory of his devotedness to this wide-spreading valley will be long and tenderly cherished ; while Oregon shall in her orphanage inquire, who will now defend her honor, her character, her interests ?—the records of the Church will testify to his virtues, his spirituality, his devotion to his God.

> " Know ye a Prince hath fallen ? Nature gave
> The signet of her royalty—and years
> Of mighty labor won the sceptred power
> Of knowledge—which from unborn ages claims
> Homage and empire, such as time's keen tooth
> May never waste—yea—and the grace of God
> So witnessed with his spirit, so impelled
> To deeds of Christian love, that there is reared
> A monument for him, which hath no dread
> Of that fierce flame that wrecks the solid earth ! "

Early and favorably impressed with the truths of the Christian religion, a close study of these truths produced, under the influence of the Holy Spirit—as was to be expected in a mind honest and sincere as his—a firm and steadfast faith as to its divine origin and its infinite interests and obligations. And his attachment to the fundamental verities of the Bible became firm and exemplary, and grew in strength and influence to the very close of his life. It is a melancholy fact that many—alas ! too many, of our distinguished men—men who are called by the suffrages of their country to occupy important and commanding positions in society, do not recognize, do not acknowledge the claims of our Holy Christianity. Nor is this, in most instances, accompanied by a wanton and wilful rejection of its truths, or an utter disregard of its appeals—or a contempt for its institutions—but, involved in multitudinous political cares, they at first find but little time, and subsequently less disposition, for matters affecting their souls' destiny ; while a few rashly prefer the glory of a day to that which lasts for ever. Not so with Dr. Linn. In the principles of the Christian faith, and in the sanctions of the Christian religion, he matured his character, secured his happiness, and founded his hopes.

The details of his conversion I have not been able to obtain. His avowed and decided preference for the Rev. Mr. Cookman, then chaplain to Congress, and pastor of one of the Methodist churches in the city of Washington, induced him in the winter of 1839 to wait upon the ministry of that great and good man, whose melancholy fate he deplored so deeply, and with whose sainted spirit he is now enjoying delightful communion before the throne of God. On the fifth day of April, of that year, he joined the M. E. Church, and from that period to the day of his death devoted much of his time to religious purposes—to the study of the Bible and the perusal of religious books.

With the minute details of his religious experience I am as unacquainted as with those of his conversion. On these points of his personal history and feelings, he was constitutionally and habitually reserved ; but when circumstances elicited remark, he was frank, and in these particulars manifested the simplicity of a child. But the genuine proofs of religion were visible to those who knew him best, and could but command their esteem and love, notwithstanding any occasional infirmity or manifestation of frailty they might discover. As a Christian, he was alike uncompromising in reference to the doctrines or duties of his faith. His experience, so far as I can learn, was not the mere triumph of joyous feeling, directly excited in the soul by an indication or act of overwhelming mercy, without any particular mental exertion or the application of sacred truth. God often vouchsafes these blessings to minds that need them—whose intellectual faculties have been so untrained, or so unfurnished with materials, as to render them most accessible to the consolations of Christianity by immediate agency on the affections. Thus the Almighty affords help and comfort to all, be their mental structures and attainments what they may. With Dr. Linn, religion was a triumph of principle, rather than the predominance of powerful emotion. Hence, he lived humbly—very humbly—and retiringly as a Christian, and as a Christian ought to live, yet very majestically, also, if I may so speak. Through the grace which was upon him—grace which could act in that particular only on a mind like his own, strong, vigorous, accustomed to close study, familiarized by habit to the most sublime and heavenly views of truth. Though well informed and firm in his religious opinions, it is not necessary for me to say that a mind so well balanced, a heart so thoroughly controlled by gentleness and kindness, could never forget the lofty and commanding position of the Christian in the restrictions of a mere sectarian. No! his was a pure catholic spirit.

For the last several months he was peculiarly thoughtful and heavenly minded. A temporary but severe indisposition, early last spring, left him with the radical and permanent impression that he would not long survive. This impression he often communicated to his family, always accompanying it with a desire to have his worldly affairs well arranged, and himself in preparation for another existence. "On the 28th of last April," says my correspondent, "late at night, he desired that his household should be called together, and, with his wife and children by his side, kneeling, in a most fervent and devout manner he dedicated himself and them to the Great Head of the Church—that, whether they lived, they should live unto the Lord, or whether they die, they should die unto the Lord ; that, whether they live therefore or die, they should be the Lord's." That solemn scene will not soon be forgotten. An offering was laid upon that altar, the perfumes of which have left a delightful fragrance behind, and in years to come, when memory shall recall that scene, how like an angel will he rise up from the dominions of death, the very personification of love, of generosity, of kindness, of friendship, of truth and heavenly ardor. But in an effort to delineate his religious character, I find myself invading that sacred enclosure, the domestic circle, where every step must wring out tears and press the bleeding hearts of the widowed and fatherless ones. Oh ! would to God that I could now retire, and let the Guardian Angel, with a feather plucked from his own bright silvery wing, describe the scenes of reciprocated tenderness and love that made his home an earthly Paradise. The image is present to my own mind with all the glowing freshness of life. Here are combined, like nestling seraphs, the graces of moral beauty, the breathing forms of holy friendship and mutual love. The majesty and dignity of giant mind turning aside from the world eager to do it homage, bending in admiration over the gentle flower at his side, while the cherub faces and merry tones of early childhood exhibit such a vision of felicity as to be cherished, loved, almost adored—while upon this already hallowed scene religion throws its radiance, like a stray sunbeam, piercing the drifted cloud and opening up another day.

This state of uninterrupted domestic bliss was the result of the happy and appropriate marriage, in 1818, of Dr. Linn and the only daughter of Mr. John Relfe, a lawyer of distinguished abilities from the State of Virginia, who died in early life, leaving but two children, Mrs. Linn and Dr. James H. Relfe, a Representative now in Congress from Missouri. Of his immediate relations, Dr. Linn left one own sister, a half-brother, Hon. Henry Dodge, and a half-sister, Mrs. Nancy Sefton, with their families, to all of whom he was tenderly attached, and among whom he felt and made no distinction. Of a large family of children, Dr. Linn left but two, a son and daughter, to mourn their loss, and soothe by their society and sympathy the aching heart of a widowed mother. God bless thee, Augustus ! God bless thee, Mary ! Yours is a rich inheritance—in your veins is coursing in blending currents the blood of a patriot and a Christian. Upon your destinies rest the blessings of a sainted father. In your behalf is enlisted the sympathy of the Church. Hearts, fond hearts, are beating high for you—prayers, warm and earnest, are offered up for you. Voices, glad voices, will welcome you at the threshold, and cheer you through the pathway of life. Go, be ornaments of society—go, and may that God who has promised to be a Father to the fatherless, shield and protect you !—go, imitate the virtues of one loved and lost !—go, and let the dawning graces of youth reflect, as in a mirror, to the anxious eye of your widowed mother the light of him who was her protector through life—whose tenderness and care constituted her sum of happiness, and who, connected with this, has only one other source of comfort—the religion of Christ. An illustrious instance for condolence and comfort is furnished us by the last words of that distinguished statesman, whose melancholy fate our country will never cease to deplore—Alexander Hamilton: "Remember," said he, with the utmost composure, to his wife, almost frantic with grief, "remember, my Eliza, you are a Christian."

The accounts published of the last moments of Dr. Linn are substantially, though not minutely, correct. Up to the evening of the 2d ultimo, he was in the enjoyment of unusually good health. Having just arrived at home, on the day previous, after an absence of twelve days, he was busily engaged in arranging some private papers, intending on the next day to visit St. Louis. During that day he had indulged much anxiety in relation to a private paper of considerable importance, that he apprehended had been mislaid. Late in the afternoon, in stooping to search a trunk, he raised his head suddenly and asked Mrs. Linn, who had been assiduously engaged in assisting her husband, if his face was not very much flushed, as he felt exceedingly dizzy, and there seemed to be a general determination of blood to the head. The painful sensation, however, passed off, and he resisted the suggestion that he should be bled during the evening, and to a late hour at night he was engaged in correspondence and in conversation with his family, whose society, he said, never seemed so sweet as upon that evening. When he retired, he was indisposed to sleep, but did not complain of being unwell. As the morning dawned, he remarked that he felt unusually sleepy. His wife, who had been accustomed to watch over him with sleepless vigilance for years, when there was the slightest indication of indisposition or undue nervous irritation, proposed to write the letters that he had dictated, and watch over him, that he might not be disturbed by the approach of any one. Whilst thus employed, she frequently turned and gazed upon him to see if he was awake—but he slept on, gently and quietly as an infant. Having finished the correspondence, and being much fatigued and oppressed for want of sleep, she concluded she would lie down by his side, to be ready, when he awoke, to wait upon him herself, as he had affectionately requested. As she drew aside the curtain to look again upon the calm and tranquil features of her loved husband—quick as thought, a dark, death-presaging shadow passed over his face! For a moment she was transfixed. It was not the painful apprehension that she was watching by the bed of death, that converted that fearful expression into the precursor of dissolution. Others might have seen it and no fear been started; but a woman's love, a wife's tenderness, marks the first indication of death, and, sleepless and vigilant, she is ever found ready to catch upon her lips the last faint breath. With Mrs. Linn vigilance had become habitual; a moment's relief suggested that all her fears might be groundless. But another look, and though her loved husband still breathed on, confirmed her fears that life, gradually sinking down into the horizon of death, was throwing its melancholy farewell rays in golden beauty over the unconscious sleeper. The agonizing cry soon filled the chamber of the dying husband and father, not only with the inmates of the family, but sympathizing friends, among whom was Dr. Sargeant, who providentially passed the house at that moment, and who was by his bedside only to see him draw a few faint breaths; and then, without a struggle or a sigh, he exchanged a life full of honors, on earth, for an eternal life, full of glory, at the right hand of God.

It certainly would have been gratifying to the Church and to his friends, to have had his dying testimony; yet this could not be necessary for the assurance of his peaceful end and eternal felicity. "They that live well shall die well," has become a religious maxim, incontestably proved by Scripture authority. Unwavering faith, ardent love, uniform piety, are the only necessary, the most desirable assurances, of a peaceful and happy death. But I will indulge no further comment upon this afflicting and unexpected dispensation. A minister of the religion of the blessed Prince of Peace, I will stoop over the bereaved, the sorrowing, the heart-stricken, and administer the consolation of the Gospel that hath brought life and immortality to light. I will suppress my own sighs and teach them to say—"It is of the Lord, let him do with us as seemeth good in his sight." I will lean over affection's dismantled harp in sad, heart-burdened silence, and point to the spirit-land where its notes in unbroken harmony will mingle with the songs of immortality. A minister of peace, I would stand upon the gloomy confines of the damp, dark grave, with the Bible in my hand, read from its heaven-inspired pages these ever enduring lines—words that shall survive when the grass has withered and the flower faded :—"Blessed are the dead that die in the Lord, even so saith the Spirit, from henceforth they cease from their labors, and their works do follow them."

The following eloquent tribute to the worth and memory of Dr. Linn fell from the lips of Col. Rollins, a whig member of the Missouri Legislature, twelve years after Dr. L. had passed away :—

Mr. Rollins said he had just heard the bill read, and his attention was called to it by the mention of the name of Lewis F. Linn. His heart was always touched, when the memory and services of our distinguished men, who had passed from the stage of action, were brought in review before him, and by none sooner than by the name of Lewis F. Linn!

Mr. Rollins said he had enjoyed but a slight personal acquaintance with that good and noble man; but it was one of the pleasing memories of his life, the day that he formed his acquaintance, now twenty-four years ago, almost a quarter of a century. Mr. R. said when he was a youth, having just left college, he paid his first visit to Jefferson City. On the hill, near the Governor's house, stood the old capitol of the State. The General Assembly was in session. Dr. Linn was a member of the Senate, the most graceful, elegant and accomplished gentleman of that body. Mr. R. said he remembered his warm and cordial reception, when he was introduced to him. An impression had been made upon his youthful heart which would never be effaced. From that time he had watched with solicitude and deep interest the career of Dr. Linn. After having served Missouri faithfully and honorably as a legislator, a vacancy occurring in the U. S. Senate, in consequence of the death of Senator Buckner, he was transferred by the appointment of Governor Dunklin, to that body. He entered that forum of distinguished men a stranger, but on account of his high and chivalrous impulses, his noble and manly bearing, the beauty and gracefulness of his whole character, he won at once an enviable position in the Senate; and Mr. R. said he would venture to say that few men had exerted a wider influence over the deliberations of the American Senate, for the length of time that he remained there, than Dr. Linn. He was a poet as well as a statesman; his character became national, and he was not only respected but beloved by all who knew him. He was twice elected to the Senate, and almost without opposition. Whilst there, and up to the day of his death, his energies and best efforts, in the vigor and prime of manhood, were devoted to the promotion of the interests of the people who had thus honored him. He was loyal and faithful to Missouri ; he was alive to every thing that concerned her honor, her prosperity and her glory, and the National statute book abounds with many acts, of which he was the author, and intended to promote our advancement.

It is appropriate, on this occasion, to mention at least one of those acts. I refer to that by which the Platte purchase was attached to our State. Without doing injustice to the honorable efforts of others, he might be permitted to say, that we were more indebted to Dr. Linn and Gen. Ashley for this beautiful addition to our State, than to any other persons. And Mr. R. said if this was all, it was sufficient of itself to entitle him to the lasting gratitude and affectionate remembrance of our people.

Look to the Platte—the six splendid counties of the Platte country—the El Dorado of our State, the most fertile and beautiful portion of Missouri—he might say of the Mississippi Valley—he might say of the Union ; a land flowing with milk and honey, as rich as the valley of the Nile, and as charming to the vision as that which opened upon the sight of Moses, when he beheld the bright and lovely heritage which God had given him. For this addition to our State, now filled with a rich, intelligent, and powerful people, we are chiefly indebted to the active zeal and devoted patriotism of Lewis F. Linn ! And now we are asked, through his warm personal friend, whilst he lived, (Mr. Bogy,) to make a small appropriation out of the overflowing treasury of this same people, whom it so much delighted him to serve, to be expended to protect from the rude decay of time the chaste and beautiful monument, erected by the hand of taste, and which marks the spot that contains his ashes. Sir, let the bill pass, and let there be no dissenting voice!

One other remark, Mr. R. said, and he was done. We are too careless and indifferent in treasuring the memory of our departed statesmen—those who aided in laying the foundations of society on this great river, and to whom we are indebted for the very State government under which we live, and have grown and prospered.

"Forget not the faithful dead" is a holy and pious sentiment, which should be deeply engraven upon the heart of every cultivated people; and it is as much by the observance of its sacred injunction, that we ourselves will be remembered and honored hereafter, as by the physical improvement of our country, and the building of it up, in all the arts of civilized life. What steps have we as yet taken to rescue from the deep sea of oblivion, the great deeds of the early pioneers of our State? Where is the Historical Society of Missouri? and where are the monuments which a grateful people have raised to perpetuate the noble deeds of the Boones, the Callaways, the Coopers, the Bartons, the Clarks, the Ashleys and the Millers of our State? These men have passed from the stage of action,

> "And memory o'er their tombs no trophies raise."

Sir, this should not be. And in passing the bill introduced by my friend from St. Genevieve, reviving as it does a recollection of the virtues of the lamented Linn, let a kindlier patriotism animate our breasts, that at no distant day we may discharge the heavy debt of gratitude due to the memory and character of other departed pioneers and statesmen.

BALTIMORE, *Oct.* 21*st*, 1843.

MY BELOVED FRIEND,—Would that it were in my power to offer consolation, that would reach the heart of one so deeply afflicted; but, my very dear friend, at the present moment I feel convinced that words were but mockery, and human sympathy vain, in view of your bereavement.

Most sincerely do I mourn with you the irreparable loss that you have sustained. The chasm has not been confined to your own bosom; the whole community feel the void that death has made, in removing from society the example of one so highly gifted in all the associations of public and private life; many, many hearts sympathize with you at this moment, but alas! the wound is too recent to admit of present tranquillity; the lacerated heart feels the insufficiency of human aid.

But, my loved friend, when the fount of earthly comfort fails and every stream is dry, we know that there is a still higher source, an inexhaustible fount of consolation in the love of Jesus. Yes, I am assured that you have often applied to that source, and from sweet experience can testify to the efficacy of its healing power. "The fountain of living waters, which if any man drinks thereof, he shall thirst no more for ever."

I do most fervently recommend my beloved friend unto Him, in whose hands are the issues of life, unto our all-sufficient God and Saviour, who alone can dry the falling tear, and soothe the lacerated bosom.

Oh! may the Sun of righteousness arise, with healing on his wings, and illumine this dark dispensation of his Providence; as with a ray of light drawn from the fount of love, impress upon the wounded heart resignation to the will of God.

Oh! my dearest friend, what a blessed hope is the

Christian's; to be enabled to look beyond this fleeting scene, and triumph over death and the grave; even from this valley of tears and mortal suffering, to behold eternal life, our own unmingled bliss for evermore in the presence of our God. Could we but fully realize this glorious prospect, oh! how greatly would it tend to reconcile us to our present warfare; we should then be enabled to place a proper estimate upon the transitory things of time and sense, and be more occupied in laying up the imperishable riches of eternal life; we should even, with the Apostle Paul, "be willing to rejoice amid tribulation, believing in the sanctifying influence of its effects upon the heart."

But it is not for me to teach you these spiritual truths, so precious to the Christian, so consoling to the mourner.

Present me very affectionately to dear Mary and Augustus. I trust that they may be ever found walking in the footsteps of their exalted father, reflecting the light of his many eminent virtues, beloved and useful members of society. They have indeed a rich patrimony to boast of, in the unblemished character of their honored father,—rich in every virtue that could adorn the man and the Christian.

How is your health at present, my dear Mrs. Linn? I hope it may not suffer under your many trials. You have a great deal to live for, and every exertion will be necessary on your part; for the sake of your precious children, you will have to exert every energy of your gifted mind. You will have to recollect also that you are now their all in all as regards earthly prospects; this consideration will strengthen you to bear up your fortitude, so that they sink not. Dear Mary is now of an age that requires all your attention, all your fond solicitation. Youth, beauty, and innocence require a guide, a mother's fostering care;

and Augustus—what could he do without you? And your friends that love you dearly. Dearest Mrs. Linn, reflect upon all this, and endeavor to preserve your health for all our sakes.

I hope Augustus has entirely recovered ere this—a present comfort near you. May God preserve and bless you all, and prove to you a help in time of need, prays your devoted friend,

JACQUELINE S. PENDLETON.

P. S.—And now, my dear friend, permit me to offer you my society, any time this winter, if it can be of the least gratification to you.

I shall await your wishes, and fly to your loved presence immediately, if my suggestion claims your approval; for language would be inadequate to express the gratitude I should experience in being the slightest comfort to you. Any way that I can serve you, command me, and be assured, dearest lady, my love is deep and lasting.

J. S. P.

ST. LOUIS, *Oct.* 13*th*, 1843.

MRS. ELIZABETH A. R. LINN,

MY DEAR MADAM,—In this season of deep affliction, my own feelings of personal friendship for yourself and family, as well as my duty to you as your pastor and spiritual guide, induces me to present my sympathy and some effort to aid in your consolation and support. The information of your husband's death fell, even upon us, as a sudden bolt from heaven, that we could hardly believe. And how much more severely must it have fallen upon a tenderly attached wife, and fond children. The circumstances are of a peculiarly painful kind, under which we learn he departed, with no previous warning to excite apprehension in your minds, and gradually prepare you for the loss you were to sustain ; not to be with him in the last expiring struggle, to speak, to hear his voice, to say farewell, or even while the spirit yet remained to lay your hand upon his brow. These are severe trials to the affectionate heart. But then, we must not look at the painful things alone. Sudden death, if we are prepared, is not in itself to be lamented. The suffering cannot be great, seeing it is one expiring effort and the cord is loosed. Better than the days and weeks of protracted anguish, which we are called often to witness without the ability to relieve. The spirit has been called into another part of the region governed by the same eternal king. I trust you are able from the knowledge of his inward workings to find evidence on which to hope, if not confidently believe that, though full of sin, he rested on the friend of sinners, who saves even to the uttermost, and now dwells with him. My lack of opportunity to know his mind prevents my aiding you in reference to this. I only know that the plan of salvation he understood, and well knew from whence deliverance must come.

But you feel that you are left with your orphans alone ; a cold, bleak world, which no sun can ever thaw or warm and clothe with flowers and verdure again, is all your mind rests on here. But sorrow blears our mental vision, and we are unable to see in its extremity the good that remains. Your children are here, and drawn the nearer because you are all of their parents left ; your friends, those really so, will not be driven off but drawn the nearer by your trials. The Saviour has not died or departed ; he who mingled his tears with those of Martha and Mary, when they wept over the untimely grave of a dear brother, is here to weep with you. There is no tear you shed he does not see, no ache of your heart he does not know; although exalted he is still accessible and is still unchanged. He counts the sighs of his children, and when their spirits are overwhelmed within them, he knows their path and adjusts the time and measure of their trials, with the same precision that he weighed the mountains in scales and hills in a balance, and meted out the heavens with a span. There is no tenderness like to that which God exercises toward his children, more than the compassion of a mother for her sucking child. Then, dear madam, carry to him your sorrows, those which you can't express to friends, that words fail to convey, with the assurance that he understands them all and sympathizes with you. If these trials thus draw you nearer to the great comforter, you will yet rejoice with David that you have been afflicted.

There are great blessings in affliction. The greater part of the promises in the Bible are directed to those who are afflicted. These, in our prosperity, remain shut up; we know them, and believe they are true, but cannot realize them in all their fulness and sweetness till affliction comes. The Lord says, "Call upon me in the day of trouble, and I will deliver." That is a city of refuge, shut up, until the hour of our calamity comes, but then we flee to it, and God is *our* God because we are in trouble. We are but pilgrims and strangers here, yet we grow fast to this earth, and forget that city whose maker and builder is God. Yet we must soon remove, and hence the trials sent seem to be to undermine the foundation we are so prone to lay here. Had Israel been in prosperity when Moses and Aaron came to them to tell them of Canaan, they would never have consented to go out of Egypt with him; but he prepared them by bondage and cruel oppression, weaning them from the land they inhabited, and making them willing to be gone. Thus God here reduces our comforts, cuts our ties, and prepares us for our removal to that city that hath foundations.

May the Lord abundantly bless, and console and sanctify you, that you may greatly rejoice in him here, and with those you love be happy in his presence for ever. Please present my love to your good mother if with you, and to the children.

With much affection,

Your pastor,

WILLIAM S. POTTS.

MY OWN DEAR FRIEND,—It is with truest sorrow, that we have heard the melancholy intelligence of the death of Dr. Linn. Believe me nothing could have occasioned deeper feeling with me, not only in reference to the long and sincere friendship which has existed between us, but more especially on account of the deep poignancy, which must have been reflected on a heart like yours, at the loss of one so truly excellent and in all the pride of honored worth. I know from my own sad experience, that our grief may be such as to incline us to shrink, even from the approach of friendship, and I know, too, that there is but little power in human consolation to mitigate the anguish of so hard a trial. May He, who in his inscrutable providence has thus afflicted, support and console you. The consolations of religion, and the healing influence of time, can alone soothe the bereaved and heart-stricken mourner. My thoughts have been much with you, dear Mrs. Linn, and with those thoughts there have mingled bright memories of other days, when we were all so happy together in Washington. My own blessed home, in which we found those abundant measures of happiness, which are looked for in vain elsewhere. Death made an inroad on them. My beloved incomparable brother, and then my precious father were taken from me. My heart rebelled and I asked, why was the angel of death sent, to change our happy home into a house of mourning? I did not know then, nor do I now, but there is one who does know; whose will I dare not question, any more than I can question his infinite goodness and mercy to us all. My dear mother's health continues very infirm; she is still a helpless invalid, whose only change of place is from her bed to "the old arm chair." It is now almost three years since she was first attacked, and the origin of all her sickness was the shock upon her nerves, occasioned by the sudden death of my father. I do not think that she is any worse within the last six months, although her physicians will not say that there has been any real change for the better; and yet there are sometimes whole days in succession, when she will appear so much recovered that our hopes and spirits rise in proportion, and we think she must be getting well again. She is now an absorbing interest with us all, and every little arrangement in our way of life depends upon her daily health, which varies more or less, as time rolls on. No murmur escapes her lips; she is the most patient and resigned spirit that ever lived, and we have a consolation above all this world can offer in her entire resignation to the divine will, and perfect assurance of a happy immortality, when she shall be summoned to bid a last farewell to all human sorrow. I am now writing in her room, and she bids me say, how deeply she mourns with you in this sudden bereavement of him, for whom we have always felt the strongest regard. The scene of your first distress is constantly before me, and I have wished that I could be with you, to soothe in some measure by my sympathy your heart's grief.

My mother and sisters unite with me in tenderest love to you and Mary. Pray write to me, whenever you feel sufficiently composed to do so, and always, my dear Mrs. Linn, believe me, very truly and affectionately,

Your friend,

ELIZABETH KANE.

NEW YORK, *Nov.* 1*st*, 1843.

From a lady, who was a great belle in the days of Gen. Washington, and often graced his drawing-room while he was President.

CUMBERLAND, ALLEGHANY COUNTY, MARYLAND,
October, 23*d*. 1843.

MY DEAR, DEAR FRIEND,—I will no longer withhold from you the expression of the deep sorrow that has so unexpectedly overtaken me. I should have done it long since, but the fear of aggravating and opening wounds I want to heal. This very day, if seventy winters had not beat upon my head, I would fly to you, you have ever felt like a daughter to me, and am I never to see her more and hear her sweet voice and converse. Although our acquaintance was made in Washington, where there is so little real friendship. The disparity too in our years. Yet we met in each other those indescribable requisites that formed the basis and union of affection, that neither distance nor time can lessen. Oh, how can I name him, who was the first connecting link to our happiness with each other. I was counting the days when I might expect him. I am sure he told you of the interesting interview we had; our parting was more like an own mother with her son; he took me in his arms, embraced me, and we invoked God to bless each other: little did I dream it was for the last time. I felt contending emotions; there was a sadness, a feeling I could not account for, when my tears flowed so unbidden before the distinguished friends he brought with him, to see his favorite relative, as he termed me. Could you be invisible, and see me seated between the pictures of our departed husbands; they seem to smile upon me, and if they could speak I know would chide me for the vain tears I shed. This sad intelligence was conveyed to me on Sunday week coming out of church; my children and friends, as they collect any further particulars from the papers, send them to me, but as yet they are unsatisfactory. I cannot ask you to give me the melancholy particulars, but will you get some friend to do it for you. I was going to write to my friend General Dodge, but on reflection remembered he was in Iowa.

I have kept all his letters to me, even the envelopes. The pen I hold in my hand was given me by him; I should like to have one of those dear curls, if ever so small. But I am wrong; I only add to your distress.

Now, let me entreat you to live for your sweet Mary and your noble Augustus. Be reconciled to the will of our heavenly Father. He will be your comforter amid the fiery trials that are about your path. Time, I know from experience, will do much for you. I was just having a beautiful pair of thread mitts ready for you and sweet Mary when you came. Pray, my dearest Mrs. Linn, excuse all inaccuracies in these sad pages; they have cost me many tears. I feel assured many of your good friends from every direction have flown to you; I feel as if I must embrace you—but to mention even my wish to go to you, my children would think me crazy. I must say farewell, oh, farewell for ever I fear,

MARY LYNN.

Just as I was about sealing my letter, the servant brought me your sweet communication; alas, a bitter sweet, but oh, it is sweet to know that in the saddest hour of distress, you thought of your aged far distant friend. I see your dear brother has franked it. I knew he would fly to you, and that dear mother. Oh, try and be comforted,—how many are left destitute! As you have known many in Missouri, I am sure, yes, and your house was their home, you and your children will be followed by their prayers. I can add no more.

M. LYNN.

PHILADELPHIA, *October 17th*, 1843.

MY DEAREST AUNT,—The mournful intelligence of the death of my beloved Uncle Lewis has just reached me. I seek to offer no consolation for a calamity so distressing; but I claim the right of mourning with you and my dear cousins. Language, at least as I could use it, would fall short of portraying the agony I feel on this occasion. I am called upon by the ties of kindred to mourn for one who has watched over me in sickness and distress; who has rejoiced with my joy and sympathized with my sorrows; who, when my spirits have been almost broken, has cheered me on and pointed out the correct path; who has always been kind, and whose assistance I have so effectually felt.

Last spring a fine son was added to my fortunes, whom I called Lewis Linn. Of this he knew nothing, and I hoped to meet you all this winter and present his namesake.—O Heaven! how vain are mortal wishes! and the presence of my boy is but the remembrance of distress.

My dear Aunt, I cannot but trust that our Almighty

Father, in depriving you of a beloved husband, has armed you with a fortitude supporting the affliction. Let us remember that we are in His hands, creatures of His will, and it becomes us to bow in humility to His mandates.

It would be a melancholy satisfaction to be informed as to how he died, and what the particulars of the case were, for I have seen nothing but newspaper paragraphs.

I will write you again very soon. Please give my love to my dear cousins Augustus and Mary; and may God in heaven bless you, my dear Aunt, is the sincere prayer of

Your most affectionate Nephew,

WM. P. MCANTHONY.

Mrs. E. A. Linn,
St. Genevieve, Mo.

WHEELING, *Sunday, October 15th*, 1843.

MY DEAR MADAM,—How solemn and impressive is the lesson we are taught by the sad tidings announced so feelingly in your respected brother's letter of the 5th to your Uncle Joseph! Truly, "In the midst of life we are in death."

Little did I imagine a few days ago, when addressing you, and communicating the fact that death's messenger had visited my little family, that so soon, so *very* soon, you would be called upon to sustain the severest bereavement which an all-wise, but all-merciful Creator can inflict upon the creature.

I know how little words (which would tend to soothe and comfort under an ordinary bereavement) will avail in expressing the deep sympathy I feel for you in your affliction, and how slight their influence will be in ameliorating the anguish you must suffer under this dispensation of a Good Providence; and yet, in His infinitely wise ordering, the very traits in the character of your lamented husband, which make your loss so irreparable, furnish some consolation. The elevation of his character, the purity and consistency of his life, the delightful amiability which characterized his intercourse with his fellow-men, heightened in an eminent degree in intercourse with each and every member of his family, cannot fail to exert a soothing influence.

In shedding tears to his memory, you necessarily cherish a lively recollection of his virtues. Thus an overruling Providence makes the afflictions with which he visits his creatures furnish to some extent an alleviation.

Death, in taking from us those we love, seems to prepare the way for an easy transit from this world of care. Each messenger from him lessens our ties to earth, and strengthens those for eternity. *They* have gone before—*we* prepare to follow after. Such is doubtless the intention of the Great Ruler ; and, in bowing with humble submission to his will, we will be strengthened and prepared for the great change which awaits us all.

Accept, my dear Mrs. Linn, my most sincere condolence in the affliction which you have suffered. That you may be supported in the bereavement you have sustained by Him who has promised to be a comforter in every time of need, that blessings may be bestowed upon yourself and your children ; that the same delightful harmony, so happily subsisting between you and your departed husband, may characterize *your* and *their* relations with each other, is the anxious desire, the sincerest wish of your friend,

S. BRADY.

Mrs. Linn.

Please remember me kindly to your mother. We are all well at present.

WHEELING, *October* 17*th*, 1843.

The intelligence of your heart-rending bereavement has just reached me. Oh! my dear coz, how deeply and truly do I sympathize with you! yet none but those that have felt the anguish of a widowed heart, can know how little consolation the sympathy of friends affords us in so trying an hour. It is then, and only then, we feel our own insignificance. How thy hand humbles, O death! and nothing short of the omniscient power that wields the mighty sceptre can heal the wound it inflicts. It was to God alone, my dear Elizabeth, that I looked for comfort, and it is to his almighty goodness and mercy I recommend you to look for help and succor. But I presume this you know yourself; and if the sympathy of friends can afford you any comfort, I can assure you that you have it. I am at a loss to know what to say on the melancholy subject. To enumerate the many manly virtues of your beloved husband, and to remind you of the deep hold he had on the hearts of all that knew him, would only aggravate your feelings; for the greater his merits, the greater your loss. I hope you will try and bear it with fortitude, for your dear children's sake. They, and your mother, and brother, will constitute your only earthly comforts; and for them let me conjure you to bear up and struggle against any inordinate indulgence of grief. It was a long time before I could bring my mind to say, "It is the Lord, and let his will be done." Our troubles and afflictions in this world have induced me to believe that the Almighty, through love and mercy, takes those who are his *especial favorites* out of it, and that it is sinful for us to wish them to remain. I can see almost daily his tender mercy in withdrawing my dear husband to himself. He was too pure and sensitive to struggle with a cold, unfeeling world, and never could have survived the many inconveniences and mortifications that he would have had to encounter in settling his affairs ; and you cannot perhaps now see why it was that He thought proper to separate you and your dear companion, who have ever been so happy ; yet the time, I believe, will come when you will think it was for the best.

I have been afflicted with a weakness for nearly three months, that has confined me to the house, and a great part of the time to bed, and I am now but very little better. You will therefore excuse my poor attempt at offering you any thing like comfort, as I feel my perfect inability to do so ; and I have, moreover, had a trying time in parting with my two daughters and my son-in-law. They left here a few days since for their residence in Mississippi. Sophy accompanied Mr. Stanton and Jane, and it seems to me "the glory of my house hath departed," and I feel almost as wretched as if I'd have buried them. They will, however, return next summer.

Mr. and Mrs. Steenrod have lost their babe ; it was about three months old when it died. Mrs. S. intends going on with Mr. S., as she has nothing now to keep her at home. Your friends are all well except Aunt Eliza. She is very feeble and has a bad cough, and I understood to-day that she was confined to bed. Mary Brady has lost her little son. Bolton Caldwell and Phebe Pearce left here last week for Vicksburg. Bolton improved very much whilst here ; he was a perfect skeleton when he arrived. Cousin Jemmy is now in St. Louis ; also Caroline's husband, Mr. Wilson, has gone there to hunt a home. Cousin Lizzy Caldwell was in from Zanesville, and spent a few weeks in the summer with us ; she looks very well. Her father, Judge Harper, has just been elected to Congress. Aunt Fanny is enjoying her usual health. Cousin John and Mary were here a few evenings since in pretty good health, and spoke of you in the most feeling manner. They are truly a worthy couple. To my dear Aunt give my most affectionate remembrance, and say, she will never be forgotten by us. Her name will be reverenced, and her memory fondly cherished, by me and my children, when time with her shall be no more. My love to your brother and your dear children. I shudder when I think of your son's narrow escape from the jaws of death, and how doubly you might have been afflicted—therefore be comforted, and still think that the Almighty has been merciful.

Yours affectionately,

E. M. Chapline.

Write me as soon as you feel sufficiently composed to do so, for I shall be anxious until I hear from you.

Cincinnati, *Oct.* 20*th*, 1843.

My dear Cousin,—We were extremely shocked to hear of the irreparable loss you have sustained—at all times and under all circumstances the Dr.'s death would have been most afflictive to you—but occurring so suddenly as it did, renders it doubly severe. I am not able to offer you any consolation, for well I know none can give any comfort ; the bereaved heart will mourn and refuse to be comforted ; it is to time alone we must look to assuage our grief. Death has indeed visited your dwelling in an awful manner, but you have the consolation of being able to think, although the summons was sudden, that he was prepared to exchange this world for the next, where he is rejoicing in the presence of God the Saviour, and entirely exempt from all the sufferings of this life. Call to mind his deep grief at the death of your daughter Jane, and feel comfort in the reflection that he is never to experience the like again. I think it is only such reflections that can soothe us; if we suffer ourselves to dwell on our own loss, we are agonized. You have two promising children left you, who can weep and lament with you, share all your grief, and be to you your only source of comfort. May they be spared to be a blessing to you, the solace of your declining years.

When you are recovered from the first severe shock, I would, my dear cousin, be gratified to hear from you the particulars of your dear husband's death, and how you and Mary are. I presume you will have many friends to condole with you; but none feel more deeply for you than I do. Mr. Neave begs me to assure you of his deep sympathy and personal interest in whatever concerns you. Give my love to Augustus and Mary, and also to Aunt if she is with you.

Believe me, your attached cousin,

JANE R. NEAVE.

KASKASKIA, *Oct. 5th*, 1843.

MY DEAR MADAM,—I heard yesterday, on my arrival at this place, of the death of my much esteemed friend, Dr. Linn. I desire most sincerely to condole with you in your heavy affliction. His loss is a great one, not only to his friends, but to the nation in whose councils he occupied so distinguished a place.

I had made my arrangements to have a personal interview with him on this day, but on yesterday the sad news reached me of his sudden and untimely death. He had attained high honors, and achieved the object of his ambition, but it availed not.

> "Or come he slow, or come he fast,
> It is *but* Death that comes at last."

I hope you bear the affliction as you should, consoled as you should be by the consciousness that you have the sympathies of many.

With high regard, your friend, and obedient,

SIDNEY BREESE.

D. APPLETON & COMPANY'S

PUBLICATIONS.

Should it be impossible to procure any of the Books on this List, they will be forwarded by the Publishers to any address in the United States, POST-PAID, *on receipt of the price affixed.*

MISCELLANEOUS.

Acton; or the Circle of Life. 12mo. . . . . Cloth, 1 25

Aguilar G. The Mother's Recompense. 12mo. . . . . Cloth, 75

——— **Women of Israel.** 2 vols. 12mo. . . . . Cloth, 1 50

——— **Vale of Cedars.** 12mo. . . . . Cloth, 75

——— **Woman's Friendship.** 12mo. . . . . Cloth, 75

——— **The Days of Bruce.** 12mo. 2 vols. . . . Cloth, 1 50

——— **Home Scenes and Heart Studies.** 12mo. . . Cloth, 75

——— The above in uniform sets, 8 vols. . . . . extra cloth, 6 00

8 vols. . . . . half calf, 13 00

Alsop's Charms of Fancy. A Poem in Four Cantos. 12mo. Cloth, 1 00

Amelia's Poems. 1 vol. 12mo. Cloth, 1 25

Gilt edges, 1 50

Annals (The) of San Francisco. By F. Soulé, J. H. Gihon, and J. Nisbet. Illust. with 150 engravings, and many fine portraits. 1 vol. 8vo. . . . . Cloth, 3 50

or in roan, marble edges, 4 00

or in half calf extra, 4 50

Agnel's Book of Chess. A Complete Guide to the Game. With illustrations by R. W. Weir. 12mo. . . . . Cloth, 1 00

Anderson's Practical Mercantile Letter-Writer. 12mo. 1 00

Arnold, Dr. History of Rome. 1 vol. 8vo. . . . . Cloth, 3 00

Half calf. 4 00

——— **Lectures on Modern History.** Edited by Prof. Reed. 12mo. . . . . Cloth, 1 25

Arthur. The Successful Merchant. 12mo. . . . . Cloth, 75

Appletons' Cyclopædia of Biography, Foreign and American. Edited by the Rev. Dr. Hawks. 1 handsome vol. royal 8vo., with over 600 engravings Cloth, 4 00

Or in sheep, 4 50

In half calf or in half mor., 5 00

Full calf, 6 00

——— **Library Manual.** 8vo. . . . . Half bound, 1 25

——— **New Railway & Steam Navigation Guide.** Published Monthly, under the supervision of the Railway Companies. 16mo. . . . . Paper, 25

——— **Travellers' Guide through the United States and Canadas.** Describing all the Important Places, their Historical Associations, &c. The whole accompanied by Routes of Travel, &c. 1 vol. 12mo. . . . .

——— **New General Catalogue.** 8vo. pp. 242. Paper. 25

MISCELLANEOUS—Continued.

Atlas. Appletons' Modern Atlas of the Earth, on 34 Maps. Colored. Royal 8vo. Half bound, 3 50

—— **Cornell's New General Atlas.** 1 handsome vol. 4to..... 1 00

Attache (The) in Madrid; or Sketches of the Court of Isabella II. 1 vol. 12mo..... 1 00

Baldwin's Flush Times in Mississippi and Alabama. 12mo. Illustrated............... 1 25

———— **Party Leaders.** 12mo. ....Cloth, 1 00

Barker (Jacob) Incidents in the Life of. 8vo. 2 portraits. Cloth, 1 00

Barth's Travels in Africa. (in press.).......................

Bartlett. Personal Narrative of Explorations in Texas, New Mexico, California, &c. &c. Maps and Illustrations. 2 vols. 8vo....................... 4 00

Bartlett. The same, in half calf extra 7 00

———— The same, in full calf extra 8 00

———— The same, cheap edition, in 1 vol., bound.................. 3 50

Basil. A Story of Modern Life. By W. Wilkie Collins. 12mo. ....Cloth, 75

Benton's Thirty Years' View; or a History of the Working of the American Government for thirty years, from 1820 to 1850. 2 very large vols., 8vo. pp. 1527, well printed, Cloth, 5 00

Sheep, 6 00

In half calf or half mor., 7 00

In full calf, 8 00

Abridgment of the Debates of Congress, from 1789 to 1856. From Gales and Seaton's Annals of Congress; from their Register of Debates; and from the Official Reported Debates, by John C. Rives. By the Author of "The "Thirty Years' View." Vol. I. (to be in 15) preparing. Price per vol. 3 00

Beyminstre. By the author of "Lena." 1 vol. (in press).......

Bridgman's, The Pilgrims of Boston and their Descendants. 1 large vol., 8vo.....Cloth, 3 00

Butler's Philosophy of the Weather, and a Guide to its Changes. 12mo...........Cloth 1 00

Brace's Fawn of the Pale Faces. 12mo.............Cloth, 75

Brownell's Poems. 12mo. Boards, 75

———— **Ephemeron; a Poem.** 12mo............Paper, 25

Bryant's Poems. New edition, revised throughout. 2 vols. 12mo. Cloth, 2 00

Extra cloth, gilt edges, 2 50

Morocco, antique or extra 6 00

Half morocco, gilt, 4 00

Half calf, antique or extra, 4 00

Full calf, antique or extra, 5 00

" In 1 vol. 18mo.....Cloth, 63

Gilt edges, 75

Antique morocco, 2 00

Bryant's What I Saw in California. With Map. 12mo..... 1 25

Burnett's Notes on the North-Western Territory. 8vo. Cloth, 2 00

Burton's Encyclopædia of Wit and Humour. Illustrated. 1 large vol. 8vo. (In press.)......

Calhoun (J. C.) The Works of (now first collected). 6 vols. 8vo. per vol........................... 2 00

———————— Sold separately:

Vol. 1. ON GOVERNMENT.

2. REPORTS & LETTERS.

3, 4. SPEECHES.

5, 6. REPORTS & LETTERS.

Or, sets in 6 vols. half calf, 20 00

" " " full calf, 24 00

MISCELLANEOUS—Continued.

Captain Canot; or, Twenty Years of a Slaver's Life. Edited by Brantz Mayer. 1 vol. 12mo. Illustrated..........Cloth, 1 25

Chapman's Instructions to Young Marksmen on the Improved American Rifle. 16mo. Illustrated..........Cloth, 1 25

Chestnut Wood. A Tale. By Liele Linden. 2 vols. 12mo...Cloth, 1 75

Clark, L. G. Knick-knacks from an Editor's Table. 12mo. Illustrated................ 1 25

Clarke (Mrs. Cowden). The Iron Cousin. A Tale. 1 vol. 12mo.......................Cloth, 1 25

Cockburn's (Lord) Memorials of His Time. 1 thick vol. 12mo. Beautifully printed..... ...Cloth, 1 25

Cooley, A. J. The Book of Useful Knowledge. Containing 6,000 Practical Receipts in all branches of Arts, Manufactures, and Trades. 8vo. Illustrated. Bound, 1 25

Coit, Dr. History of Puritanism. 12mo ....Cloth, 1 00

Coleridge's Poems. 1 neat vol. 12mo. ....Cloth, 1 00
Gilt edges, 1 50
Morocco antique, or extra, 3 50

Coming's Preservation of Health and Prevention of Disease. 12mo................ 75

Cornwall, N. E. Music as It Was, and as It Is. 12mo. Cloth, 63

Cousin's Course of Modern Philosophy. Translated by Wight. 2 vols. 8vo........Cloth, 3 00
Half calf, 5 00
Full calf, 6 00

Cousin's Philosophy of the Beautiful. 16mo........Cloth, 62

Cousin's Lectures on the True, the Beautiful, and the Good. Translated by Wight. 8vo.
Cloth, 1 50
Half calf, 2 50
Full calf, 3 00

——— The Youth of Madame De Longueville. 1 vol. 12mo.........................Cloth, 1 00

Cowper's Homer's Iliad. Revised by Southey, with Notes by Dwight. 1 vol.............Cloth, 1 25
Gilt edges, 1 50
Antique or extra morocco, 4 00

Creasy (Prof.) Rise and Progress of the English Constitution. 1 vol............... 1 00

Croswell. A Memoir of the Rev. W. Croswell, D.D. 1 vol. 8vo..................Cloth, 2 00

Cust (Lady.) The Invalid's Own Book. 12mo.......Cloth, 50

D'Abrantes (Duchess.) Memoirs of Napoleon, his Court and Family. 2 large vols. 8vo. Portraits...................Cloth, 4 00
——— The same, in half calf extra or antique......... 7 00
——— The same, in full calf extra or antique.......... 8 00

De Bow's Industrial Resources, Statistics, &c., of the United States. 8vo. 3vols. bound in 1 vol..............Cloth, 5 00

De Custine's Russia. Trans. from the French. Thick 12mo. Cloth, 1 25

Dew's Digest of Ancient and Modern History. 8vo. Cloth, 2 00

Don Quixote de La Mancha. Translated from the Spanish. Illustrated with engravings. 8vo.
Cloth, 2 00
Half calf, 3 00
Full calf, 4 00

MISCELLANEOUS—Continued.

Drury, A. H. Light and Shade; or, the Young Artist. 12mo.................Cloth, 75

Dix's Winter in Madeira, and Summer in Spain, &c. 12mo. Illustrated.................Cloth, 1 00

Dumas (Alex.) The Foresters. A Tale. 12mo.............Cloth, 75

——— **Philibert; or, the European Wars of the 16th Century.** 12mo....Cloth, 1 25

Dumont's Life Sketches from Common Paths. A Series of American Tales. 12mo.....Cloth, 1 00

Dupuy, A. E. The Conspirator. 12mo...............Cloth, 75

Dwight's Introduction to the Study of Art. 12mo.....Cloth, 1 00

Ellen Parry; or, Trials of the Heart. 12mo........Cloth, 63

Ellis, Mrs. Hearts & Homes; or, Social Distinctions. A Story......................Cloth, 1 50

Evelyn's Life of Mrs. Godolphin. Edited by the Bishop of Oxford. 16mo..............Cloth, 50

Ewbank. The World a Workshop. 16mo..............Cloth, 75

Fay, T. S. Ulric; or, the Voices. 12mo. ....Boards, 75

Farmingdale. A Tale. By Caroline Thomas. 12mo........Cloth, 1 00

French's Historical Collections of Louisiana. Part III. 8vo.... ....Cloth, 1 50

Foote's Africa and the American Flag. 1 vol. 12mo. Illust. Cloth, 1 50

Fullerton, Lady G. Lady Bird. 12mo..............Cloth, 75

Garland's Life of John Randolph. 2 vols. in 1. 8vo. Portraits 1 50
Half calf, 2 50
Full calf, 3 00

Gibbes' Documentary History of the American Revolution, 1781, 1782. 1 vol. 8vo. Cloth, 1 50

——— The same. 2d vol. 1764 to 1776. 1 vol. 8vo..........Cloth, 1 50

Ghostly Colloquies. By the Author of "Letters from Rome," &c. 12mo.................Cloth, 1 00

Gil Blas. Translated from the French by Le Sage. Illustrated with over 500 spirited engravings. 1 large vol. 8vo.......Extra cloth,
Gilt edges, 3 00
Half calf, 3 50
Full calf, 4 00

Gilfillan, Geo. Gallery of Literary Portraits. Second Series. 12mo..............Cloth, 1 00

Goddard's Gleanings. Some Wheat—Some Chaff. 12mo. Cloth, 1 00

Goethe's Iphigenia in Tauris. A Drama in Five Acts. Translated from the German by C. J. Adler. 12mo.............Boards, 75

Goldsmith's Vicar of Wakefield. 12mo. Illustrated. Cloth, 75
Gilt edges, 1 00

Gore, Mrs. The Dean's Daughter. 12mo........Cloth, 75

Gould's (W. M.) Zephyrs from Italy and Sicily. 12mo. Colored plate, 1 00

Grant's Memoirs of an American Lady. 12mo.........Cloth, 75

Griffith's (Mattie) Poems. 12mo.......................Cloth, 75
Gilt edges, 1 25

Guizot's History of Civilization. 4 vols. 12mo.....Cloth, 3 50
Half calf, 8 00

——— **Democracy in France.** 12mo.......................Paper, 25

MISCELLANEOUS—Continued.

Gurowski's Russia As It Is. 1 vol. 12mo................Cloth, 1 00

Hall, B. R. The New Purchase; or, Early Years in the Far West. Illustrated. 12mo. Cloth, 1 25

Harry Muir. A Scottish Story. 12mo.............Cloth, 75

Hamilton's Philosophy. Arranged and Edited by O. W. Wight. 1 vol. 8vo........Cloth, 1 50

———— The Same, in full calf, 3 00

Heartsease; or, The Brother's Wife. By the Author of "The Heir of Redclyffe." 2 vols. 12mo. Cloth, 1 50

Heir of Redclyffe (The). A Tale. 2 vols. 12mo...............Cloth, 1 50

Heloise; or, The Unrevealed Secret. By Talvi. 12mo..... Cloth, 75

Holmes's Tempest and Sunshine; or, Life in Kentucky. 12mo.....................Cloth, 1 00

———— **The English Orphans.** A Tale. 12mo. Cloth, 75

Home is Home A Domestic Story. 12mo............Cloth, 75

Home; or, The Ways of the World. By Mrs. Reeves. 1 vol. (In press.).........................

Household Mysteries. By the Author of "Light and Darkness." 1 vol. 12mo...................... 1 00

Hunt's Pantological System of History. Folio, ...Cloth, 3 00

Iconographic Cyclopædia of Science, Literature, and Art. Systematically Arranged. Illustrated with 500 fine steel plate engravings. 6 vols. Half morocco, 40 00

———— Or in full morocco,..... 50 00

———— Or in separate divisions:—

The Laws of Nature; or, Mathematics, Astronomy, Physics, and Meteorology Illustrated. With an Atlas of twenty-nine steel plates, containing twelve hundred illustrations. 2 vols.......................Cloth, 5 00

The Sciences; or, Chemistry, Mineralogy, and Geology Illustrated. With an Atlas of twenty-four steel plates, containing one thousand illustrations. 2 vols. Cloth, 3 00

The Anatomy of the Human Body; or, Anthropology Illustrated. With an Atlas of twenty-two steel plates, containing six hundred illustrations. 2 vols. Cloth, 3 00

The Countries and Cities of the World; or, Geography Illustrated. Including a Complete German and English Geographical Glossary. With an Atlas of forty-four steel plates, containing Geographical Maps and Plans of Cities. 2 vols..............Cloth, 5 00

The Customs and Costumes of People of Ancient and Modern Times; or, History and Ethnology Illustrated. With an Atlas of eighty-one steel plates, containing fourteen hundred illustrations. 2 vols............Cloth, 8 00

The Warfare of All Ages; or, Military Sciences Illustrated. With an Atlas of fifty-one steel plates, containing fifteen hundred illustrations. 2 vols...Cloth, 5 00

MISCELLANEOUS—Continued.

The Navigation of All Ages; or, Naval Science Illustrated. With an Atlas of thirty-two steel plates, containing six hundred illustrations. 2 vols ....Cloth, 4 00

The Art of Building in Ancient and Modern Times; or, Architecture Illustrated. With an Atlas of sixty steel plates, containing 1100 illustrations. 2 vols....................Cloth, 6 00

The Religions of Ancient and Modern Times; or, Mythology Illustrated. With an Atlas of thirty steel plates, containing eight hundred illustrations. 2 vols.......................Cloth, 4 00

The Fine Arts Illustrated. Being a Complete History of Sculpture, Painting, and the Graphic Arts, including a Theory of the Art of Drawing. With an Atlas of twenty-six steel plates, containing five hundred illustrations. 2 vols. Cloth, 4 00

Technology Illustrated. Being a Series of Treatises on the Construction of Roads, Bridges, Canals, Hydraulic Engines, Flouring and Spinning Mills, and on the Principal Proceedings in Cotton Manufacture, Coining, Mining, Metallurgy, Agriculture, &c. With an Atlas of thirty-five steel plates, containing 1,100 engravings. 2 vols.......................Cloth, 4 00

A very few copies only remain of the above. Early orders are necessary to secure them.

IO. A Tale of the Ancient Fane. By Barton. 12mo. Cloth, 75

Irish (The) Abroad and at Home, at the Court and in the Camp. 12mo.........Cloth, 1 00

Isham's Mud Cabin; or, Character and Tendency of British Institutions. 12mo. Cloth, 1 00

James, Henry. The Nature of Evil, considered in a Letter to the Rev. Edward Beecher, D.D. 1 vol. 16mo. Cloth, 1 00

James, G. P. R. and M. B. Field. Adrien; or, The Clouds of the Mind. 12mo. Cloth, 75

Jameson (Mrs.) Commonplace Book of Thoughts, Memories, and Fancies. 12mo.....................Cloth, 75
Half calf extra, 1 75

Johnson, A. B. The Meaning of Words. 12mo.......Cloth, 1 00

Johnston's Chemistry of Common Life. Illustrated with numerous woodcuts. 2 vols. 12mo. Cloth, 2 [illegible]
In sheep, 2 25
In half calf, 4 00

Juno Clifford. A Tale. By a Lady. With illustrations. 12mo. Cloth, 1 25

Kavanagh, Julia. Women of Christianity, Exemplary for Piety and Charity. 12mo. Cloth, 75

——— **Nathalie. A Tale.** 12mo.....................Cloth, 1 00

——— **Madeleine.** 12mo. Cloth, 75

——— **Daisy Burns.** 12mo. Cloth, 1 00

——— **Grace Lee.** ..Cloth, 1 00

——— **Rachel Gray.** 12mo. Cloth, 0 75

——— The same. 6 volumes. Half calf, 10 00

Keats' Poetical Works. 1 vol. 12mo......................Cloth, 1 00
Gilt edges, 1 50
Antique or extra morocco, 3 50

www.ingramcontent.com/pod-product-compliance
Lightning Source LLC
LaVergne TN
LVHW021132110826
845150LV00005B/1003

* 9 7 8 1 4 2 5 5 4 9 7 8 7 *